Stuart Piggott
Marlborough
12 August 1971

Man and his habitat

Emyr Estyn Evans, C.B.E., M.A., D.Sc., Sc.D., D.Litt., F.S.A., M.R.I.A.

Man and his habitat
Essays presented to
Emyr Estyn Evans

Edited by

R. H. Buchanan
Emrys Jones &
Desmond McCourt

Routledge & Kegan Paul   London

First published 1971 by
Routledge & Kegan Paul Ltd
Broadway House, 68–74 Carter Lane
London E.C.4
Printed in Great Britain by
Alden & Mowbray Ltd
at the Alden Press, Oxford
© Routledge & Kegan Paul 1971
No part of this book may be
reproduced in any form without
permission from the publishers, except
for the quotation of brief passages in
criticism
ISBN 0 7100 6908 1

Contents

		page
Introduction *Emrys Jones*		ix
1 Emyr Estyn Evans: A personal note *H. J. Fleure*		1
2 Man's occupance of the soil *Bruce Proudfoot*		8
3 Plants, animals and man *Carl O. Sauer*		34
4 Tools and man *Axel Steensberg*		62
5 Society, man and environment *John Mogey*		79
6 Fields and field systems *Harald Uhlig*		93
7 The dynamic quality of Irish rural settlement *Desmond McCourt*		126
8 Hamlet and village *P. Flatrès*		165
9 The dispersed habitat of Wales *E. G. Bowen*		186
10 Mountain glory and mountain gloom in New England *J. K. Wright*		202
11 The Canadian habitat *Andrew Clark*		218
12 The future habitat *Emrys Jones*		247
13 A bibliography of the writings of E. Estyn Evans *M. L. Henry*		264
Notes on contributors		277

List of illustrations

		page
Frontispiece	Emyr Estyn Evans	ii
Figure 1	Triangular blade, *c.* 2400–1900 B.C.	65
Figure 2	Danish wheelbarrows	70
Figure 3	Co-ordinates for classifying the curve of sickles	73
Figure 4	Rural settlement patterns, 1832–40	138–9
Figure 5	Distribution of clachans, *c.* 1900	146–7
Figure 6	Distribution of raths	154–5
Figure 7	Distribution of place names containing the elements 'bally' and 'ton' or 'town'	158–9
Figure 8	Squatters in the Penuwch area of central Cardiganshire, 1834	193
Figure 9	Llandulas, 1834	197
Figure 10	Llandulas, 1968	198

Introduction
Emrys Jones

Embarking on a volume of essays in honour of an eminent person is a dangerous task. Perhaps its greatest difficulty lies in finding some kind of cohesion which will overcome the natural tendency of such a work to be a number of disparate contributions with nothing in common but authors' admiration for the recipient of the essays. Whether successful or not, the editors of this volume have tried to link the following essays along a broad and evolving theme. Estyn Evans approached geography through man, and more specifically through man's works—his tools and buildings, fields and furrows—and the way in which he comes to terms with his habitat. It seems fitting to have as a theme a series of reflections on man and his habitat, keeping in mind that historical continuity which gives Estyn Evans's work such depth.

The form of the contributions varies considerably, from the well-documented study pushing forward the frontiers of our knowledge to the reflective essay which hides—or reveals—a lifetime of experience, or the summary of years of research. They represent different approaches, but all of them will be appreciated by the recipient, who has shown himself the master of all approaches. In some cases they also strongly reflect the personality of the writer and the way in which he interprets his links with Estyn Evans. This is particularly so with J. K. Wright's essay and with H. J. Fleure's personal note. Both these contributors died shortly after writing. This great loss to geography is tempered only by the extent of their contribution to the subject. Their deaths are a more personal loss to Estyn Evans; nothing could have gratified them more than being represented in this tribute to him. All the contributors have or have had a close link with Estyn Evans, some as colleagues, some as pupils, one as a teacher—all as friends; and all are aware of having gained enormously from their contacts with him, sharing his learning, his wit and his companionship. The result, not surprisingly, has an international flavour, for his intellectual impact is appreciated in Europe and North America as much as it is in Britain.

This is no place for an evaluation of Estyn Evans's work and his contribution to archaeology and geography. H. J. Fleure reflects a little on its breadth and depth, and some idea of its magnitude is given in the Bibliography. The latter is in no way complete: it excludes reviews—many of which were themselves contributions to knowledge—as well as articles in newspapers and periodicals, and many broadcasts. The first item in the Bibliography is significant, a pointer to the unparalleled contribution that Estyn Evans has made to the archaeology of Ulster. From the early 1930s it is clear that he took to the spade, unravelling Ulster's prehistory by himself revealing many of the clues. It is not surprising that so many items in the Bibliography are records of field excavations: the evidence had to be uncovered before the story could be told. The wider interests of the geographer take over at intervals, as in his *France* and in his later books: but he was never an armchair intellectual. Estyn Evans has never lost touch with the reality of the habitat. One of the things which no bibliography can reveal is his brilliance in the field. He holds his own as a naturalist, and his capacity for sizing up the total situation in the field—flora and fauna, nature and man—can only be partially conveyed through the printed word. It was surely the significance of the small and ordinary things in the countryside that led to his deep appreciation of peasant life in Ireland and convinced him that this was a continuation of the prehistoric story. Spade work and observation go hand in hand, and the result is the masterly *Irish Heritage*, and also *Mourne Country*, the latter probably the best regional study in the language. The sense of continuity is very strong and the concern with habitat a constant one. This attitude is best summed up perhaps in his presidential address to the anthropology section of the British Association in 1960, entitled 'The peasant and the past'.

H. J. Fleure referred to Estyn Evans's contribution to the teaching of geography. He not only laid the foundation of our knowledge of prehistoric and peasant Ireland, but he also built up a department of geography in Belfast from its very beginning. He established a school and a tradition by his ability to communicate his enthusiasm. Estyn Evans talks as delightfully as he writes and he enlivens the most scholarly observations with rare wit. By writing and teaching he inspired many with his learning and his humanity. Those who have written the essays which follow are a few of those many.

1
Emyr Estyn Evans:
A personal note

H. J. Fleure

Emyr Estyn Evans, Estyn to friends, colleagues and disciples, was born at Shrewsbury on 29 May 1905, one of a family of four sons and one daughter, of the Rev. G. O. Evans.

Estyn was educated at Welshpool County School and this is surely more than a formal item in his career, for the school, a small one, in the first quarter of this century sent on to the University College of Wales, Aberystwyth, a remarkable series of exceptionally able students: E. C. Price became a Sheriff of the City of London, E. C. H. Jones Secretary of the National Savings Organization, F. N. Price Keeper of the Classics Department of the British Museum, R. U. Sayce Director of the Manchester Museum, and Sir William J. Pugh a Professor of Geology at both Aberystwyth and Manchester University, before his appointment as Director of the Geological Survey. Others became H.M. Inspectors of Schools and members of university staffs.

Havelock Ellis once wrote to ask me whether I would agree with his opinion that Norfolk and Salop were among the most notable British nests of ability and did I think race or environment was specially involved. I replied that I had had occasion to note these foci but I did not feel that race in the physical sense had much part in the result. Norfolk, with its admixture of Neolithic, Celtic, Saxon, Dane and Norman elements had later received a number of self-conscious emigrants from Flanders, with skill in textiles. It was possible that they soon acquired the faculty of looking at England as Flemings, as well as at Flemings as Englishmen. So far as Salop was concerned, years of happy contact with intelligent young people of both sides of the Salopian and Welsh border had shown me that many of them could at one time feel themselves on the Welsh side of the border and look at England from outside, and just as naturally do the reverse. This objectivity is a factor that promotes general ability, if it does not spoil itself by the false conceit of *nil admirare*. Estyn is a clear example of this quality.

In October 1922 Estyn entered the University College of Wales, Aberystwyth, as a student in the Faculty of Arts. His professors in the first-year courses in Latin and French would have welcomed him to their respective honours schools, but he chose geography. At that time Liverpool and Aberystwyth were the only two universities that had honours schools of geography (both honours schools established in 1917), though the University of London was moving in the same direction. The young honours schools had to meet a strong barrage of opposition, so there was an element of adventure involved in joining them—an element which contributed greatly to their vitality and value.

During his undergraduate years Estyn contrived to spend part of a vacation in France and so gained knowledge of and affection for the country and its language. A later visit to Spain and France with our mutual friend J. B. Willans, further enriched this knowledge and affection for the civilization and tradition of France and its appeal to his temperament, steeped in the love of historic beauty. One eventual outcome of this was the publication of a little book on France in 1937, small in size but rich in thought. The physical and cultural aspects of the country are thoughtfully set forth, and to all this is added an expression of Estyn's feeling for literature and history, making the book a choice example of human geography. May it live long and prosper into many editions!

In 1925 Estyn graduated with first-class honours at Aberystwyth. His first task after graduation was assisting in a new edition of *Encyclopaedia Britannica*, rather dull work which often he enlivened with witty, almost mischievous, sallies. In 1928 he was elected to a lectureship at the Queen's University, Belfast, to inaugurate a new department of geography. So began a lifework of study of Irish life.

When Estyn went to Belfast, the effort for geography in education was still in its early stages and many diverse views were urged by teachers who approached the problem from different standpoints or with different knowledge and experience. Maps and mapmaking, especially topographical mapping, had powerful claim to specialized attention, but was ill adapted to elementary instruction which was much more likely to profit from interpretative work. Mapping of geological, climatic and other data had claims that grew in importance as comparisons between distributions, for example of climates or of populations, were studied and refined. Syntheses of these data led to improved accounts of regions, and data for diverse periods helped to amplify the regional study of social evolution. The field was wide, the labourers as yet few, their preparatory studies and intellectual interests were varied. So there was much not very profitable discussion about the content of geography in education. About 1923 the Geographical Association had sent a deputation to the Board of Education, and as a result geography came to have a reasonable place in sixth-form teaching and examinations in schools. This improvement in school geography was increasing the number of university candidates for a degree, and especially for an honours degree in geography.

Estyn had to meet this demand single-handed, and with his humanist interests, naturally designed courses in which the relations of human groups to their special environments were emphasized. He gave special attention to France among foreign countries. To ensure better quality in teaching it was necessary to organize refresher courses for teachers in the school holidays and especially in summer, and Belfast had many attractions of scenery and history to offer. Estyn's succession of summer schools became well known and vitalized the teaching in many a school.

In the summer of 1929 Estyn widened his experience by taking part in the South African meeting of the British Association for the Advancement of Science. Glimpses of Rhodesia, Zanzibar and Kenya were added to a more detailed observation of the Cape peninsula.

In 1936 Estyn and I jointly led a group of members of Miss Tatton's Le Play Society in a study tour of Romania. River steamer took us down the Danube from Passau to Linz, Vienna, Budapest, Belgrade and the Iron Gates and so into Romania. Here we studied the social structure of several towns, notably of Brasov and Sibiu, where there persists the distinct nucleus of the city of medieval Saxon immigrants.

Estyn's knowledge of rural life in Wales, England and Ireland and experience of Romanian and French villages led him to write an important article in *Geography* in 1939 on 'Survivals of the Irish openfield system'. To appreciate this study we need to look back over discussions of the rather untidy tangle of problems involved.

Arthur Young (1741–1820) emphasized the contrast in France between the compact farm of the more Roman south and the strip-system, with communal control of cultivation, in the Frankish north, and he condemned the latter. This was the attitude of British experts too, and the change from strips to block farms (between the sixteenth and the early nineteenth centuries) was held to be a great economic advance; this was the enclosure movement. There was a widespread feeling that the strip system was a Germanic feature and in 1895 Meitzen published a monumental study, *Siedelung und Agrarwesen*, which presented an immense wealth of detail very admirably supporting this view and showing that the strip system, with an irregular cluster of houses, the *Haufendorf*, had probably spread from Germany with the Anglo-Saxons, the Franks and other groups in post-Roman times. As a study of the *Haufendorf* and its derivatives, Meitzen's work was of great value, but his theory raised many difficulties and much rather unprofitable discussion—one specialist was so troubled about it all that he said, 'Il n'y a pas de géographie historique de l'habitat rural.' Meitzen was especially wrong in his views about Ireland where not only do we find diverse systems of considerable antiquity, but where we also have to take account of climatic change, with the spread of peat over large areas in the last millenium B.C., during a succession of cold, wet summers around 700–400 B.C., reaching a maximum about 500 B.C. There is a probability that this cold, wet time began earlier on the continent, where it gave adequate rain in Mediterranean lands and was a factor in the rise of Classical civilization.

The story of rural settlement and farming is clearly different in different regions and among peoples of different backgrounds, but it varies also according to implements and domestic animals available, as well as according to seeds, cultivable or producible. And not all change is necessarily improvement; sometimes conquerors have imposed unfamiliar techniques or implements upon the conquered, and sometimes a progressive mind has failed to get innovations accepted by traditional communities.

Estyn and his students have begun to review these problems afresh in the light of Irish evidence. One of the widespread traditional Irish systems is that of a small cluster of houses where one may still find lingering remnants of old habits of communal civilization of strip holdings. This system they have called the 'rundale' system, and the settlement, the 'clachan'.

Another form of rural settlement in Ireland is the 'rath', of which about 40,000 are estimated to have survived into the last century. A few occur in Pembrokeshire and are usually ascribed to the immigrants who came from Ireland to South Wales in the latter half of the Romano-British period. Estyn thinks that the earliest raths are immediately pre-Roman, and that they were built thereafter for several centuries. They are usually considered to have been farmsteads with a family habitation and possibly other structures within an enclosure, the whole being often a little higher than the surrounding lowland. Are they the result of a valleyward movement from peat-covered moorlands of the cold damp centuries, or do they represent some class-distinction between landowners who built them and labourers who may have been grouped in clachans? Estyn's students have been trying to interpret the distribution of these two different types of rural habitation, finding more of one and more of the other in a particular area, and looking forward to the dating evidence that the Carbon-14 method may provide. Simple holdings with communal control of cultivation are probably an ancient scheme that must be considered as probably preceding the plough, and it is interesting that traces of early groups in several cases in Ireland have within or near them some prehistoric stone monument.

We hope Estyn will continue to write about habitat and peasant work. His studies in this field have led him to observe many aspects of popular tradition on rural Ireland, and his *Irish Heritage* has been enjoyed by many readers as a fresh introduction to a new field of study. It was followed by *Irish Folkways*, which pictured for us the survival of many a prehistoric feature and custom. In such studies Ireland is especially important, for it is one of the richest of all European lands in great stone monuments dating from a wide period beginning, it seems, about 3000 B.C. and continuing until our era, with ritual celebrations that have probably not completely ceased. It is also distinguished for its prehistoric craftsmanship, especially in gold.

B

Estyn's artistic mind, infused with strong human sympathies, has made him think of Ireland as much more than a field of surviving antiquity. It is alive with many-sided activities and all this is captured for us in *Mourne Country*, a labour of love for its author who enjoyed a rural retreat on the wooded southern slope of Slieve Donard facing the Irish Sea. This beautiful book is enriched by many sketches and maps from Estyn's pencil, always aimed at showing some feature of place, earth sculpture or man's effort. The role of tradition is portrayed with great sympathy in the chapter on the Elder Faiths, while stories of modern minds trying to hide old beliefs, and references to smugglers and pedlars all combine to make the book a synthesis of the scientific approach of the naturalist and of the reactions of man evolving the present from the past. *Mourne Country* owes much of its distinction to its being a revelation of a rich, free-ranging, unselfconscious personality who has walked and climbed among its glens and summits and learned its lore.

In getting to know Ireland, Estyn excavated and recorded many prehistoric monuments and laid the foundations of an attempt to synthesize a picture of Ulster's evolution, distinctive in many ways from the earliest Neolithic times onwards. Among these prehistoric sites one of the most notable was that of Lyle's Hill, north-west of Belfast. This had often been thought of as an earthwork of the pre-Roman Iron Age, but Estyn's excavation yielded masses of potsherds and parts of what must have been at least a thousand vessels. These pots are of Neolithic type and probably of Neolithic age, and were accompanied by quantities of worked flints. Some finer pots that can be classified as late Neolithic were different from the mass, but no find of any sort suggests Iron Age connections. The site is a large one, by far the most important Neolithic occupation site so far known in Ireland. Estyn has compared it with the Neolithic site of Le Lizo in Brittany, near Carnac, distinct from, though near to, the famous prehistoric tombs of the area west of Le Morbihan. The sorting and study of the material from Lyle's Hill occupied his spare time for many years, the account of the site being published in 1953.

Ireland has been looked upon as an ultimate corner of western Europe, a treasury of the past, the last place to which a culture would spread and the last place in which an out-of-date culture would linger. The spread of fine craftsmanship in gold from Ireland to Britain, even if only a spread of jewellery and not of skills, could be advanced against this theory. So could the influence of the Celtic saints reaching from Ireland to Atlantic Britain, Brittany, Gaul, Basel and even Vienna. It seems that there is more to be considered than an occasional blossoming. Ireland is on the sea route from the Mediterranean and Spain to north-west Europe via the many inlets of the Irish coast, the Minch, perhaps the Pentland Firth or the Great Glen and Moray Firth. The proportions of the A and O blood groups in Ireland and Iceland strongly suggest a close link and make it probable that Vikings married Irish women and had to move to Iceland as a result of the Irish resurgence of the eleventh century. At the same time the old sea-routes of the Atlantic fringe were declining as climate worsened after the tenth century and seafaring became much less attractive.

Estyn's thought and work have played their part in this development of thought about prehistoric Ireland and its role in Atlantic Europe. We note also his efforts to reinstate and foster the Ulster Journal of Archaeology, his co-operation with the Belfast and Dublin Museums and the emphasis he has always maintained on attempts at synthesis of past and present in the life of the people, remembering that new communications corrupt old customs. The local feature gives way before the assault of the motor-car and the aeroplane. Presidential addresses to Section E in 1959 and Section H in 1960 of the British Association have been eloquent efforts in the same direction, especially to direct thought to prehistoric Irish rural economy. *Prehistoric and Early Christian Ireland* (1966) gives a summary of Estyn's thought about ancient Ireland followed by a guide reviewing the antiquities of each county and of their ancient monuments. The Ulster Folk Museum was also established largely as a result of Estyn's pioneer work. All these activities have led to the new Institute of Irish Studies at Queen's University, Belfast, which has been placed under his direction. Estyn Evans has done more than anyone to lay the foundations of geographical, archaeological and folk studies in Northern Ireland, and has ensured, through his teaching, a continuation of this work which we trust will be as fruitful as his own.

2
Man's occupance of the soil

Bruce Proudfoot

Since man's achievement of humanity with the deliberate and
conscious use of tools in the early Pleistocene, the soil has been
continually modified by human activities. Soils have been destroyed
and created, they have been a source of food and of other raw
materials. Man has altered the soils he has occupied both directly
by economic activities such as ploughing and digging clay for
bricks, and indirectly by changing such soil-forming factors as
vegetation, drainage and micro-climate. We can study in contemporary situations the effects of, for example, forest clearance
and cultivation, and from descriptions of near contemporary yet
technologically simple societies obtain some idea of the changes
that must have taken place in earlier times.

High- and low-energy environments

On a world scale we can distinguish between high- and low-energy
environments.[1] In low-energy environments soil erosion by natural
agents is rare because local relief is slight, rainstorms are of low
intensity, the waste-mantle is stable, and vegetation cover is
continuous. High-energy environments are characterized by
considerable local relief, intense rainstorms, and large-scale mass
movement. As a result of these characteristics soil erosion by
natural agents is a frequent occurrence, and today is often greatly
aggravated by human action. This distinction between high- and
low-energy environments is important because it makes clear that

8

under certain circumstances soil erosion is a natural phenomenon —the 'geologic norm' of Lowdermilk and Sharpe.[2] In high-energy environments where natural soil erosion occurs it is extremely difficult to disentangle the human and natural causes of erosion.

Where vegetation cover is not continuous, as would be the case even without human interference in arid and some semi-arid areas, accelerated erosion may be a natural feature. In these areas, as in all other high-energy environments, periods of little erosion would be followed by short periods of intense erosion, and these alternations might be periodic, on a seasonal or longer-term basis. Today some of the most difficult problems in land management occur in high-energy environments, and research into the history of land use, soils, and geomorphology is only slowly enabling us to distinguish between natural erosion and humanly-aggravated erosion.[3] Carbon-14 dating has added a much needed chronological framework to such research, but over most of the world it is difficult to find areas that may not have been occupied by man during the last 30,000 years. It is ironical that in the New World where Carbon-14 dating has been used to provide a chronological basis for geomorphic studies of landslides, alluviation and gully infilling in high-energy environments, such as parts of California and Colorado, the same technique should concurrently be establishing the reality of human occupance in the New World in the same areas and at the same time as these periodic geomorphic events were occurring.[4] In New Zealand, where the first human occupance occurred only a millennium ago, we have a nearly ideal situation in which to study both natural erosion and humanly accelerated erosion in a high-energy environment. In south-west Fiordland, for example, Wright and Miller have suggested that forest slides or debris avalanches are a feature of the normal erosion of the region.[5] When the plant cycle nears the climax form, the increased weight of forest vegetation and moisture-retaining soil renders the steep slope unstable, and a debris slide breaks away to leave a prominent scar in the landscape. Elsewhere in New Zealand Selby has demonstrated that mass movement occurred between 15,000 and 1,900 years ago, in an upland area of weathered greywacke, where mass movement today occurs periodically as a result of high intensity rainstorms.[6] Such storms do less damage in areas of forest than in areas of pasture, so that human alterations of the landscape significantly affect the location of accelerated erosion.

Under a continuous vegetation cover in low-energy environments soil erosion proceeds so slowly that it does not interfere greatly with the normal processes of soil formation. Balance is attained between the soil-forming processes—breakdown of rocks and minerals by physical, chemical and biological action, formation of new minerals, especially clay minerals, and accumulation of organic matter—and the soil-destroying processes—splashing by raindrop action, soil creep, surface or sheet wash, windblow and gully erosion. Since soils, vegetation and slopes are all interrelated, changes in plant species or even in vegetation density will cause changes in the rate at which soils are being formed and destroyed. Soil-forming processes can only act slowly, soil-destroying processes may act rapidly. Human actions, by changing vegetation, by altering the structure of the soil with cultivation, by damming rivers and digging new drainage channels, thus altering the slope of the land and the water channels running across it, are therefore potent causes of soil erosion.[7]

Crucial stages in man's changing relationships with the soil have been nine in number:

1. The first use of fire.
2. The domestication of plants and animals.
3. The invention of irrigation.
4. The creation of soils, for example, by terracing or draining swamps.
5. The widespread use of iron ploughshares and coulters, and iron spades, which enabled sod grassland and heavier soils to be extensively cultivated.
6. The spread of commercial economies—in antiquity as well as in modern times.
7. The improvements in European agriculture in the post-medieval period and, with European expansion overseas, the spread of temperate European practices to other areas.
8. The increasing mechanization of agriculture which began with steam traction in the nineteenth century but has increased many-fold with the heavy diesel engines of the mid-twentieth century.

9. The increasing urbanization and industrialization of human societies, with large areas used for non-agricultural purposes, including recreation, and increasing pollution of the total environment with waste materials.

Early changes

In early times, and until recently amongst those peoples who retained simple food-gathering economies, modification of the soil by man must have been mostly indirect and unintentional, being induced largely by vegetation changes, many of them caused by fire. Evidence for vegetation change has become available through pollen analysis of sediments of many types, and sites such as Hoxne in Suffolk, England, which show changes in vegetation from forest to grassland at the same horizon as evidence for burning and human occupation, provide tangible support for Vidal de la Blache's prescient comments of 60 years ago on the relations between early man and his habitat.[8] Areas for camp sites would have been cleared by cutting and burning. Fire would also have been used to improve collecting and hunting grounds, and for chasing game or concentrating animals for slaughter, practices well attested from the hunting and collecting societies of native North America.[9] There would have been selective use of plants for food, fuel and house construction, and a wide range in type of plant material used—bark, bast, leaves, stems, roots, fruits and tubers. For religious and for economic reasons certain plants might well have been specially protected against damage from grazing animals and over-utilization, as happened more recently in parts of West Africa and China for example.[10] Digging for small animals and reptiles, roots and tubers would have had some direct effect on the soil around camp sites and near trails linking these together. Even where populations were relatively small, and technologies simple, these effects might, cumulatively through time, be considerable. An estimate of the changes brought about over a very short period of time can be obtained by studying, for example, surviving Australian Aborigines but the effect of such changes being made annually or seasonally over a long period of time is more difficult to assess.[11] Other changes also occur at camp sites—considerable areas of soil may be disturbed by scooping out sleeping-hollows, and the accumulation of organic debris selectively enriches the soil. Such enrichment can be long persistent, as witness the high phosphate values of soils overlying Swedish Mesolithic sites, a feature which enabled Arrhenius to localize the actual sites in the 1920s.[12] This local enrichment may permit or even encourage the establishment and persistence of particular plant species such as the nettles, *Urtica* spp., which spread rapidly in nitrogen-rich soils.[13]

Even before formal domestication of stock had occurred man may have protected those animals which he hunted, and is likely to have encouraged the formation of single or few species herds, like the buffalo herds of North America. Many of the animals he hunted were herbivores, and the concentration of such animals, and man's actions in managing these herds is likely to have altered the original woody vegetation of many areas selectively in favour of grass. Continuous trampling by man or the animals he hunted would have led to the formation of trails where patches of broken ground would have permitted the spread of light-demanding species into otherwise shady woodland.[14] Intensive use of such trails, especially around waterholes in drier areas, may have modified both vegetation and soils to such an extent that the surface of the soil would have become compact and impermeable with virtually no surface vegetation so that surface run-off would have increased and local erosion ensued.[15] On the North American Prairies, where buffalo trails were often cut into the edges of the deeply incised valleys and converged at convenient crossing places, there was often considerable local erosion, the trails acting as watercourses in wet weather and sites for landslides which scarred the valley walls.[16] The wallowing of animals in muddy waterholes, or their rolling in dusty depressions as with the buffalo, especially during the height of the fly season in summer, again must have upset locally the structure of soils, their infiltration capacity and vegetation cover. On occasions waterholes themselves may have been infilled by erosion.

Cumulative modifications of vegetation by all these means would have favoured grasses and shrubs at the expense of trees, especially in areas marginal for tree growth as along the dry edges of the Tropical Forests or in drier mid-latitude areas such as the central and western United States. Regular burning of forest is known to reduce the amount of organic matter and nitrogen in the soil, thus reducing its fertility.[17] Burning also destroys the surface layer of litter which develops below the forest canopy, and consists of decaying and decomposed leaves and plant remains, together with an abundant flora and fauna. Change from forest to grassland, provided vegetation cover remained complete, may not have altered soil conditions markedly if analyses of contemporary 'virgin' timber and 'virgin' prairie soils from adjacent areas of Minnesota are to be taken as a guide.[18] Organic matter in the soil is likely to have been increased with change to grassland, and to have been more deeply distributed through the soil profile, while leaching, the washing down or out of soluble materials in the soil, is likely to have been slowed down. Much would depend on the original character of the forest vegetation. If tree species producing acidic litter layers likely to promote leaching were originally present, then change to continuous grassland might well represent a marked change for the better.

Since the first domestication of plants and animals there has been increasing intensity of utilization of natural resources, caused not only by increasing numbers of the human population but also by the increasing material complexities of human cultures. Until the discovery of fossil fuels, vegetation was increasingly used, at first simply for domestic fuel, charcoal burning and the baking of pottery on a small scale in kilns; later, it was also used for glazed pottery manufacture, for the smelting of metals and the manufacture of kiln-treated bricks, all of which required higher temperatures and more fuel. Vegetation was also used with increasing intensity for construction purposes, in larger and more complex buildings, and for ships. Such increasing use can be documented both archaeologically and from written sources for many of the centres in which early civilizations developed. Deforestation of uplands, brought about by increasing use of wood and by pressure of grazing animals inhibiting woodland regeneration, has been a major factor in the stripping of soil from many of the upland areas around the Mediterranean and in the Middle East.[19] Often the eroded soils were the red Mediterranean soils known as *Rotlehm* and *Terra rossa*, products not of post-Glacial weathering and contemporary soil forming factors, but of older Pleistocene Pluvial conditions.[20] Once eroded they have been replaced only by thin brown soils. This man-induced erosion of these upland areas is additional to the natural erosion found in all such semi-arid and arid areas, as discussed earlier. Deforestation of the uplands has caused excessive run-off which in turn has made river-flow more erratic and exposed the lower reaches of the river-valleys to increased risks of flooding and the deposition of water-borne sediments over the rich lowland soils. The original soils have been lost to sea or have contributed to the new alluvial areas of which the Tigris–Euphrates and Indus are the outstanding examples. In some lowland areas and notably in the Nile, annual increments of alluvium have sustained soil fertility for millennia of cultivation. More often alluviation of the lowlands has led to the silting up of drainage channels, the growth of vegetation on sand bars in the lower courses of rivers, the formation of marsh and the disruption of both artificial and natural drainage.[21]

Agriculture in the drier areas of the Middle East, where grain cultivation seems to have originated, similarly led to vegetation changes and to consequent changes in soils. In many areas clearance of the natural vegetation and its replacement by cultivated grain crops must rapidly have led to further accelerated erosion as continuous vegetation cover was broken, at least temporarily for some months after the grain was sown. As the natural grasses which seem likely to have been the predecessors of many of the cultivated grains were native to the upland areas flanking the valleys of southwestern Asia and to some of the higher intermontane basins of such areas as Anatolia, earliest domestication of grains is likely to have taken place in environments whose stability was easily disturbed by man and by a concentration of his domesticated grazing stock, particularly by his sheep and goats native to similar mixed tree and grass habitats.

Presumably before irrigation and manuring were practised cultivation was on a 'shifting' basis, in which a patch of land would be cleared and cultivated for a number of years, then abandoned as crop yields fell, to be cultivated again later after the forest or bush had regrown.[22] Under orderly management such a system is better known as bush fallow in recognition of the long-term rotation of crops and trees. The larger the trees, within the size-limits imposed by the available tools, the easier the clearing, the larger the increment of wood ash and the better the yield of crops. Provided only small areas are cleared at a time and sufficient length of time is allowed for plant regeneration to occur, then this type of cultivation permits tillage in steeply sloping areas and protects the soils from widespread erosion. Such has been the case in parts of Burma, south-east Asia and Mexico for example, but more often, as in much of contemporary tropical Africa, population pressures are such that plots are again required for cultivation before woody vegetation has been able to re-establish itself fully, with the result that burning gives little ash, and crop yields are therefore smaller, and the plot can be used for fewer years. Moreover, plots are so numerous that there is steady impoverishment of vegetation and this, together with frequent burning, leads to a general reduction in the organic matter of soils and increased soil erosion. Zeuner, and Nye and Greenwood have pointed out that the soils of the cultivated plots are changed by tillage.[23] After the fallow is cleared and burned, the surface of the soils is bared to the sun and rain until the first crop forms an effective cover. Any unhumified organic matter decays rapidly and there is increased loss of soil by sheet wash and wind erosion. These changes in soil constitution are inimical to colonization by the former vegetation and when regeneration of cultivated plots occurs the original vegetation is usually replaced by one of a drier type.

Similar impoverishment has undoubtedly been induced in many areas by man's domestic animals. Over-grazing and over-cultivation lead to patches of bare ground easily susceptible to erosion. Thomas and Gradwell have emphasized the part played by trampling in damage caused by over-grazing in general.[24] Cattle, although they do not graze so closely as sheep or goats, tread more heavily. In temperate countries winter frosts, by heaving the surface, remedy the effects of excessive trampling. But in hot countries, where frosts do not occur, trampling by cattle may make the surface so compact that rain cannot penetrate the soil, the pastureland is ruined, and erosion ensues. Sheet flooding washes thin films of soil successively from the surface, water concentrated into rills and channels cuts into the soil and subsoil dissecting, grazed and cultivated lands. Wind erosion is able to blow away the finer soil material no longer aggregated by organic matter into the crumbs which form under grass or forest, crumbs which not only give stability to the soil but also help to retain moisture in the soil during the dry season.

The effects of over-grazing, intensive cultivation and deforestation of the uplands were already becoming apparent in the Mediterranean area on a wide scale by late Classical times with the silting up of many harbours and conversion of valley floors to marshland.[25] The role of climatic change in this widespread erosion of late Classical times is difficult to evaluate. Vita-Finzi has drawn attention to the widespread occurrence in the valleys of the Mediterranean basin of valley-floor alluvium deposited in post-Classical and late Classical times.[26] He and others have argued that this widespread occurrence of deposits of similar age and lithology suggests that climatic fluctuation was primarily responsible.[27] To counter this argument it has to be pointed out that in detail the valleys of the Mediterranean are climatically disparate so that climatic fluctuations are unlikely to have produced the same results everywhere. Moreover, the area as a whole was united politically and economically in Classical times until the collapse of the Roman hegemony so that the occurrence of widespread erosion at the same period is as likely to have been induced by human activities as by climatic fluctuations.

Detailed chronologies for similar landscape changes in other areas are slowly being established but the same difficulties arise in the assessment of the various causal factors involved. Land reclamation, irrigation and soil deterioration have a long history throughout south-western Asia and similar semi-arid areas. The environment as we see it there today is one much modified by man. In many areas rural populations are smaller than they were in the past, as indicated by archaeologic evidence of settlement size and distribution of agricultural systems. In upper Khuzestan in southwest Iran, for example, population seems to have reached a maximum in the Sassanian period from the third to the early seventh centuries A.D., with the imposition of a unified system of irrigation and drainage over an area of broken topography.[28] All the evidence suggests centralized planning and the development of such new and highly specialized cultivation techniques as growing rice and sugar cane. There was discontinuous but cumulative decline in population size, production and commerce after the Arab invasions of A.D. 639. Large areas of good land on the upper plains were abandoned, while new lands of marginal quality appear to have been irrigated for the first time, only to fall rapidly into disuse. Archaeologic and historic evidence here combine to indicate the complex sequence of occupance in this area.

European influences

Within the last five centuries local sequences of occupance have everywhere been interrupted by the intrusion of Europeans. The transfer of temperate European farming techniques to the warmer and drier parts of the rest of the world has had dramatic effects. Tobacco planting had exhausted many soils in Virginia by the middle of the nineteenth century, by which time the upland cotton lands of Georgia were also being dissected by gullies.[29] By the 1890s the western grazing lands, formerly the habitat of great herds of buffalo, were subject to intensified erosion by wind and water, perhaps as a result of the combined effects of climatic fluctuation, over-grazing and the attempted cultivation of unsuitable cereal crops.[30] Three decades later the dust bowl of the drier western states developed alarmingly during the 1920s and 1930s, less than a century after much of the land had been first cultivated by the European settler.[31] Even in areas climatically more akin to those of Europe, the new settlers often allowed land to deteriorate rapidly. Along the fertile banks of the St Lawrence the *habitants* practised intensive cultivation of wheat and other crops, but neglected to replenish the soil with manure, and failed to allow land to lie fallow. As a result, by the 1680s much of the land which had been continuously cropped for 20 years was completely exhausted.[32]

As well as deliberately transferring plants all round the world Europeans accidentally transferred living organisms associated with the plants, some of which radically altered the soil environment, enabling the transferred plants to thrive in their new environment. Such is the case with mycorrhiza which were introduced into Australia with living plants in pots.[33] Their existence in some areas has been reflected in the successful growth of introduced conifers, whereas the same species have failed to thrive in other areas where the mycorrhiza are absent.

Probably none of the practices transferred from temperate Europe to the warmer parts of the world has given rise to as much discussion as green manuring.[34] While there is no doubt as to the efficacy of green crops in protecting the soil surface from erosion, the usefulness of ploughing the green crop into the soil to increase the humus or nitrogen content, or assist in improving soil structure, has been strongly disputed. Results have certainly been equivocal and the interpretations of experimental data purporting to explain why green manuring is not always valuable have ranged widely. Perhaps a significant general point is that reasonable amounts of calcium, potassium and phosphates are needed by legumes for adequate growth and the fixation of enough nitrogen to make their cultivation worthwhile, and such nutrients may initially be inadequate in many tropical soils. Nevertheless, green leguminous crops can be particularly valuable in saline soils because they take their water from the subsoil and shade the surface. In comparison with fallow they therefore reduce the evaporation from, and hence the salt content in, the surface soil. Moreover, when they are ploughed-in their residues help to increase the availability of phosphate and trace elements to the succeeding crop because of the lowering of the soil pH brought about by the carbon dioxide produced during the process of decomposition.

Other European practices transferred abroad have been much modified. In the drier areas of the northern United States and adjacent parts of Canada, traditional Old World techniques of dry farming have undergone radical change, especially since the dry erosive years of the early 1930s.[35] Increased emphasis has been placed on incorporating a cover of plant debris into the fallow land throughout the dry summer period, thus giving protection against erosion, and conserving moisture for the following crop, yet maintaining weed control. In areas such as southern Alberta experimental evidence has shown the superiority of this method over the earlier system of clean fallowing.[36] Here as in so many areas of North America during the last century new machines have been developed to reduce labour costs and enable larger areas to be cultivated.

New and larger machines have not been entirely advantageous in all environments. It is especially fortunate that in most of the agricultural areas of North America and western Europe, where larger and heavier machinery has been developed, soils have been structurally strong and stable. Such effects as compaction caused by the concentrated operation of farm machinery between tree-rows have been shown to be relatively short-lived in orchards in southern England.[37] Elsewhere in areas where soils are structurally weaker and less stable the widespread use of heavy machinery has brought new problems.[38] The traditional light plough used in many areas of thin, stony soils in the Old World did little more than scratch the surface of the soil and was generally used only in the limited areas which were to be currently cropped. The large mechanized plough is often used more widely and with less discretion, thus encouraging soil erosion by increasing the area of bare ground liable to sheet wash, gullying and windblow. Such ploughing allows too much evaporation of valuable moisture and induces the formation of an impermeable plough pan at the base of cultivation, hence making the soil less permeable to the often heavy intermittent rainfall, and again increasing soil erosion.

Soil erosion

In the temperate European homeland soil erosion had always seemed less of a problem, or even no problem. An evenly distributed rainfall and moderate summer temperatures had allowed, even encouraged, continuous vegetation cover. A continuing emphasis on animal products necessitated cover crops that could be grazed for much of the year, and provided animal manure to maintain fertility.[39] Over much of the lowlands, primary deciduous forest was replaced intermittently from Neolithic times onwards by crops, grass or heathland.[40] Where conditions were marginal for deciduous tree growth, as in the wet western uplands of the Atlantic fringe, or in the sandy and dry loessic areas of the North European Plain, primary colonization by Neolithic settlers often had dramatic effects on vegetation and soil history. Whereas formerly under deciduous woodland there had been slow cycling of nutrients after their incorporation from the parent material through the soils and vegetation thence returned to the soils, cultivation disturbed this natural regime of the forest soils and rapidly used up the plant nutrients, a process aided by burning of woodland and soil surface during clearing. Grazing animals, particularly under marginal conditions, inhibited forest regrowth, and disruption of woodland cover allowed windblow and rainwash to remove some of the silt and clay fraction of the soil. Soils rendered slightly sandier than before would have been impoverished, less fertile and more easily leached. These processes have been studied in North America where Evans and Dahl, for example, have compared the soils of woodlands and adjacent fields, now abandoned, in Michigan.[41]

The results can also be seen in the stratigraphy of archaeological sites in Europe. At Goodland, in an area of high rainfall in the north of Ireland, for example, one can follow the sequence from the slow leaching of soils under open deciduous woodland, through Neolithic occupance and tillage, to podsolization and the initiation of wet grassland and finally blanket peat.[42]

Elsewhere, increasing amounts of silt-sized material in ditch fillings must represent material deposited after windblow from adjacent cleared areas.[43] In the successive Neolithic camps at Les Matignons near Cognac in western France fluctuating amounts of silt in the ditch fillings can be interpreted ecologically in terms of changing vegetation and soil conditions.[44] As the ditches of the first camp were nearly filled the amounts of silt in the ditch fill increased noticeably, reaching a maximum when the fine silty fill at the top of the ditch was deposited. It is suggested that this occurred as a result of woodland clearance at the time the camp was built, and of subsequent tillage of areas at least several acres in extent around the camp. With continuous tillage, and especially if the ground were left bare or fallow during warm, dry weather, the soil surface would have been liable to erosion, and silt blown from the surface would have been deposited in the ditches. The initial fill of the ditches of the second camp contains deposits with very little silt, while the amounts of silt in the ditches of the second camp on the southern flank of the hill remained small throughout the period during which the ditch was being filled. However, the general increase in the silt percentage of the deposits elsewhere in the ditches of camp 2, and the high silt values recorded for the pit filling of Bronze Age date, suggest that when the second camp succeeded the first and the site was later reoccupied in the Bronze Age, windblow was still carrying considerable amounts of silt-sized material from disturbed ground near Les Matignons.

Like many early sites, Les Matignons is in an area of relatively light soils. Prehistoric European cultivators using stone axes would clear the woodlands on such soils and utilize the cleared areas.[45] Pollen evidence suggests that many such clearings were temporary and that early agriculture in Europe was of shifting cultivation type.[46] Why this should have been so is problematical. In some of the marginal areas where forest soils were rapidly podsolized it is easy to postulate that yields fell quickly after the initial clearance and planting. Yields may have fallen especially quickly where burning was associated with the clearance, as suggested by documentary evidence for clearing of this sort in the nineteenth century and by current experiments in the Danish forests at Draved.[47] It is difficult to postulate such rapid falls in yields in areas of fertile loessic soils. Perhaps cultivation was rendered difficult by the rapid growth of grassland or heathland, rather than of shrubs and trees, after initial clearance and planting.[48] Not until iron tools became widespread was it possible to utilize more fully areas of grassland and heavy soils.[49] Neolithic man could have cleared woodland on heavy soils but he did not have digging tools to cope with such soils, as anyone who has ever used an antler pick in clay will testify. Clay soils with their higher adsorptive capacity were inherently more fertile than many of the soils previously cultivated and have supported crops longest under cultivation. Iron ploughs, fitted with iron coulters, and iron spades made possible the cultivation not only of such heavy soils but also enabled a closely grown grass sod to be cut and cultivated. Moreover, these tools also enabled the depth of cultivation to be increased. A selection of soils developed on glacial drift over Silurian bedrock from County Down in the north of Ireland is instructive.[50] None of the early soils here seems to have been cultivated; at best they can only have had their surfaces scratched. The organic rich A_H horizons are less than 4 inches (10 cm.) thick and the total A and B horizons vary from less than 4 inches (10 cm.) to no more than 12 inches (30 cm.) deep. In comparison, a modern cultivated soil on the same parent material may be cultivated to a depth of 12 inches (30 cm.), then have below this a zone of weathering some 8 inches (20 cm.) or 10 inches (25 cm.) deep before the unweathered till is reached. The rounded shape of the stones in the cultivated soil, compared with the angular nature of the stones in the buried soil, suggests the effects of mechanical disturbance as well as the greater effects of weathering in the cultivated soil. Support for the hypothesis of greater weathering in cultivated soils has come from recent studies of the incorporation of radioactive elements in soils. These studies have clearly shown that the rate of mixing of soil materials is much greater under tillage than under undisturbed forest or grassland.[51]

However, the cultivation of soils has had not only beneficial effects, such as deepening the soil and making more plant nutrients available, but it has, in other areas, led to soil erosion, even in such countries as the British Isles. As increasing attention is paid by archaeologists, geomorphologists and pedologists to the origins of the strata exposed in the sections they examine, more detailed evidence is becoming available of the influence of man on the soils of Britain. On the edge of the chalk escarpment at Brook near Ashford, Kent, excavation through the filling of one of the coombes or dry valley heads has shown that 5 feet of hill wash accumulated during the post-Glacial period near the head of the coombe.[52] About half of this accumulation is likely to have taken place following drastic woodland clearance which probably marks the beginning of early Iron Age agriculture about 500 B.C. The presence of lynchets on the chalk lands of southern Britain is in itself evidence as to the reality of soil movement on even gentle slopes in this region of moderate climate.[53] Avery has pointed out that, as a result of erosion, many of the agricultural soils in the Chilterns have come to differ markedly from their semi-natural counterparts on similar sites.[54] In old woodland on upper slopes and spurs the clay-with-flints which mantles the chalk is normally covered by a layer of flinty loam, whereas in adjacent long-cultivated fields the profile has commonly been truncated by erosion, thus exposing the clay subsoil or, where this is thin, the chalk below.

Evidence for soil erosion, presumably induced by human activities, has been recorded on many archaeological sites elsewhere in Britain. Colluvial deposits in the forecourt of the Monamore Neolithic chambered cairn at Lamlash, Isle of Arran, are probably eroded podzolic B_2 horizon material, washed downslope in the third millennium B.C. as a result of human activity uphill from the cairn.[55] In Ulster, Pollock and Waterman have described the way in which occupation on a Bronze Age habitation site at Downpatrick was interrupted at least in part by a spread of hill-wash of sandy boulder clay.[56] Occupation resumed above this layer but was itself overlain by 3–4 feet of hill-wash, which must have been formed rapidly, since the junction between the occupation layers and hill-wash was very sharp. Presumably this erosion was the result of woodland clearance and cultivation of the slopes above.

It would be wrong to assume that under present conditions soil erosion has ceased, although in many areas the rate of erosion is now much less than in the periods immediately following the clearance of extensive woodland cover. Careful survey of a field enclosed in the eighteenth century at Codsall in Staffordshire has shown that soil has been lost from the field along the line of section at a rate of between 0·04 and 0·06 inches (0·1 cm.) per annum.[57] Presumably this has been lost by windblow, gentle sheet wash, and by the removal of soil on root crops, farmworkers' boots, horses' hooves and on the wheels of carts and other vehicles and implements. More rapid losses of soil than these have been reported elsewhere in Britain within the last decade. In March 1968 in the eastern county of Lincolnshire there was one of the most recent occurrences of soil erosion by wind when more than 20,000 acres (8,000 hectares) were affected.[58] It is estimated that in the worst affected areas a depth of about 2 inches (5 cm.) of soil was lost. Liability to wind erosion has increased within recent years and areas of Lincolnshire where no previous wind erosion had been recorded suffered considerable soil loss in 1968. A major cause of this increased liability is probably the intensification of arable cropping during the last 10–20 years, which has been made possible by the widespread use of chemical fertilizers. Erosion following a grass fire on the limestone uplands of Derbyshire has also been recently described in some detail.[59] An area burnt clear of vegetation in 1959 was stripped of soil after the frosts of the winter of 1959–60 were succeeded by a series of easterly gales. Subsequently wind and sheep disturbed the few small patches of thin soil and recolonized vegetation, and exposed further areas of bare limestone. In the summer of 1963, and through the winter of 1963–4, there was more extensive recolonization by vegetation and the surface had generally become more stable. Clearly, however, the balance between man-maintained pasture and bare limestone is tenuous indeed.

Producing new soils

If cultivation has often led to soil erosion it has, perhaps equally often, been the incentive to produce soils. Irrigation, terracing, the draining of fens and marshlands, and the reclamation of coastal areas are all themes in the history of land use as significant as the clearing of the woodlands and the ploughing of the prairies. Some of these practices are certainly of considerable antiquity, and the case of the Paiute Indians in Owens Valley, California, who irrigated and weeded the plants from which they collected seeds later in the year without any formal cultivation or domestication of the plants, suggests that the origin of irrigation may be found even among Mesolithic rather than Neolithic peoples.[60] The great tanks found by Kathleen Kenyon at Jericho, built against the massive stone tower backing on the defences of the settlement, are logically interpreted as a source of irrigation water for the cultivated areas on which the town must have depended, at least in part, during the seventh millennium B.C.[61]

As soon as attempts were made to distribute irrigation water in orderly fashion over the cultivated ground primitive terracing must have developed. However, the history of terracing has scarcely been examined in any systematic manner save in south Asia, where Spencer and Hale's study of the spread of terracing indicates some of the problems involved.[62] Early terrace systems have been widely reported from the Americas, and some from Africa, but the absolute chronology of such systems is almost unknown. Most such systems have been built during periods of population increase when there was a large surplus of labour available to undertake the vast amount of construction work.

Similarly, Slicher van Bath has argued cogently that the expansion of farming in western Europe into physically marginal areas, and the reclamation of fens and marshes, occurred during times of high agricultural prices, prosperity and expanding populations.[63] Techniques of land reclamation learned in Europe were transferred overseas. The Dutch, for example, seem to have been largely responsible for coastal reclamation and land drainage of the lowlands of Guyana.[64] Earliest settlement was along the river banks but the mangrove-lined coastal lowlands have been embanked and drained since the eighteenth century. To ensure that each planter had an equal share of the fertile alluvial soil along the coast and equal shares in the development and maintenance costs, the land was parcelled out into rectangles and parallelograms running inland from the shore. Each planter was initially offered a frontage to the sea of about 400 yards (365 m.) and a depth of 3,000 yards (2,750 m.), giving him an area of about 250 acres (100 hectares). The first necessity was a sea wall behind which the mangrove trees could be cleared, and the land drained. It has been estimated that each square mile of arable land needed on an average some 49 miles (79 km.) of drainage canals and 16 miles (26 km.) of high level irrigation canals. Such construction work was feasible only with the large labour force provided by the massive importation of slave labour. This one example serves to illustrate something of the effort and investment involved in land improvement.

Problems of irrigation

Improvement is of necessity a continuing process. Irrigation without maintenance of drainage can lead swiftly to the production of saline soils impossible for cultivation, especially if no crop rotation or intercropping is practised. In the coastlands of southern Turkey one can find areas which were reclaimed from marshland 10–15 years ago and then cultivated continuously with cotton and irrigated, but not drained, so that today they are too saline for cropping.[65] Moreover, this is an area which is only seasonally dry. In the arid or semi-arid inland areas of Asia, salinization is a problem on an even greater scale, and must always have arisen when cropland was irrigated. Jacobsen and Adams have examined the historical role of soil salinization in ancient Mesopotamia and recognized three major occurrences.[66] The earliest and most serious affected southern Iraq from 2400 B.C. until at least 1700 B.C. A milder phase of salinization occurred in central Iraq between 1300 and 900 B.C., and a third phase is indicated by archaeological evidence which suggests that the Nahrwan area east of Baghdad became salty only after A.D. 1200.

Probably the largest area in the world today where salinization problems occur is in West Pakistan.[67] Estimates of the area in West Pakistan lost to cultivation annually from this cause are as high as 100,000 acres. Attempts are continually being made to offset this loss and currently about 29,000 acres are annually being restored by increased irrigation and the consequent leaching of the salts down to a depth of 5 feet (1·5 m.) or more. However, this type of reclamation is not a lasting one as the salts are bound to reappear after some years when the amount of irrigation water used decreases again. To combat these problems an integrated plan has been drawn up by the Dutch firm, International Land Development Consultants N.V., who carried out the 'Indus Special Study' in West Pakistan, which was commissioned by the International

Bank for Reconstruction and Development. The plan proposes further development of both surface- and ground-water resources to increase available water supplies, a partial remodelling of the existing canal system to obtain a more efficient distribution of water supplies, and a lowering and stabilizing of ground-water tables at a safe depth through a tubewell drainage system and additional improvement of surface drainage.

An entirely different approach to problems of salinity is currently being tried in the Negev desert in Israel, where crops are being grown on highly permeable sandy soils using saline sea water for irrigation.[68] This salt water agriculture is possible on such sandy or gravelly soils because the salts do not accumulate as they do in conventional agricultural soils which contain clays. Normally the clays would adsorb sodium ions from the salt water, deflocculate, and swell, making the soil impermeable. The sand particles do not adsorb sodium, the soils remain permeable and their voids are filled with air. Further addition of saline irrigation water dissolves any accumulations of sodium and magnesium chloride which are harmful for plant growth from the surface layer of the soil, and the salts are rapidly washed down into the sand. Less soluble components of sea water remain in the surface layer for a longer time and provide a balanced nutrient supply for the growing plant. Eventually the salt water drains away from the cultivated soil and flows back to the sea.

Elsewhere in the Negev, studies of older methods of land use are providing useful models for contemporary development schemes.[69] Parts of this now barren desert area have been inhabited by flourishing agricultural civilizations. In historical times the northern Negev was first settled during the Chalcolithic period in the fourth millennium B.C.; then during Middle Bronze Period I, from the twenty-first to the nineteenth century B.C., there was quite dense settlement throughout the Negev. The next period of sedentary settlement dates from the end of the tenth century B.C. to the beginning of the sixth century B.C., the period of the Judaean Kingdom (Israeli II–III). The last and most flourishing period was that between 200 B.C. and A.D. 630 when the area was successively ruled by the Nabataeans, Romans and Byzantines. After the Arab Conquest, from the seventh century A.D. until the present, the Negev was occupied only by nomadic Bedouins. Archaeological survey of surviving field remains has enabled several different types of irrigation systems to be recognized.

The loess-mantled slopes of small watersheds were used to provide run-off for subsequent use in nearby fields. A relatively large area provided water for a much smaller cultivated area, subdivided by low terrace walls which retained the flood water on the field, where it could soak into the soil and be stored for subsequent use by the crops. In the larger watersheds attention was focused on the use of water from the large flash floods which occur. Initially, cultivated fields on the wide shallow wadis were stabilized by stone walls which were later extended to spread the water over larger sections of the flood plain. At some stage these flood-plain, water-spreading systems and the wadis cut deep gullies through the flood plain. Later, diversion structures were developed higher up the wadis to water areas below the diversions, making use of a considerable knowledge of hydrology and hydraulics. Finally, perhaps because of silting or serious flood damage, these large systems were replaced by small run-off farms which made use of small watersheds only, before being abandoned during the seventh century A.D. Today carefully instrumented experimental farms have been established, making use of the kinds of systems that survived only as archaeological remains. Successful crops have again been raised in this difficult desert environment.

Here, as elsewhere, the study of older methods of land use can sometimes provide useful models for contemporary development schemes, and can always provide illustrations of practices best avoided. Man's use of the soil has been a chequered process in the attempt to feed an ever-growing population on a limited area of the earth's surface. This essay is offered as a tribute to a scholar who has, in combining a variety of disciplines, done much to aid our understanding of this process.

Notes

1. Compare J. L. Davies, 'A morphogenetic approach to world shorelines', *Zeitschrift für Geomorphologie* 8 (1964), 127*–142*.

R. Common, following on earlier work by Peltier, has mapped some of the climatic variables which may be of general significance in geomorphology, 'Slope failure and morphogenetic regions' in G. H. Dury (ed.), *Essays in Geomorphology*, London, Heinemann, 1966, 53–82.

2. W. C. Lowdermilk, 'Acceleration of erosion above geologic norms', *Trans. American Geophysical Union* 15 (1934), 505–9.

C. F. S. Sharpe, 'Geomorphic aspects of normal and accelerated erosion', *Trans. American Geophysical Union* 22 (1941), 236–40.

See also, A. N. Strahler, 'The nature of induced erosion and aggradation', in W. L. Thomas, Jr. (ed.), *Man's Role in Changing the Face of the Earth*, Univ. of Chicago Press, 1956, 622–3.

3. For a general survey of present knowledge, see L. D. Stamp (ed.), *A History of Land Use in Arid Regions*, Arid Zone Research, 17, UNESCO, 1961. An outstanding critical evaluation of evidence from part of the south-west USA is Yi-Fu Tuan, 'New Mexican Gullies: A critical review and some recent observations', *Annals Assoc. American Geographers*, 56 (1966), 573–97.

4. For example, R. Berger and W. F. Libby, 'UCLA Radiocarbon dates V', *Radiocarbon* 8 (1966), 468–72.

R. Berger and W. F. Libby, 'UCLA Radiocarbon dates IX', *Radiocarbon* 11 (1969), 194–5.

V. Haynes and G. Agogino, 'Geological significance of a new radiocarbon date from the Lindenmeier Site', *Proc. Denver Museum Nat. Hist.* 9 (1960), 1–23.

Discussion on early man in America: A. L. Bryan, 'Some problems and hypotheses relative to the early entry of man into America', *Anthropologica* N.S. 10 (1968), 157–77.

A. L. Bryan, 'Early Man in America', *Current Anthropology*, 10, iv (1969), 339–67.

5. A. C. S. Wright and R. B. Miller, *Soils of South West Fiordland*, N.Z. Soil Bureau Bulletin, 7, 1952, 30.

6. M. J. Selby, 'Soil slumps and boulder fields near Whitehall', *J. of Hydrology (N.Z.)* 5 (1966), 35–44.

M. J. Selby, 'Aspects of the geomorphology of the Greywacke ranges bordering the Lower and Middle Waikato Basin', *Earth Sci. J.* 1 (1967), 47–56.

M. J. Selby, 'Erosion by high intensity rainfalls in the Lower Waikato', *Earth Sci. J.* 1 (1967), 153–6.

J. Healy, 'Recent erosion in Taupo Pumice, Central North Island, New Zealand', *N.Z. J. Geol. and Geophysics* 10 (1967), 839–54.

7. S. L. Vendrov, 'Geographical aspects of the problem of diverting part of the flow of the Pechora and Vychegda Rivers to the Volga Basin', *Soviet Geogr.* 4, vi (1963), 29–44, esp. 33, 38.

S. L. Vendrov, 'A forecast of changes in natural conditions in the Northern Ob' Basin in case of construction of the Lower Ob' Hydro-Project', *Soviet Geogr.* 6, x (1965), 3–18.

8. R. G. West, 'The Quarternary deposits at Hoxne, Suffolk', *Phil. Trans. Roy. Soc. London* 239B (1955), 265–356, esp. 336–8.

P. Vidal de la Blache, *Principles of Human Geography*, ed. E. de Martonne, trans. M. T. Bingham, London, Constable, 1926, esp. 11–12, 23–4, 46–8.

9. Well summarized by O. C. Stewart, 'Fire as the first great force employed by man', in W. L. Thomas, Jr. (ed.), *Man's Rôle in Changing the Face of the Earth*, Univ. of Chicago Press, 1956, 124–9.

10. R. S. Rattray, *Ashanti*, Oxford, Clarendon Press, 1923, 121–32.

J. M. Hunter, 'River blindness in Nangodi, Northern Ghana...', *Geogr. Rev.* 56 (1966), 408 and Fig. 6.

Yi-Fu Tuan, 'Discrepancies between environmental attitude and behaviour: examples from Europe and China', *Canadian Geographer* 12 (1968), 188 and Fig. 4.

11. Apart from written accounts, outstanding sources for material on the Australian Aborigines are recently made documentary films.

Specific comments on tool making and use are to be found in D. F. Thomson, 'Some wood and stone implements of the Bindibu tribe of Central Western Australia', *Proc. Prehist. Soc.* 30 (1964), 400–22.

12. K. D. M. Dauncey, 'Phosphate content of soils on archaeological sites', *Advancement of Sci.* 9, xxxiii (1952), 33–6.

13. H. H. Mann, 'Weed herbage of slightly acid arable soils', *J. Ecol.* 45 (1957), 149–56.

14. G. H. Bates, 'Track making by man and domestic animals', *J. Animal Ecol.* 19 (1950), 21–8.

A. S. Thomas, 'Sheep paths', *J. British Grassland Soc.* 14 (1959), 157–67.

15. A. S. Thomas, 'The tramping animal', *J. British Grassland Soc.* 15 (1960), 89–93.

16. F. G. Roe, *The North American Buffalo*, Univ. of Toronto Press, 1951, 100–5.

J. D. Soper, 'History, range, and home life of the Northern Bison', *Ecol. Monographs* 11 (1941), 349–412, esp. 385–7.

17. For a general discussion on the effects of fire on forests see K. P. Davis, *Forest Fire: Control and Use*, New York, McGraw-Hill, 1959.

18. H. Jenny, *Factors of Soil Formation*, New York, McGraw-Hill, 1941, 220–3.

19. The most recent summary of the Classical evidence is presented briefly by A. H. M. Jones in *The Decline of the Ancient World*, London, Longmans, 1966, esp. 304–9.

Among regional and local studies mention should be made of W. C. Brice, 'The history of forestry in Turkey', *Orman Fakultesi Dergisi, Istanbul Universitesi* 5 (1955), 29–38 and J. M. Wagstaff, 'A small coastal town in southern Greece', *Town Planning Rev.* 37, iv (1967), 255–70, esp. 259–60.

20. W. L. Kubiena, 'Über Reliktböden in Spanien', *Aichinger Festschrift, Mitteil Inst. für angew. Vegetationskunde*, Klagenfurt, 1 (1954), 213–24.

K. W. Butzer, 'Palaeoclimatic implications of Pleistocene stratigraphy in the Mediterranean area', *Annals, New York Acad. Sciences* 95 (1961), 449–56.

21. T. Jacobsen and R. M. Adams, 'Salt and silt in ancient Mesopotamian agriculture', *Science* 128 (1958), 1251–8.

22. Many of the practices grouped together as 'shifting cultivation' have been described by J. E. Spencer, *Shifting Cultivation in Southeastern Asia*, Berkeley, Univ. of California Press, Univ. of California Pubs. in Geography 19, 1966.

23. F. E. Zeuner, 'Archaeology and geology', *South-Eastern Naturalist and Antiquary* 55 (1950), 12–16.

P. H. Nye and D. J. Greenwood, *The Soil under Shifting Cultivation*,

Technical Comm. No. 51. Commonwealth Bur. Soils, Commonwealth Agric. Bureaux, 1960, esp. Chap. 5.

24. A. S. Thomas (1959), *op. cit.*

M. W. Gradwell, 'Compaction of Pasture Topsoils under winter grazing', *Trans. 9th International Congress of Soil Science, Adelaide, 1968*, vol. 3, pp. 429–35.

25. References as in Note 19.

26. C. Vita-Finzi, 'Synchronous stream deposition throughout the Mediterranean area in historical times', *Nature* 202 (1964), 1324.

27. E. S. Higgs and C. Vita-Finzi, 'The climate, environment and industries of Stone Age Greece: Part 11', *Proc. Prehist. Soc.* 32 (1966), 25–7.

D. R. Harris and C. Vita-Finzi, 'Kokkinopilos—A Greek Badland', *Geogr. J.* 134 (1968), 537–46, esp. 545.

28. R. M. Adams, 'Agriculture and urban life in early southwestern Iran', *Science* 136 (1962), 109–22.

29. R. H. Brown, *Historical Geography of the United States*, New York, Harcourt, Brace & World, 1948, 133–4.

C. O. Sauer, 'The agency of man on earth' in W. L. Thomas, Jr., *op. cit.*, 64–5.

30. J. C. Malin, 'The grassland of North America . . .' in W. L. Thomas, Jr., *op. cit.*, 358–9.

A. H. Clark, 'The impact of exotic invasion on the remaining New World Mid-Latitude grasslands', *ibid.*, 741–6.

R. B. Held and M. Clawson, *Soil Conservation in Perspective*, Baltimore, Johns Hopkins Press, 1965, 79–86.

31. Maps of Soil Erosion in the USA produced by the US Soil Conservation Service have been widely published, see, e.g. *Soils and Men—The Yearbook of Agriculture*, 1938 (USDA, 1938) 93, *Soil, The Yearbook of Agriculture*, 1957 (USDA, 1957) 307.

32. W. J. Eccles, *Frontenac: The Courtier Governor*, Toronto, McClelland & Stewart, 1959, 6.

33. L. D. Pryor, 'How important is mycorrhiza to introduced conifers?', *Australian J. Sci.* 20, vii (1958), 215–16.

34. E. W. Russell, *Soil Conditions and Plant Growth*, 9th ed., London, Longmans, 1961, 255–63.

J. J. Ochse *et al.*, *Tropical and Sub-Tropical Agriculture*, New York, Macmillan, 1961, vol. 1, pp. 233–57.

Sir H. Tempany and D. H. Grist, *An Introduction to Tropical Agriculture*, London, Longmans, 1958, 105–13.

35. D. T. Anderson, 'The cultivation of wheat', *Proc. Canadian Centennial Wheat Symposium, U. of Saskatchewan, 1967*, Saskatoon, 1967, 338–55.

36. D. T. Anderson, 'Surface trash conservation with tillage machines', *Canadian J. Soil Science* 41 (1961), 99–114.

37. D. A. Holland, 'Environmental modifications resulting from the culture and grubbing of trees', *J. Applied Ecol.* 4 (1967), 353–62.

38. S. G. Willimott *et al.*, *Conservation Survey of the Southern Highlands of Jordan*, London, UK Ministry of Overseas Development, 1964, 64–7.

J. C. Eyre, *The Development of Dry Land Farming in Jordan* [Privately circulated], Middle East Development Division, Beirut, Lebanon, 1963.

39. B. H. Slicher van Bath, *The Agrarian History of Western Europe A.D. 500–1850*, trans. O. Ordish, London, Edward Arnold, 1963, *passim*.

40. Since the classic work of Iversen in the 1930s and 1940s pollen analysis has been widely used to establish local sequences of vegetation history. J. Iversen, 'Landnam i Danmarks Stenalder', *Danmarks Geol. Undersøgelse* R11, Nr. 66 (1941).

41. F. C. Evans and E. Dahl, 'The vegetational structure of an abandoned field in south-eastern Michigan and its relation to environmental factors', *Ecology* 36 (1955), 685–706.

42. V. B. Proudfoot, 'Problems of soil history...', *J. Soil Sci.* 9 (1958), 186–98.

V. B. Proudfoot, 'Soils and soil history' in H. J. Case, *Excavations in Goodland Townland, County Antrim* [*Archaeol. Res. Publications*, Govt N. Ireland, forthcoming].

43. I. W. Cornwall, 'Soil science and archaeology with illustrations from some British bronze age monuments', *Proc. Prehist. Soc.* 19 (1953), 129–47. Cornwall emphasizes the importance of a drier and perhaps warmer bronze age climate but we now know such climatic change is not necessary for erosion to occur in Britain, see below: Notes 50–7 and text pages 21–3, and the same features have been widely reported in a range of chronological contexts.

44. V. B. Proudfoot, 'Etude des sols' in C. Burnez and H. J. Case, 'Les camps néolithiques des Matignons à Juillac-le-coq', *Gallia*, 9, i (1966), 200–9.

45. Early comments on prehistoric distributions in relation to environment in C. Fox, *The Archaeology of the Cambridge Region*, Cambridge, CUP, 1923.

J. G. D. Clark, 'Farmers and forests in neolithic Europe', *Antiquity* 19 (1945), 57–71.

For an important extension of these arguments to the importance of contrasts between soils with different drainage characteristics, and for useful discussion, see C. B. Crampton and D. Webley, 'The correlation of prehistoric settlement and soils in the Vale of Glamorgan', *Bull. Board of Celtic Studies* 18, iv (1960), 387–96.

46. For north-west Europe there is a short summary by H. Godwin, 'The beginnings of agriculture in North West Europe', in Sir J. Hutchinson (ed.), *Essays on Crop Plant Evolution*, Cambridge, CUP, 1965, 1–22. Unfortunately palynological data for eastern and south-eastern Europe are scanty and in the absence of extremely close sampling for radio-carbon dating we are uncertain as to the length of time represented by the breaks between the numerous successive layers in well-stratified tell and other sites in south-eastern Europe. For a broad chronological framework see H. T. Waterbolk, 'Food Production in Prehistoric Europe', *Science* 162 (1968), 1093–1102.

47. A. Voelcker, 'On paring and burning', *J. Roy. Agric. Soc. England* 18 (1857), 342–68.

The experiments at Draved are briefly mentioned in A. G. Smith and E. H. Willis, 'Radiocarbon dating of the Fallahogy Landnam Phase', *Ulster J. Archaeol.* 24/25 (1961–2), 16–24.

32 BRUCE PROUDFOOT

48. For development of heathland, G. W. Dimbleby, *The Development of British Heathlands and their Soils*, Oxford For. Memoirs 23, 1962.

49. The Irish evidence is well described in M. V. Duignan, 'Irish agriculture in Early Historic Times', *J. Roy. Antiquaries Irel.* 74 (1944), 124–45.
   G. F. Mitchell, 'Post Boreal pollen-diagrams from Irish raised-bogs', *Proc. Roy. Irish Acad.* 57B (1956), 245.
   G. F. Mitchell, 'Further identifications of macroscopic plant fossils . . .', *Proc. Roy. Irish Acad.* 55B (1953), 276.
   At the other end of the Old World, in China, the widespread use of iron for agricultural tools in the 6th century B.C. coincided with the extensive development of large-scale irrigation and a commercial economy; Kwang-Chih Chang, 'Archaeology of Ancient China', *Science* 162 (1968), 524–5.

50. Detailed discussions by V. B. Proudfoot, 'Audleystown: the pre-cairn soil', *Ulster J. Archaeol.* 22 (1959), 26–7. 'Soils and stratigraphy at Castle Skreen', *Ulster J. Archaeol.* 23 (1960), 74–5. 'Soil samples from Lismahon', *Medieval Archaeol.* 3 (1959), 171–3. 'Lisnagade 2', *Ulster J. Archaeol.* [forthcoming]. F. W. Boal and M. K. Moffitt, ' A partly destroyed rath in Killarn Td. Newtownards, Co. Down', *Ulster J. Archaeol.* 22 (1959), 107–11.

51. R. F. Reitemeier *et al.*, 'The extent and significance of soil contamination with radionuclides', in N. C. Brady (ed.), *Agriculture and the Quality of our Environment*, Washington, Amer. Assoc. Adv. Sci. Pub. 85, 1967, 269–82, esp. 274, 276–7.

52. M. P. Kerney *et al.*, 'The Late Glacial and Post-Glacial history of the Chalk escarpment near Brooks, Kent', *Phil. Trans. Roy. Soc. London* 248B (1964), 135–204, esp. 190–1.

53. H. C. Bowen, *Ancient Fields*, London, British Assoc. Adv. Sci., 1964.
   C. C. Taylor, 'Strip Lynchets', *Antiquity* 40 (1966), 277–83.

54. B. W. Avery, *The Soils and Land Use of the District around Aylesbury and Hemel Hempstead*, London, Memoirs Soil Survey, HMSO, 1964, 48.

55. J. C. C. Romans, 'Soil analyses', *Proc. Soc. Antiquaries Scotland 1963–64* 97 (1966), 30–4.

56. A. J. Pollock and D. M. Waterman, 'A Bronze Age habitation site at Downpatrick', *Ulster J. Archaeol.* 27 (1964), 31–41.

57. G. T. Warwick, 'An attempt to measure accelerated erosion at Codsall, Staffordshire', in D. I. Smith (ed.), *Rates of Erosion and Weathering in the British Isles*, Inst. Brit. Geographers/British Geomorphological Research Group Symposium, 1965, Bristol, 1965, 44–6.

58. D. N. Robinson, 'Soil erosion by wind in Lincolnshire, March 1968', *East Midland Geographer* 4, vi (1968), 351–62.

59. T. D. Ford, 'A recent example of soil erosion on the Derbyshire Limestone', *Mercian Geologist* 1 (1964), 31–3.

60. C. D. Forde, *Habitat, Economy and Society*, London, Methuen, 1934, 35–6.

61. K. M. Kenyon, 'Jericho and the origins of agriculture', *Advancement of Sci.* 17 (1960), 120.

62. J. E. Spencer and G. A. Hale, 'The origin, nature, and distribution of agricultural terracing', *Pacific Viewpoint* 2 (1961), 1–40.

P. Wheatley, 'Agricultural terracing', *Pacific Viewpoint* 6 (1965), 123–44.
63. B. H. Slicher van Bath, *op. cit.*, Note 39, e.g. 116–31.
64. P. Simms, *Trouble in Guyana*, London, George Allen & Unwin, 1966, 345.
R. T. Smith, *British Guiana*, London, OUP, 1962, 16–17, 26.
M. Swan, *British Guiana*, London, HMSO, 1957, 36.
65. Fieldwork by the writer.
66. T. Jacobsen and R. M. Adams, *op. cit.*, Note 21, 1251–8.
67. H. Schroo, 'Notes on the reclamation of salt-affected soils in the Indus Plain of West Pakistan', *Neth. J. Agric. Sci.* 15 (1967), 207–20.
68. H. Boykos (ed.), *Salinity and Aridity: New Approaches to Old Problems*, Monographiae Biologieae 16, 1966.
69. Conveniently summarized in M. Evenari *et al.*, 'Ancient agriculture in the Negev', *Science* 133 (1961), 979–96.

3
Plants, animals
and man

Carl O. Sauer

The paleogeography of man, which deals with the whole span of his existence, asks whence he came, the manner of his dispersal, and in what lands new ways of living were learned. It tries to understand the changing outlines and patterns of the *oikoumene* and also of the natural world, the spread and wasting of ice sheets, fall and rise of sea levels, climatic changes, alteration of vegetation and fauna. As a human geographer I have considered such topics from time to time. They are restated here in condensed and revised form. Also I have thought that enough is now known of the age of cultural innovations and of the course of the Ice Age to link Old and New World cultures in longer perspective.

Far reaches of human time[1]
The human lineage has now been traced back to beyond 2 million years. *Pithecanthropus erectus*, the 'erect ape man', since determined to have lived half a million years ago, was not the intermediate he was thought to be at the time of his discovery, but a rudimentary human inhabitant of Java. *Australopithecus* of South Africa, named 'the southern ape', is now recognized as hominid. When the Leakeys later found their famous and vastly old fossil at Olduvai it was placed in the human family tree as *Zinjanthropus*, 'East Africa man', found by the Potassium–Argon clock as living $1\frac{3}{4}$ million years ago. The course of human evolution has been distinct from that of the anthropoids and began its particular direction before a time of which we have knowledge, perhaps, it has been suggested, to diverge before the apes began.

34

The human body differs in significant ways from the other Primates, apart from cranial topography. The trunk and limbs are proportioned so that man stands, strides, and runs erect, using the legs alone for locomotion, the arms freed to serve whatever the hands find to do. The only real biped among his kindred, he has been a dweller and forager on the ground. To this terrestrial adaptation Sir Alister Hardy has added an appraisal of human anatomy, skeletal, muscular, and epidermal, as apt for swimming and diving and has therefore suggested a partly aquatic habitat in his evolution. The hypothesis is attractive and has not had the attention it deserves. Some Primates cannot swim, others do so reluctantly and frantically. Humans learn to swim readily and may do so as early as they learn to walk. When the Spaniards came to the tropical New World they were amazed by the daily swimming of the natives and their proficiency in water. The Tasmanians, one of the most primitive cultures, astonished the European visitors by their skill at swimming and diving, by which means they got much of their food. The symmetry and grace of the human body, so different from the other Primates, Professor Hardy suggests, may have developed in part by an ancestral habitat in water as well as on land.

The other Primates are mainly vegetarian. Man, although lacking the powerful jaws and teeth of apes, is one of the most omnivorous of creatures. He eats, likes and is able to digest a great diversity of foods and is not driven thereto by famine as civilized observers have concluded at times from their own fastidiousness. The human stomach and intestines are extraordinarily competent and tolerant, somewhat limited in ability to consume raw starch in quantity. Sensitive to lack of iodine and of high intake of salt, mankind suggests an old affinity to the sea. Needing to drink often, the more so the drier and warmer the air, man could not range far from fresh water. This most naked of warm-blooded creatures, thin and sensitive of skin, lacking fang, claw and horny extremities, was restricted to a particular habitat outlined in his anatomy and physiology.

An African origin is generally accepted, present evidence favouring East Africa. The physical geography of equatorial eastern Africa is not greatly different from that of millions of years ago. The highlands of the African Shield bordered upon the Indian Ocean by an intermediate coastal lowland, growing broader or narrower as Pleistocene sea levels rose and fell. Vulcanism was active; in Olduvai Gorge, for example, the age of human sites has been determined by overlying volcanic beds. Climate is least subject to change in equatorial latitudes and in these parts it may have remained rather constant under the control of the seasonal reversal of monsoon circulation across the Indian Ocean. Thus the sedimentary beds exposed in Olduvai Gorge show evidence of minor climatic changes from somewhat more to somewhat less arid than at present. Olduvai has long been notable for its great number of vertebrate remains, indicating a scrub savanna within which there were gallery forests and marshes about water courses and ponds. The early Pleistocene landscape resembled the present, a major difference perhaps being that grass savannas have largely replaced the mixed assemblage of drought-tolerant shrubs, trees, herbs, and grasses. The replacement continues at present by the practice of burning, carried on by man for a long time.

Olduvai has become the classic site that has reoriented thinking about human beings. It has brought us closer in time and location to the ancestral home but the habitat lacks the primal advantages which once favoured man. The dry season is long and extreme. The herd animals, their predators and scavengers move far in search of food, as illustrated in the modern game reserve of the nearby Seringeti plain. The famous primordial camp site of Olduvai was at the edge of a small body of shallow water, with remains of the young offspring of large animals, of small waterside creatures, and of fish, all of which would be taken by hand or knocked down by club. A temporary camp at a watering place, its open situation was attractive as well to the herbivores and predators of the plains.

It is unlikely that such a marginal, exposed, and seasonally limited environment should have provided the sustenance and protection needed for the origin of the human lineage. The hominids whose presence has been found about Olduvai had stone implements of recognized type. They camped in the open and therefore knew how to safeguard themselves against the great cats for which they were attractive prey, easier to take than the fleet herd animals of the savannas. Olduvai man was in possession of developed skills that enabled him to venture into a land of hazard and seasonal provision. His presence became known by burial under a blanket of volcanic ash. He came from elsewhere.

The African savannas are currently in vogue as the first habitat of mankind, despite their severe seasonal limitations. Perhaps then, as now, they held great herds of large game. Primordial man, lacking the physique and the weapons to live by hunting-skill, is imagined as trailing after the moving herds, picking off injured, infirm, and dead animals, competitor of jackal and hyena rather than of the feline predators. Thus he has been construed as living in small mobile bands dominated by the strongest and most aggressive male, with submissive females and their young in his keeping. The inferred first basis of human society is masculine authority, band not family, and mobility not habitation.

The evidence of the human female is that human origins and society took a different course and came about in an environment other than that of the savannas. The period of gestation is about the same for humans and apes, but the human pelvis failed to enlarge so as to accommodate the foetus to physical maturity. The human infant is born in complete dependence on maternal care and long remains so. It does not cling to its mother, but must be carried; it is slowest in becoming ambulant; it must be fed longest. The juvenile stage is longest by far. Dependence becomes participation by continuing association of mother and offspring. Unlike other animal societies there is no break when mother and offspring lose such mutual recognition. When or whether the male parent became identified as such is less important. The enduring family is unique to mankind, and the recognition of kinship was first established maternally. Consanguinity, whether fact or fiction, is most elaborately structured among primitive peoples, suggesting that the recognition of relatedness was a basic concern, from the immediate to the extended family and to the community.

It was the role of the mother to see to providing the young with food and drink; to shelter them from harm by cold, heat, or wet; to keep them from straying and from accident. She taught them to recognize what was good or harmful and trained them until the boys were taken into the activities of the adult males. The men might roam and do whatever they wished, the women were constantly engaged in the care of their offspring, until the youngest became adult.

Mobility might suit the males but was a disadvantage to the women, who were responsible for the welfare of the family, as the keepers of the household. The primitive home, it may be stipulated,

D

was as permanent as possible. The selection of a suitable site was of primary concern, to have food and drinking water close by and protection from weather and enemies. If supplies were available the year round and there was good shelter, the women stayed put with their brood, sessile home-makers.

The biogeographer Moriz Wagner proposed a law of migration as a supplement to Darwin's *Origin of Species*. Evolution, Wagner thought, would not produce diversity if the progeny stayed in the same habitat, divergent forms being suppressed by the dominant established kind. If variants moved into a new environment favourable to their deviation they might survive, increase, and become a successful new entity. The hominid Primate departed far from his kindred. Premature birth, slowest and longest adolescence, lack of a pelt except for the head of hair, living on the ground, walking erect, a body well designed to swim, omnivorous habit, in addition to a mind that has the capacity of thought, tell of a different destiny determined in a distant time. They supply clues also to a place suited to his origins and the development of human ways. Accepting the present evidence for an African origin in low latitudes, and holding the concept of bands roaming about the savannas as incompetent and irrelevant, a suitable ecologic niche is required and indicated.

The attractive sea coast

The African shores of the Indian Ocean have advantages for human beginnings that are lacking in the savannas of the interior. Waves have fashioned a varied coast line, trimming back headlands and building strands along the lowlands, the stand of the sea being notably higher at the time we are now considering. Good tidal range gave daily access to diverse foods available at the water's edge and at all seasons. The beachcombing life knew no lack and at times enjoyed additions to the daily fare of shellfish: sea turtles came to lay their eggs in the beach; sea mammals and fish were stranded occasionally; sea cows pastured in estuaries. Landward there was plant food to be had, in particular where surface stream, spring, or underground seep issued from the mainland behind. Here there was water to drink in dry as well as rainy season. The environmental setting is in strongest contrast to the savannas: there was no need to wander, no season of hunger, no tracking of mobile and elusive game. And there was almost no competition for food or danger from predators. Here was an ample and comfortable niche awaiting occupation and ready to provide the opportunity to increase in numbers and develop human society. This was the promised land for the Primate variants who would survive by taking a course that was reserved to them alone.

As a student of the forms of life in the sea Professor Hardy was impressed by the design of the human body and its remarkable adaptation to swimming, thus extending the evolutionary perspective to include natation as well as erect carriage on land. This gets farther away from the old and familiar picture of primitive man as a shuffling, clumsy, ape-like creature.

A tidal, tropical sea-shore habitat satisfies all ecologic essentials including the provision of shelter. Cliffed coasts are likely to have recesses; driftwood piles up on low shores and marshy ground has stands of rushes and reeds. There was no need to wander. In choosing a place to live the first consideration was a dependable supply of fresh water. Next would come the appraisal of sufficient and varied food at all times, having the choice of a productive beach, tide pools, and perhaps tide-washed rocks and the presence of an adequate shelter. A well chosen place was permanently habitable, a home where the mother raised her brood. Local resources permitting, the family became a family cluster and perhaps a community in which living in association began the process of social organization. This seems to me a better-founded view of the origins of society than the contrary view of a wandering band held together by force.

As the sea coast was superior to the savanna in food, water and shelter, it also offered more advantage of materials for the practice of manual skills. The tidal sea washes many kinds of objects ashore: shells, stones, wood, seaweed, the jetsam that rouses the curiosity of the beachcomber, young or old, an ever changing assortment of things to pick up, play with, and keep as useful or ornamental. Salt-seasoned wood provided shafts for tools of many purposes, for digging, throwing, prising. Shells of many forms, sizes, and colours served as containers, tools and decorations. Headlands supplied stone shaped by waves into cobbles, rounded and selected for toughness by continued abrasion. Cobbles of a size to fit the hand were ready made tools. The earliest known artifacts are such cobbles, also called pebble tools, partly dressed to have a cutting edge or a pointed tip, by repeated directed blows of another rock. In materials and models the sea coast is a workshop, well stocked for the beginnings of technics. The protein and fat of marine animals was abundant and continually available. The coast was least pre-empted, being mainly beyond the range of other Primates as well as of the great cats.

The use of fire

The earliest certain use of fire was by Peking Man during the Second Interglacial period, at a time when winters in north China were much like the present. It does not follow, as has been suggested, that this is approximately when man began to keep fire. Nor does the oldest record of cooking, which is by Neanderthal man, necessarily suggest a deferment of such use until that late time, as has also been inferred. These finds were made in caves that gave good protection. Sites in the open air do not retain proof that fire was used over long periods. Now that the age of human existence has been so greatly extended, the question of eoliths needs to be restudied, for example those of the Red Crag on the East Anglian coast. The flints in question have been described as artifacts though this has been questioned or denied by some. Some of the flints are fire-crazed which has been attributed to natural fires, on the assumption that lightning might have had such effect; supporting evidence however is not given. The objection that the flint objects are too old to have been shaped by human hands no longer holding, the resort to an unknown and improbable effect of lightning is gratuitous.

The capture of natural fire came about when human curiosity replaced the animal fear of fire. Of the two agencies, lightning and vulcanism, the latter may be the more likely. In East Africa very early hominids lived in a land of volcanic fire; the camp at Olduvai was buried by hot volcanic ash. The step from watching a land ablaze to taking a brand and using it may have been decisive of the course of mankind and history. Its ritual memory is continued in fire worship of various forms, in the keeping of sacred fire, in the priestly services of fire sacrifices, incense, and eternal flame.

Lacking fire, man was limited to living in lands without extreme cold. The alternative, that he covered himself with skins, implies that he was a fairly competent hunter and that he, or rather the women, knew how to dress skins so that they were soft and stayed thus, a craft beyond the capacities of rudimentary cultures. Possessing fire he could venture into harsher environments on his way to the ends of the earth and its domination. That he did so at an early stage is recorded in the distribution of his remains and stone tools, fairly legible across Eurasia as far back as the Second Interglacial (Swanscombe Man in England, Peking Man in north China), half a million years and more ago. It is suggested as a reasonable thesis that the presence of man beyond the tropics implies his utilization of fire.

The hypothesis of his seaside origins points the way as well to the routes of his dispersal. He could skirt the shores of desert interiors, discovering the same supply of food and other materials at all seasons and also finding water to drink. He could continue thus into temperate latitudes and beyond, depending on the harvest of sea shore before he learned how to live inland, where seasonal contrast of supply was marked. (Also, in addition to his early presence by or near the sea, there are such interior sites as Heidelberg, Steinheim, and Choukoutien that raise questions about his ability to store food.)

Fire may be held as the greatest cultural achievement. It enabled the dispersal of mankind, which need not have been due to pressure of population, but to an inclination of a group to detach itself and find a new home, perhaps a pioneering bent that has been inherent in man and which has never been explained adequately in economic terms. Fire provides a place where the cognate group gathers after dark for companionship. Tropical nights are longer than is needed for sleep and nightfall brings the household together about the hearth for some time before it retires, as I well recall from Indian communities. The fireplace draws people into its circle of light and warmth to attend to small jobs, to talk or keep silent, to relax in company, to share a sensible propinquity that may be the oldest of social satisfactions.

It is incredible that early humans, whatever the disputed quality of their brains, should have sat about the fire generation after generation without experimenting with it, especially in relation to food. Roasting over coals or baking in hot ashes changes the taste and texture of animal foods. A place of high antiquity may be suggested for the clam-bake as a 'sociable'. Starchy roots and tubers were made easily digestible by heat, bitterness was removed from seeds and roots and some poisonous plants were found to be nutritious after baking. Dry heat was introduction to an empirical chemistry that enlarged the range of what was edible. Steam cooking antedated the fashioning of containers, perhaps by wrapping food in succulent leaves, encasing it in mud, or placing it in a covered pit of coals. The techniques can be inferred from the cooking skills of historic primitive peoples. Using fire, man learned to identify palatable plants and how to prepare them. The collecting of plants and the preparation of food for the household was the business of the women, who were the first botanists and organic chemists. They had to recognize the kinds that were safe to eat, the kinds that could be made palatable, and those that were to be left alone. The most primitive aborigines have this competence, a knowledge that was of survival value wherever a land became inhabited.

The contained fire of the hearth carries us back very far in human time. Its dispersal by setting fire to vegetation as a means of procuring food is perhaps also an ancient practice. Primitive people in modern times have done so where vegetation and climate permit, an effective means of collecting that does not require special hunting skills or arms. The spreading fire overtakes slow animals and suffocates others in their burrows. Repeated burning changes the character of the vegetation and may increase the harvest of animals and useful plants. In East Africa humans witnessed the killing of living things by volcanic fires and perhaps this set an example. However, we do not know that man altered vegetation extensively until the advent of the hunting societies that depended on big game.

The long span and slow pace of early mankind

The major divisions of prehistoric time were formulated a century ago by archaeologists in western Europe as a succession of skills applied to stone and then to metals. The Old Stone Age included the time before stone was ground and polished. A very long period of rudimentary dressing of stone was recognized as Lower Paleolithic. This was followed by the Middle Paleolithic, represented by Mousterian culture and Neanderthal man, in its turn succeeded by Upper Paleolithic, introduced by Aurignacian culture and Cro-Magnon man, the first fully accepted representative of *Homo sapiens*. This third 'stage' is now considered to have begun between 30,000 and 40,000 years ago and continued to within 10,000 years before the present. The antiquity of human lineage now carries back about 2 million years. All but the last 150,000 years are assigned to the Lower Paleolithic, and the greater part of the remainder to the Middle Paleolithic.

The status of Lower Paleolithic man is read almost wholly from his stone implements. These were made by percussion, shaping the desired object by blows from another stone. Archaeology has been able to determine how they were made, largely how they were used, and in part the cultural inventory to which they belonged. Temporal and regional complexes and connections have been recognized. There was some innovation of pattern, improvement in workmanship, and introduction of new tools. Percussion continued to be the basic technique, though this did not produce specialized hunting implements such as blades or spear points.

The extremely slow rate of innovation is considered by some to reflect the capacity of the primitive brain. In this respect the origin of speech has been of particular interest but it now appears to be admissible anatomically as primordial. Certainly implements of Paleolithic age which belong to the same type and are recognized over a wide area imply communication. In distinctive association they are called cultures, and some of the earliest, such as the pre-Chellean, are widely distributed. The testimony of the rudest lithic cultures is that their makers had use of speech.

The time it took mankind to get to the end of his first chapter is greater than we had thought, possibly because the human brain was slow in developing. Stone implements continued to be made by percussion, with some improvement of skill and diversity of form. They may have served the needs of the users adequately, and in the absence of other criteria it is unwise to use them as a measure of intelligence. The bias of the lithic stages of culture is obvious. Lower Paleolithic man extended his occupation to far parts of Eurasia and Africa, hot, temperate, and cold, implying the use of fire and foresight in gathering stores against the seasons of want. The archaeological record does not reveal his thoughts, or tell what he learned in fashioning wood and fibres to his service.

Nor may we postulate that population was sparse everywhere. Resources available to his skills set the limits to his numbers. Water-side habitats were most richly and continuously rewarding on tidal coasts; Mediterranean shores, lake and stream sides were also attractive. Such habitats could support goodly numbers and community living. During the glacial stages sea levels were low; their coastal plains are now submerged and lost to our knowledge. Also the valley floors of such times have been buried by the aggradation that followed from rising interglacial seas. The world-wide swings of sea level during the Pleistocene have largely concealed the places most advantageous to human occupation.

A world-wide middle Paleolithic?

With Neanderthal man and Mousterian culture a major change must be recognized. The type skeleton was found in a cave in the Ruhr region, the culture was established from caves in the Dordogne of south-west France. *Homo neanderthalensis* became the prototype of the cave man, brutish, ugly and backward, to disappear when *Homo sapiens* came on the scene. It was thought that perhaps he succumbed to the readvancing ice and superior sapient man. The older version has been under revision, and needs more. He has now been advanced to the status of *Homo sapiens neanderthalensis* and is given a span of about 100,000 years, beginning in the warm Third Interglacial (Eem) and continuing into the cold Fourth Glacial (Wurm/Wisconsin), less than 40,000 years ago. Also the physical type and a generally Mousterian culture have become known far from the narrow part of western Europe to which they were thought to have been restricted. Mousterian culture ranged from Portugal into south-west Asia and far into Russia.

In Eurasia the continental ice cap and mountain glaciers had their greatest extension in the Third Glacial (Riss). Boreal vegetation was established over unglaciated lowlands between northern ice cap and interior mountains, persisted in part in the following interglacial, and again occupied the northern lowlands in the Fourth Glacial. Mousterian culture appeared during the Third Integlacial and continued long into the following glacial time. Across the northern lowlands of Eurasia the vegetation was more boreal, in part tundra, in part moor and heath, with low forest of willow, aspen, birch and northern conifers, browsed upon by reindeer, bison, forest horse, woolly mammoth and rhino. Marsh, lake and stream were populous with water fowl and beaver and there were salmon to be taken. Food and pelts were available for men who knew how to hunt and fish and how to get through the winters. These people did so, and they had northern Europe to themselves for a long time.

These are the earliest people known who are properly called hunters. They lived largely by the pursuit and killing of large game, an enterprise requiring co-operation. The animals were not in large herds nor do they appear to have been widely migrant. Hunting seems to have been a matter of bringing in game as needed to the place of living. Where available the people occupied rock shelters (abris) some of which were permanently occupied. Their implements show refinements and innovations, the most significant being the making of points for spears. The regional differences in kind and style suggest that there was provincial grouping. Ceremonial burials, from France to the Zagros Mountains, give the first indications of religion.

Neanderthal/Mousterian is now known to have been present also from Morocco east to the Zagros Mountains beyond Mesopotamia, over a long belt of summer dryness with plants and animals differing markedly from those north of the Alps and Pyrenees. The old view of a habitat at the edge of tundra forest is expanded to extend to the edge of desert lands. Instead of an origin in western Europe the bearers of this culture perhaps came west into Europe out of south-west Asia.

Recent archaeological work has located Mousterian sites far to the north-east, in the Altai of the U.S.S.R. and in Chinese Mongolia.[2] In time they appear to correspond to Mousterian in western Europe. There is no report of human skeletons. The great culture of the Middle Paleolithic thus appears to have been established across the north of Eurasia from the Atlantic into Mongolia. At the time in question the Scandinavian ice reached slightly across the Baltic Sea and eastward somewhat into Russia.[3] An ice-free lowland bordered widely on the Arctic Ocean to the east of Scandinavia, the great plains of Russia and Siberia being then covered by tundra and boreal forest. Here the woolly mammoth ranged, feeding in the open tundra on shrubs and herbs and retreating in winter into the woods for shelter and scant subsistence. The large historical commerce in its fossil ivory, taken for centuries from Siberia into

China, attests its presence in numbers on Arctic plains in late Pleistocene time. Mousterian sites in European Russia indicate major dependence on mammoth-hunting. The people who could live on hunting, fishing, and plant food in north-western Germany practised a similar economy across Siberia. There is also some evidence of greater and more diverse plant growth at the time of the mammoths and of a milder climate in Arctic lowlands. This accords with a current theory of Pleistocene climates proposed by Maurice Ewing and William Donn, who suggest that the Arctic Ocean was open during glacial stages, ice-covered during interglacials. The Lamont Geological Laboratory dates the start of the Fourth Glaciation at somewhat more than 100,000 years, with a notable recession about 50,000 years ago.

For long, most authorities accepted a post-glacial entry of man into the New World. The last major recession of the ice now is placed as within 11,000 years. There was no difficulty in getting across Bering Strait. Mousterian culture had reached north-east Asia at a time when the woolly mammoth thrived on the Arctic plains, and the time is thought to fall within the span of European Mousterian. The unglaciated corridor south of the Arctic Ocean was never blocked. The reasons for denying earlier entry to the New World are various and obscure. The extension of Mousterian culture into farther Asia was not known until lately. The difficulty of migration by skirting the Sea of Okhotsk and Kamchatka was evident, the habitability of the Arctic Plain and coast was not considered. Authority continued to reject the reports of early man in the New World, but this position is now untenable with the evidence provided by radiocarbon dating. It is now possible to determine age to about 40,000 years, or into the last part of Middle Paleolithic time and mid-Wisconsin glaciation (by the Lamon calendar). There is good evidence that men were living in North America that long ago, in particular in California and Texas.

The Santa Barbara channel coast of California has a long record of human occupance which the Santa Barbara Museum of Natural History has kept under close attention for many years, yielding a long and nearly continual record of human presence on mainland and channel islands. Santa Rosa Island, inhabited by endemic dwarf mammoths, has been examined most closely. Their bones are exposed by the erosion of marine terraces, some found in fire-baked, pit-like depressions. These have been proved to be baking pits in which parts of mammoths were roasted, the oldest beyond the range of radiocarbon dating. It has also been shown that the channel by which the island was reached was then almost as wide as at present and that water craft were needed to cross it.[4]

The Mojave Desert has long been of interest for a number of sites having implements of primitive workmanship and occupied at a time of notably moister climate. Excavation of one of these, at Yermo, is now nearly complete, and the consensus is that its age is no later than mid-Wisconsin.

In northern Texas, excavation for the Lewisville Dam north of Dallas exposed an ancient site with at least fourteen hearths and numerous bones of extinct and living animals. The charred wood samples were beyond the limit of the radiocarbon testing, then given as 37,000 years. The number of hearths and bones indicated a community that was more than a casual camp. Gravel pits in the highest terrace of the Trinity River to the south-east of Dallas have yielded three crudely-carved limestone boulders. Two represent human heads, the third may have been intended to do so. They were taken at different times from the bottom of the pit, bones of elephants, horse, camel, and ground sloth being found in the same horizon.[5] The height of the terrace and its fauna indicate pre-Wisconsin age, probably the Third Interglacial. The Trinity site resembles the situation at Frederick, Oklahoma, in the valley of the Red River, which adjoins that of the Trinity to the north. Here sand and gravel pits were worked commercially, also on the highest terrace. The extinct fauna was the subject of paleontologic study, but an earlier generation of anthropologists considered that the artifacts could not be contemporary in view of the then-current theory of man's post-Glacial arrival.

Both in Texas and in California the presence of man has now been established beyond the limits of radiocarbon dating, which in terms of archaeology is within Middle Paleolithic time. In both states, geomorphological evidence also points to human presence well before the end of that period, high river terraces in the south-west indicating inter-glacial entry. No remains of human skeletons have been found, but in both the Old and New World mammoths were hunted and other big game of extinct forms. In late Pleistocene times the Mojave was not a desert and had surface streams flowing into lakes. The Santa Barbara coast was rich in shellfish and fish, and the land abounded in oaks bearing sweet acorns and in diverse nutritive shrubs and herbs. The valleys of North Texas about Dallas had woods of oak and nut trees, fish in the rivers, and small and large game. Pleistocene folk found good places to live in the New World at the time of Neanderthal/Mousterian in the Old World.

Hunters of the end of the Ice Age

The rapid melting of ice sheets between 11,000 and 10,000 years ago accompanied the shift to the modern pattern of climate with its extremes of hot and cold, wet and dry. It was at the waning of the Ice Age that the people of the *grande chasse* took over in Europe and also in North America. In both continents they were immigrants, perhaps from unknown areas of the interior of Asia. They followed the moving herds of big game as organized hunting parties, and in Europe the later ones are known to have used skin tents. Their new technique of shaping stone by pressure-flaking produced blades and points of superior execution and design. The use of a new weapon, the dart thrower, was added to that of the spear. It gave precision at longer range to the practised marksman and was useful for hunting both large and small game. These Paleolithic hunters engaged in mass hunts, driving a herd to a place convenient for mass killing, inferentially by fire drive.

They engaged mainly in hunting large game of kinds now extinct. Quarry and hunter ranged plains from south-western France across Russia and Siberia into Texas and beyond, and apparently disappeared together. In north-west Germany and Texas they survived to about 9,000 years ago. Each culture was somewhat specialized in its pursuit of a dominant game. For example, the Gravettian people of Eastern Europe and Siberia largely hunted mammoths, the Solutreans the forest horse, Magdalenian and Ahrensburg hunters followed herds of reindeer in France and on the north German lowlands. In the United States people belonging to the earliest known culture of the kind, makers of the fluted Clovis points, have been called elephant hunters because they hunted mammoths as well as other game. Their range was wide and centred on the high plains of New Mexico. They were succeeded by the

Folsom hunters of giant, extinct bison, their name taken from the place in north-eastern Mexico where a Folsom point was first found embedded in the skeleton of such a bison. The Folsom points are small and fluted, well designed for use by dart thrower. Their area of use centred on the Rocky Mountains side of the high plains, from Colorado southward. A third hunting culture, called Plainview from a locality in the Llano Estacado of Texas, came a little later. Here a kill of a hundred giant bison was found in an area of 500 square feet. Plainview points have been found from Alaska to Mexico and east to Ontario.[6]

It is not likely that this hunting complex of vast extension across Eurasia and North America developed independently in different places. In every known case it employed the new, demanding technique of pressure-flaking to shape thin and sharply edged implements of specialized design. The laurel leaf blades in Texas are nearly identical in pattern with those of Solutrean France and quite as elegantly made. The introduction of the dart thrower, or throwing board, and the attachment to darts of points designed for greater penetration represents another technical advance that seems to have a single origin. The American participants came somewhat later than those in Europe; their end seems to have been at about the same time.

The reason for the disappearance of hunter and hunted has been sought in change of climate. Aridity became more widespread in the American south-west, between the Rio Grande and the Gulf of California, and this may have driven the mammoths from these parts. The same thing perhaps happened in inner Asia. The plains of North America east of the Rocky Mountains, however, continued to grow a great deal of palatable vegetation. The proposal that hunting was so severe as to kill out the game lacks merit. There was an ecologic upset later restored by a different fauna and vegetation. The disturbance became a continuing crisis; the repopulation of the plains set in slowly, for plants, animals, and man. The one agency that could operate thus is fire. The older fauna, mammoths, horses, reindeer and bison, inhabited woodland, brush and tundra, browsing rather than grazing. Hunters could prowl about such a herd and pick off individuals but not cause them to stampede. Mass kills are characteristic of the Upper Paleolithic hunters, and can be accounted for by fire spreading over a wide front, before which the animals fled in panic. I know of no other competent explanation. The hunters had learned the art of setting fire during dry weather so that it spread downwind, driving the game before it to a place where it would bog down or fall over a cliff or be trapped by a barrier. The use of fire drives has been known generally to hunters in historic time. Its continued employment suppresses the reproduction of trees and other woody growth, which are replaced by grasses, annual and perennial, and by annual herbs. Plains woodlands thus became steppes and prairies, occupied by a different fauna. The competent agent was man, organized for mass hunting; the time when the practice was instituted I suggest as Upper Paleolithic.

The grasslands of the New World are plains, semi-arid, sub-humid, and humid, whatever the season of rain. They do not extend into arid lands but, as in the western Llanos of Venezuela and the eastern United States, they did develop in areas of abundant rainfall. The common quality is that they are plains. They end where the terrain changes to steep and irregular slopes. Wherever valleys have been cut into grassy plains between the Appalachians and Rocky Mountains, the valley sides remain wooded, usually to the top. The early white visitors and settlers knew that the prairies and their western extension across the high plains were caused and maintained by burning. Indians set fires; the hazy sky of late autumn is still known as Indian summer, recalling the time when that was the season of Indian burning.

The alteration may be outlined roughly thus: the American hunters, from Clovis to Plainview, had possession of the plains for perhaps 3,000 years, in the course of which the vegetation of trees and shrubs, and the browsing game it supported, were converted to an altered biome dominated by grass and herbs. Herds of other grazing animals multiplied, such as the plains bison, known as buffalo in the American vernacular, the prong-horn antelope, and the American elk. Low growing, spreading grasses, such as buffalo grass and the grama grasses, palatable green or dry, and a lot of annual weeds were symbiotic with the later grazing herds and fire. Burrowing rodents, such as the prairie dog, became numerous. The older cultures were replaced by more 'localized' Archaic hunting and gathering cultures that had domestic dogs, used mortars and pestles, and to some extent polished stone. Bow and arrow were introduced later into the New World, in Texas, according to Newcomb, after the beginning of the Christian era.

Divergent ways of culture

The division of human time based upon different types of stone artifacts was conceived in western Europe. It was proper there, holds across northern Asia, and appears to relate to the early migrations into North America. But it is not valid for the world as a whole, nor is it a general evolutionary series of stages. Atlantic Europe lay at a remote end of the habitable world. Its history during that vastly disproportionate time called Paleolithic is one of immigrations from the south-east, south and east; it is not endemic in origin. There is a bias in the European Paleolithic scheme in its stress on the masculine provider as dominating society, culminating in the collective hunters of terminal Pleistocene time. Its record deals with interior lands and takes little account of the water side, salt or fresh.

The Upper Paleolithic hunters did not carry on as bearers of change into Mesolithic and Neolithic times. Some may have sired later reindeer-hunting tribes of the far north, others became lost in the spreading farming populations. They were the last of their kind, not the link to the new era. In north-west Germany, for example, the Ahrensburg reindeer hunters were contemporaries of farmers and town builders in Anatolia. The Plainview hunters were killing giant bison on the Llano Estacado when different people were cultivating plants in Pueblo and Oaxaca.

The new way of life, centred on tilling the ground, has been moved back in time by recent archaeological discoveries in upland localities of the Near East and Mexico and these earliest records date back from 9,000 to 10,000 years. They do not establish either the place or the time of agricultural origins, using agriculture to include the cultivation of plants of any kind by any means.

When the last deglaciation began, somewhat more than 10,000 years ago, the sea level stood about 100 feet lower than at present, except for high, northern latitudes. Continued melting of ice raised the level of the sea until it reached its present state about 3,600 years ago, the approximate age of the present coast lines in major outline. Low coastal plains, such as those fringing the South China and Java seas, were submerged and salt marshes spread about their margins. Rivers were embayed except where they carried the greatest loads of alluvium, and upstream alluvial deposits buried the earlier valley floors. Over this span of 7,000 years the lowland habitations of man are lost, in part submerged under the sea, in part covered by alluvium. In the lower parts of the great alluvial valleys they were more recently buried, as has been demonstrated in the Mississippi River delta.

It is improper to infer from archaeological sites that the origins of agriculture were in upland regions and are post-glacial. Nor are they to be tied into the lithic stages of cultural succession. A quite different cultural and physical context is required and is available. I refer to the invitation of living by the waterside, which I proposed as the primordial human habitat. Such opportunity continued through Pleistocene time, in time of high or low sea level, offering sustenance and security at all seasons. It gave invitation to take a fixed abode, a prerequisite to farming life. By turning from salt to fresh water man had to acquire a new manner of living. The chronometer of the tides was replaced by the rise and fall of streams, the seasons of growth and harvest, the time of flooding and drying of land. Water resources were still of major importance, those of the land adding new attractions. The changing course of streams, the margins that were marsh and swamp, the fertile flood plains, and the bordering uplands formed a different habitat which man might learn to know and utilize. He could explore and exploit it from a permanent base, learning steps in elaborating more varied skills and interests. Living in families is stipulated, with the women having charge of the household and being mainly responsible for procuring the plant food and learning to know the kinds and properties of plants. The bilateral nature of waterside living is the provision of animals from the water, of plants from the land.

There is no longer a place for a Mesolithic stage of cultural evolution from Paleolithic hunting to Neolithic farming. The great hunters of old were not ancestors of the tillers of the soil. While specialized hunters ranged the plains other kinds of people lived in other places and with different ways, collecting what their land and waters produced, including particular devices for taking animals on land and in water. The archaeological record being scanty, primitive peoples that survived into historic times provide insights into ancient and widely distributed skills that give information of cultural directions other than the lithic categories of conventional archaeology. To what extent were such artifices a cultural heritage communicated from a common ancient source? The question here concerns the context of simpler waterside cultures, remote from each other but of similar practices.

In America, the most primitive natives of whom the Spaniards had early knowledge were the Karankawas and their neighbours on the coast of Texas, the main account of which was related by Nuñez Cabeza de Vaca as a result of the wreck of the Narváez expedition in 1528.[8] These tribes moved according to the season from island and lagoon to mainland and streamside, collecting, fishing and hunting. In winter tubers (duck potato, *Sagittaria*) dug from the mud bottom of fresh water were a staple, in autumn they gathered acorns. Oysters at one season, blackberries at another were mainstays. Fishing was practised in stream, estuary and lagoon, by spear and net, by weirs built of canes and by brush dams, from dugout canoes. Canoes were used for spearing fish at night by torchlight. Medicine men prepared plants to stupefy fish, which were preserved by smoking. Cooking was done in pits. Baskets were made by twining and mats were used to cover their conical huts. Some of these artifices recurred widely throughout the world among waterside peoples of advanced as well as of simple cultures, and adumbrate a large and old dispersal of a way of life other than the lithic orientation of archaeological sequence.

The geographic distribution of water craft and the use of *barbasco* are of particular interest. The Spanish–Portuguese term *barbasco* applies to plants used to stupefy or kill fish in mass without impairing their quality as food. Plants of many kinds have been found to have such effect, commonly by paralysing the gills. Root, bark, leaves, or fruit of a suitable plant are mashed and strewn on still or slowly moving water, and the fish are collected as they float to the surface, belly up. The operation is organized and often ceremonially directed. The active substances lose potency by dilution and loss of stability, and thus have a short-term effect. Under social control the practice provided and conserved a supply of food. Whatever the plant employed, the procedure was similar and distinct from the use of bait or any mode of attracting fish. The range of the practice does not coincide with that of *barbasco* plants,

E

which have a wide distribution. This manner of fishing was commonly used by the natives of Mexico, Central America and the Pacific coastlands of the United States but not in the Mississippi valley or in the Atlantic coast states, where proper plants and suitable clear and quiet waters are present. In South America, *barbasco* was prepared by many tribes in the Amazon basin, including those possessing a most primitive culture. In the Old World it was important in lands around the Pacific and Indian Oceans. This then was an ancient art, rooted in a substream of waterside habitats that were carried far about the world, with competent identification of drug plants. In more sophisticated kindred societies, plants found to be narcotic to man were adopted into ceremonial use.

The hunters of big game were not discoverers of plant drugs, nor did they build water craft. Beyond the depth in which poles may be used, paddles or sweeps were needed to propel the craft, whether it be steered raft, dugout, reed bundle, bark, or plank boat. Boat and propulsion are associated artifacts of distinctive types.[9]

Dugout canoes were the most widely used means of water transport, and in many parts the only one. The name *canoa* was adopted by Spaniards from the Island Arawaks, who fashioned elegantly made boats of tree trunks. They were seaworthy, fast and expertly manœuvred, the paddlers ranging up to several score in boats of state. Dugouts of elaborate design and large size were also used by Indians of the Pacific north-west. In simple form and small size they were the water craft of primitive peoples from California to the Amazon and La Plata basins. In the Old World they survived most strongly in Africa and around the Indian Ocean. The idea of paddling a hollowed tree trunk may have occurred independently to different peoples, but the patience and skill required to make a serviceable boat out of a tree, and to propel and steer it by properly designed paddles, require competent workmanship. Shaping a dugout was an exacting and tedious task of charring and scraping inside and outside to get balance, displacement, and steerage. A common and ancient origin is suggested.

Reed bundle floats were another approach to being water-borne. They were made of reeds, rushes, sedges or the like, tied into bundles, these in turn lashed into the shape of a slender boat, coming to a peak at one or both ends, somewhat like a gondola.

The occupants are partly immersed in water but unlikely to sink or capsize. Propulsion is by paddles. Such floats, of very similar construction and pattern, have a greatly disjunct distribution, especially around the Pacific and Indian Oceans and their interiors. Considerable antiquity is inferred from their great geographic range, from New Zealand, Tasmania and Australia, Lake Chad, the Nile, Mesopotamia and Afghanistan, the Gulf of California, the coasts of Peru and Chile, Lake Titicaca, and Argentina:[10] from their use by very primitive peoples such as the Tasmanian, Seri and Uru; and their representation in the ancient art of Egypt, Mesopotamia and Peru. They are also said to antedate other boats on the Nile. Being a distinctive and complex artifact, independent invention seems as unlikely for the reed bundle float as for the dart thrower or bow and arrow. That they are a substitute for the dugout in a country that lacked suitable trees appears to be an inadequate explanation—the Tasmanians, for example, with tall and straight eucalypts at hand, made floats closely resembling those of Lake Titicaca. Dugout and bundle float are two different concepts adopted by different peoples.

Agricultural origins

The earliest farming known to archaeology dates back to between 9,000 and 10,000 years both in the Old and New World, in Anatolia and South Mexico. It is found in interior locations, in climates of long, marked dry seasons, and it set seeds to harvest seed. This was the period when Upper Paleolithic hunters of big game still held the plains of Russia and Texas. The omission of the waterside people who fished, made boats and nets, dug tubers, processed plants for fibres and drugs, and had houses is a discontinuity of sequence. The rise of sea level with deglaciation submerged coastal lowlands and raised valley floors with alluvial deposits and thereby covered most of the early record of this other manner of living.

In superior locations, food was available to waterside peoples the year round both from water and land. Living in permanent communities gave them the benefit of shared learning. Sedentary fishers, attentive to the uses of plants, are indicated as the first farmers. The waters yielded animal protein and fat, fleshy roots and shoots of plants, starch, sugar, and other supplements to diet.

Digging roots is a transition from collecting to cultivating. A patch that has been dug for a particular kind of root is likely to leave parts that reproduce as individual plants; the more often the plot is dug the greater the reproduction. Root digging is incipient tillage. The next step was to take pieces of a desired plant to a convenient location and begin cultivation.

Vegetative propagation results from observing that a piece of a plant will grow and reproduce itself. Primitive garden culture was established by assembling desirable plants, which would grow from a tuber or part of root or stem. Attention is directed to the individual plant; an attractive variant is selected and multiplied. In the course of long selection some plants have lost the ability to bear seed and became dependent on propagation by man. The plants adopted are perennials and may be used at all seasons as wanted, without need of storage. Such a planting economy is largely independent of a season of harvest.

The two great areas of this vegetative planting complex are south-east Asia with the islands beyond and the lands around the Caribbean Sea. In both the interest in plant food has been directed mainly to starch and sugar. Mainland south-east Asia and Indonesia were the home of the ancestral yams (*Dioscorea*), aroids including taro, *Musa*, sugar canes and other plants that supplied starch or sugar. Bamboos and pandans were planted for diverse uses. Vegetatively cultivated fish poisons include the famous *Derris* which yields rotenone.

In the New World tropics around the Caribbean, a great variety of roots was taken into cultivation and ameliorated for human use. Manioc (*yuca* in Spanish, *cassava* to the English) is a singular achievement, the greatest producer of starch, source of sure poison, with the capability to keep indefinitely when baked in cakes, and with extraordinary tolerance of dry weather and of wide variations of pH values in soils. The list of superior cultigen tubers is large and includes sweet potatoes, the taro-like *Xanthosoma*, at least one *Dioscorea*, arrowroot, *Arracacia*, and *Canna*. The pineapple was developed by vegetative selection. Diverse drug plants were grown for ceremonial use as narcotics and hallucinogens. Curare was prepared to poison darts. The great attention to toxic plants carries back perhaps to the ancient practices of drugging fish, some, such as *Lonchocarpus nicou*, having been vegetatively reproduced to the extent that their propagation depends on man.

Both great regions of vegetative planting cultures in Old World and New were much alike in food economy, plant techniques, and habitation. They lived in permanent villages, easily provisioned from water and land, and with competent water transport. They built houses of wood, cane, and thatch; made nets, mats, baskets and wooden bowls, and experimented with plant poisons. Their economy was strongly focused on the use of plants.

In South America the practice of vegetative reproduction extended through and along the Andean lands, adding there such cultigen tubers as oca (*Oxalis*) and ulluco (*Ullucus*) and the great assemblage of potatoes, ranging from diploids through fertile and sterile polyploids. Northward the vegetative cultigen complex was replaced by the maize–beans–squash seed complex, beginning in the highlands of Central America. In Costa Rica vegetative propagation is still much used, and the markets are well supplied with its products. A perennial cucurbit, chayote (*Sechium*), which may be grown by cutting or seed, is a favourable vegetable, both as fruit and root. The pejibae (peach palm), an ancient tropical cultigen, is selected by planting suckers as well as by seed. Vegetative propagation is practised in Central America and from here south to the limits of agriculture in southern Chile. Costa Rica, at the meeting of the two agricultures, uses both kinds of propagation for the same plants.

The northern agricultural complex of maize, beans and squash reached from Central America to the Gulf of St Lawrence. The southern root crops dropped out to the north, not because of climatic limits, but because the northern plant breeders were interested in seeds. The vegetation to the north did not lack edible roots. Mexico and the adjoining American south-west, for example, have wild potatoes, of current interest to potato breeding. These were dug and eaten but they were not cultivated or made the object of selection. Northward attention centred on the cultivation of annuals, plants of rapid growth in the season of summer rains, maturing with the onset of the dry or cold season. Planting and harvest time regulated the calendar of work and ceremonial. The plants grown provided a reasonably adequate diet. This manner of seed growing for seed harvest is known as the *milpa* system by its Mexican name, in contrast to the vegetative propagation by *conucos*, a term taken from the Arawaks of the West Indies.

The origin of the *milpa* is obscure. Recent excavations at Tehuacan and Oaxaca in Mexico have shown it to be far older than had been thought. In both places, plants grown by inhabitants of rock shelters included beans and squash, at a time when giant bison were still hunted in Texas. There was no maize, and when it appeared later its yields were for a long time so poor that this could hardly be its attraction. Collecting and hunting would seem still to have provided the chief means of subsistence, although the bow and arrow were not as yet known. That seed plants were grown meant permanent residence, at least from planting to harvest. These high interior basins with their short rainy season do not impress one as a place where a great departure in plant domestication would begin. Yet they are not far distant from coastal lowlands where fishing and *conuco* farming were practised. The wild kindred of the squashes and beans are native to southern Mexico and northern Central America, especially in the higher and drier lands. The position of the most ancient *milpas*, marginal to lowlands of *conuco* farming, suggests that as agriculture moved inland and upland away from productive streams and lakes, wild cucurbits, beans and other plants populated the clearings, were found useful, and became the object of attention and propagation. The cucurbits spread their vines over the cleared ground, the beans climbed up supporting stalks. Chayote, *Cucurbita ficifolia*, resembling a watermelon, and the scarlet runner bean (*Phaseolus coccineus*) are perennial vines with edible fleshy roots, perhaps linking them to *conuco* origins. Except for some cucurbits, the plants at hand gave little promise of becoming important crops. With patience, wild *Phaseolus* were bred into high quality and heavily yielding cultigens, the kidney and navy, lima and other beans of commerce. Four of the five cultivated species of squashes and pumpkins are attributed here, and, after a long time of indifferent success, maize was made into the great staple grain.

The maize–beans–squash complex afforded a balanced diet that needed little supplementing by animal food. The plants also served as green vegetables, roasting ears of corn, green beans, green squash and squash blossoms. *Milpa* agriculture follows practices like those of *conucos*, probably derived from the latter. Selection is by individual plant, the desired pumpkin, ear of corn, or bean pod, choosing certain colours and large-sized seeds. The seeds are thrust into the ground in determined numbers and spacing. The planting is by heaping the earth into mounds. Until the agricultural revolution of the late 1930s, the American farmer followed the Indian manner of growing corn, placing the grains by mechanical planter and 'hilling' the plants by cross-cultivation.

The earliest agriculture known in the Old World is in Anatolia and adjacent areas; the growing of small grains and pulses, keeping sheep and perhaps other domestic animals, the people living in villages or towns with cult shrines. Their condition was far removed from the beginnings of agriculture. There are wild relatives of wheat in those parts, some, such as einkorn and emmer, taken into cultivation. The breeding of bread wheats came later. Vavilov pointed out that in the domestication of small grains and pulses the elimination of shattering of the ripe seed heads and pods was important and that such change of cultivated forms increases westward from India. The hypothesis may be suggested that seed cultivation had its beginnings in the less-rainy monsoon land of India, in which attractive annual weeds, grasses and pulses had an advantage over perennial roots and stems and thus moved west through lands of scantier summer rain into the winter rain lands of the Levant. The amelioration of the seed crops was not by individual but rather by mass selection. The small grains, *Phaseolus* beans, peas, and lentils of the Old World were not increased in seed size nor diversified in colour as was the case in the New World. Broadcast sowing is indicated before the plough was used.

The thesis of Eduard Hahn was that animals were domesticated for religious reasons, as symbols of a divinity or as themselves sacred, as necessary to the observance of cult, perhaps for sacrifice. Starting out to study the economic geography of dairying, he found that milking began as a ritual act, and only later came to be regarded as a source of food. His exploration of sexuality in religions as represented by particular animals opened new insights that still hold good. With few exceptions the domestication of animals, including herd animals, was done by agricultural peoples in ceremonial context. Ease of taming and propinquity to man were not involved in their adoption. Their profane uses derived from ritual origins. The man-avoiding jungle fowl of south-east Asia appeared in Homeric Greece as a means of divination and in the ritual of cock fighting before it was bred to produce eggs. Horned cattle were kept as sacred animals before they found a place on the farm. That hunters penned game to assure themselves of meat and thus became stock raisers is a myth invented by materialist imagination. I know of no evidence which suggests an economic basis of the origin of animal domestication.

The history of mankind can now be seen in relation to the history of the Ice Age. The repeated spread and recession of glaciation successively changed the extent and aspect of the habitable world, and the chronology of these changes now can be determined in part. There still are greatly differing interpretations of the alterations of the climatic patterns, oversimplified as 'cold' or 'warm' stages. The most important fact of the rise and fall of sea level has had the least attention concerning its effect on the history of mankind. This concerns coastal lowlands and as well the valleys that are dependent on the level of the sea. The oldest known agricultural sites are in high interior locations. It does not follow, as has been thought, that agriculture began in such situations. At that time the sea stood about 100 feet below its present state and the associated valley floors were correspondingly lower. At the last glacial maximum, sea level was 300 feet or more below the present. The superior attractions of waterside living that I have inferred for the beginning of human kind apply also, I submit, to the origins of the agricultural way of life at a time well before any archaeological record.

Notes

1. See selection of my writings made by John Leighly under the title *Land and Life*, Part Three: 'Human Uses of the Organic World', and Part Four: 'The Farther Reaches of Human Time' (Berkeley, 1963, in paperback 1967). The Bowman Memorial Lectures (American Geographical Society, 1952), and *Agricultural Origins and Dispersals*, reprinted as a paperback (Cambridge, Mass., MIT Press) with addition of three more articles. The references given in these two collections are not repeated here.

Knowledge of the relevant past is enlarging greatly. Karl W. Butzer, *Environment and Archaeology, An Introduction to Pleistocene Geography*, Chicago, 1964, is the latest synthesis. His emphasis is on the western part of the Old World, where the data are best and where he has contributed geomorphic field studies of notable originality on the association of land forms, soil development, and climate. Karl J. Narr, *Urgeschichte der Kultur*, Stuttgart, 1961, has stressed the ethos of cultures, the indications that material remains recovered by archaeology give of ancient cultures, spiritual as well as material. Properly and prudently Narr has therefore also considered persistence in modern peoples of ceremonial traits concerning life and death, the spirit world, and 'good' and 'evil'.

2. C. Chard, *Saeculum* 14 (1963), 170–2.

3. K. W. Butzer, *op. cit.* (1964), Fig. 63.

4. Phil. C. Orr and Rainer Berger, 'The Fire Areas on Santa Rosa Island', *Proceedings of the National Academy of Sciences* 56 (1966), 1408–16, 1678–82. The geochronology is summarized by Orr in *Proceedings of the Symposium on the Biology of the California Islands*, Santa Barbara Botanic Gardens, 1967.

5. The heads are in the Texas Memorial Museum and are reproduced in Plate I, W. W. Newcomb, *The Indians of Texas*, Austin, 1964, which gives also an account of this site and of Lewisville.

6. *Ibid.*

7. In Africa the savannas are still expanding by the practice of burning. They too are plains, they range from high to low rainfall, and their vegetation is considered to be the result of periodic burning. That this has gone on for a long time is suggested by their grasses, the most nutritious pasture of low latitudes. As our bison spread and increased the buffalo and grama grasses, so African grazing animals are thought to have been selective agents in the dispersal and perhaps in the evolution of nourishing grasses. More recently, the introduction of African grasses into the New World is causing a revolution in tropical cattle raising in Brazil and around the Caribbean.

8. *Ibid.* See Chapters 3 and 12 for a summary of the customs of the Texas coast tribes.

9. Clinton Edwards, 'Aboriginal Water Craft on the Pacific Coast of South America', *Ibero-Americana* 47 (1965), includes notes on wider distributions of the several kinds.

10. *Ibid.*

4
Tools and man

Axel Steensberg

From the earliest Pleistocene time man has been a user of tools, though they have not been exclusive to him. Professor W. Köhler has shown that some Primates can occasionally improvise a tool to meet a given situation. But a chimpanzee has not sufficient foresight to be able to shape a stone or a stick for use in an imagined future, and as far as lower beings are concerned it is difficult to say how much of their planned work is due to inherited co-operation and how much to a real evaluation of the possibilities in a special case.

However, we must accept that man without some kind of tools would be an impossibility. Even Diogenes may have had a knife in his tub, and the most spiritual persons in modern time make use of pencils and typewriters. In prehistoric time personal utensils used to accompany men and women to their burial places, and tools are often the only visible traces of man's past.

Tools in the form of pictographs were an indispensable part of the earliest written sources. Their purpose may be immediately understandable, but without knowing the context a full explanation is impossible. Real tools are themselves signs which have to be interpreted in a context similar to the smallest elements of language. The problem is to interpret them rightly, and they cannot be interpreted without taking into consideration other aspects of the cultural environment. We may recognize a mattock or a spade as a hoeing or a digging tool, but how the hoe was treated in cultivation, or whether the spade was used for digging or traction, claim research in the culture as a whole.

Concerning the study of ancient tools we are nearly in the same situation as a linguist or a geologist. The linguist must build exclusively upon signs that are not immediately understandable, and the geologist has to consider what the conditions were when his ammonite died and was imbedded in some sort of clay. The ammonite is just as mute as the hieroglyph or the casual tool, but the tool has the advantage that it may be copied as a model and treated in systematic experiments in order to learn something essential about its use.

A collection of facts and an analysis of characteristic traits are equally necessary for an ethnologist, a historian and a natural scientist working on material from ancient times. But since the days of Herodotus the historian has been asking 'Why?' If he did not, he would remain on an archivist's level, and so would an ethnologist. However, an object collected without a historical background will often require another form of treatment. A purely heuristic classification may reveal important phases of its development, especially when one pays attention to apparently unimportant details such as relics preserved from stages when environmental conditions were different.

Wear marks as a proof of the kind of use

A rough classification of tools and implements may be based on their shape. Normally it is easy to distinguish a plough from an ard or a sickle from a knife. If the ard was used as a right-handed implement of tillage, this can be revealed by examining the share, and if a flint knife had harvested grain it should be possible to prove it from the brilliant gloss produced along its edge by the organic silica in the ripe straw. Deliberations of this kind were relevant for F. C. J. Spurrell when in 1892 he proved that the famous Polada sickle was a harvesting implement, not a saw.[1] When in 1937 attention was drawn to an ard-share from Borris, Jutland, the wear marks of which clearly proved a right-sided use, it added new information to our knowledge.[2] Later P. V. Glob published a couple of similar examples,[3] and at Sergejevsk in the Ukraine a ploughing implement was recently found on the right side of which a mouldboard had been sculptured.[4] This example shows how difficult it may be to distinguish between implements of a similar shape, because superficially the Sergejevsk plough looks like a Triptolemos ard.

A number of triangular blades made of limestone or basalt were excavated at Hama in Syria. They could be dated to a time between *c*. 2400 and *c*. 1900 B.C. From wear marks on both sides of the hafting pivot I have assumed that the blades had not been attached to the traction element at a fixed angle like an ard-share, but that they were pulled by a rope, which allowed a certain amount of flexibility between the means of traction and the blade. Signs of wear along the edges of the blades are usually more pronounced on the front towards the corners, while at the back the traces are nearer the point, apparently due to the fact that nearly all the raised soil passed the corners while the point was worn only by soil in the middle of the furrow. The back of the share was protected from wear, apart from an area at the point which was worn because the implement was held obliquely backward (Fig. 1). Imitative experiments carried out by a hafted copy of one of the limestone blades produced wear marks at exactly the same places on the blade as on the originals. The blades from Hama proved to be the shares of a rope-traction ard, an implement consisting of a spade-like element pulled by traction ropes instead of a wooden beam. Apparently the implement was operated like an ard, pulled continuously forward, while a traction spade would be pressed down and pulled off by repeated movements.[5]

Observations of wear marks may often, therefore, throw light on the character of a tool and its purpose. This can be further illustrated by three wooden implements found by Professor H. Schwabedissen in Satrup Moor, Schleswig, and dated to *c*. 3000 B.C.[6] He interpreted them as spades, but some other archaeologist doubted that they were strong enough for that use. Could they be a type of oar? One of them had its shaft preserved in full length, and when I examined it thoroughly I observed slight concavities into which my fingers fitted exactly when they were placed as on a spade while digging. Those marks were apparently made by means of a burning stick. Curiously enough they were placed rather high up on the shaft, as if the tool had been used for shovelling, not for digging. But the triangular blade which was cut in one piece with the shaft was perforated by two holes which could have been intended for the attachment of traction ropes like those on the Hama implements.

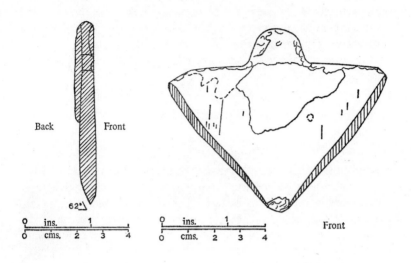

Back   Front

ins.   1
cms.   2   3   4

ins.   1
cms.   2   3   4   Front

62°

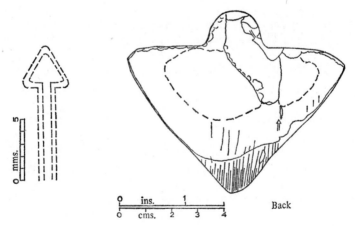

mms.

ins.   1
cms.   2   3   4   Back

Figure 1   Triangular blade, *c.* 2400–1900 B.C.

Unfortunately this spade had *not* been used. Dr J. Troels-Smith observed on the surface of the blade fresh marks from the edge of a flint scraper and no wear marks are to be seen at all. Therefore it is impossible to prove how this spade was operated in detail, and none of the other two spades was perforated, nor had they fully preserved shafts.

Relation of shape and material to environmental conditions

Obviously a certain adaptation to geographical conditions is reflected in the character of tools and implements as well as in other man-made elements of the environment. A threshing sledge is characteristic of dry climates and a flail would be used in temperate zones, for you have to thresh the corn in the barn because of the rainy weather in autumn and snow in winter. The mouldboard plough is unfitted to arid conditions but necessary when a tough, matted sod needs to be turned over. The coulter to cut this sward is therefore characteristic of the plough, not of the ard. The blade of the grass-scythe was developed to its full size in the northern half of the Roman Empire, not in Africa or Asia. The longest scythe blades I have seen are in English museums. But tools also reflect topographical differences. In Scandinavia the wheel plough was not generally accepted north of the plains of Scania. The spade is used in many places where there is not enough space to manœuvre a plough, although the plough is otherwise the implement generally used. The Káfirs in the Hindu-Kush plough with an ard when possible, but near the fairly broad U-shaped valleys suitable for ploughing with an ard are V-shaped valleys with terraced sides. On the small terraces the seed is covered by means of a fork-shaped traction spade; one woman digs the spade into the ground and another pulls it up, this process being repeated until all the seed is covered, after which water is led through the irrigation system among the terraces.[7]

The idea of traction is not directly connected with the shape of the working part of the spade which in fact differs according to practical demands within the distribution zone of the traction spade. This covers a wide area in Asia from Japan and Korea to the Middle East; in neither Europe nor Africa has it been generally accepted.

Therefore I have elsewhere put forward the idea that the ard originated from some kind of traction spade inside Asia, perhaps in widely separated areas and at different points in time.

The working part of a tool will normally be better adapted to the working conditions than its other parts. For example the oar-shaped spades of the Faroe Islands have been developed for turf cutting on raised cultivation beds, and there is also a special spade for cutting heather turf in Jutland, just as the Jutish peat spade has been adapted for cutting blocks out of deep peat bogs. The latter is presumably a descendant of narrow wooden spades with a transverse handle at the upper end of the blade which have been found in great numbers in Jutish peat bogs and some of which are dated to the Iron Age.

Concerning harvesting implements, rice in Indonesia is cut with a special rice-knife instead of a real sickle which would not be useful for this purpose, and in Iran the small sickle is used in parts of the field where the bigger one—the *mangal*—could not be swung. Alexander Fenton has mentioned that questions of demography may sometimes influence the manner in which hand tools are used or adapted:[8]

In Scotland the scythe with a Y-shaped handle first came into extensive service as a tool for cutting grain crops (as opposed to hay) in the north east. This was an area of small family-sized farms, where the surplus population had been drained off by emigration to other lands or into the industrial towns and villages. Reapers were scarce at harvest time and the scythe began to replace the sickle, since it could do more work with reduced manpower. At the same time, since the scythe is primarily a man's tool, this marked a stage in the specialisation of farm labour as a male prerogative. On the other hand, in more advanced farming areas like the Lothians, where local labour was more plentiful and where there was an annual influx of cheap seasonal labour from Ireland, the sickle remained in use until well into the second half of the nineteenth century, being replaced eventually by the reaper rather than the scythe. The retention of the more primitive tool in such areas is obviously not an indication of a more primitive economy.

In Denmark there is a connection between the introduction of the balanced sickle and of winter rye about A.D. 1200, and there is a clear causal link between the simple, round handle and the balanced sickle just as there is between the elaborate grip of the angular sickle and its unbalanced shape.[9]

The study of the adaptation of tools to environmental conditions is one approach amongst several, and it is always attractive to show how balanced it can be. Sometimes good explanations can be given of archaeological finds in that way, but one must guard against exaggerations. Cultural intermingling is complicated, and a simple explanation may rarely be true.

Typology and classification

Ancient tools tell much about man's occupance of his various habitats, and recent tools are among the most characteristic of his cultural traits. Therefore it is important how we record them.

Since the early nineteenth century scholars have been arranging tools such as the plough in an evolutionary sequence. In 1815 Mongez advanced the idea that the plough had been developed from the hoe,[10] and in 1845 K. H. Rau showed how this could have happened.[11] As late as 1919 Franz Nopcsa attempted a development scheme based on modifications of two original types: the staff-plough and the crooked plough.[12] However, he had elaborated his system without taking the work of the tools into consideration. A plough cannot be treated scientifically in the same way as a number of heads of Roman emperors in art history. The plough has a practical purpose which may have influenced its form. Therefore the form alone cannot be the only criterion of classification. On the other hand life is full of inexplicable matters, and formal considerations will be just as relevant as genetic and functional ones.

A simple description of a tool including measurements, drawings, and photographs of it should always be the starting point for an investigation. The drawing of complicated implements may be difficult but should nevertheless be undertaken for the most characteristic examples, since it is impossible to photograph all the parts without hiding some or distorting others. Moreover, a drawing will in nearly all cases reproduce more clearly in print than a photograph. When in the late 1930s I published some articles on

Danish ploughs I drew a number of them both in elevation and in plan[13]—they often occur in books and papers on the subject—and this method proved to be acceptable, but unfortunately other scholars have done little work of the same kind. In reality each implement should be drawn from both sides and in section, as was done in the paper on the Hama implements mentioned above. When I was drawing one of these basalt blades I observed, in the photograph I was working from, a very small and almost invisible figure which had hitherto escaped attention. It proved to be an incised spade-like symbol of 'The God with the Mace'.[14] Such details may in most cases continue undiscovered if the publisher of the tools has not been encouraged to explore its smallest details by the act of drawing. The exactness of drawings should generally be related to the size of the implement and the scale of its measurement. A bad drawing may be better than nothing, but an exact drawing demands much time and often complicated equipment. Moreover, a minute description of wear marks will in many cases be impossible without the aid of a microscope. All this sounds troublesome, but it is always better to build upon a small number of well-elucidated and fully examined objects than to draw wide-ranging conclusions from copious but badly treated material. A conclusion is never better than its premise, even if it may be a result of logical and highly theoretical deliberations.

In former times students of the genetic aspect have often presupposed that the least complicated and simplest tools were the most primitive—those which stood nearest the original types. This is a false generalization. Numerous examples could be given of misunderstandings of this kind. Recently Alexander Fenton produced evidence to suggest that the famous Scottish *caschrom*, or foot-plough, was presumably developed in connection with the introduction of the potato culture.[15] This is a purely functional proof; it should be mentioned that in China a 'spade-plough' (Le-si) has been used by farmers in the same way in order to turn the soil, though not in combination with the cultivation of potatoes.[16] Jaroslav Kramařík of Praha has shown that some primitive-looking agricultural implements from Czechoslovakia are of recent origin, for example the *Hakenpflug* of northern Bohemia, while the more complicated ploughs of middle and south Bohemia are more ancient.[17]

F

However, a functional explanation is relevant in many cases. For example, the *socha* with two mouldboards is characteristic of the transition area between the wooded country in the north of Poland and the steppe in the south.[18] In Denmark two types of wheelbarrow for manure were formerly in use. The one in the eastern part of the country was shaped like a normal wheelbarrow with two legs, but the body frame was surrounded by vertical boards (Fig. 2). In

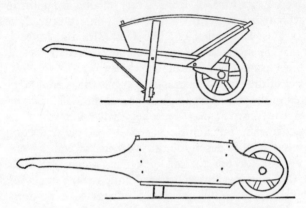

Figure 2   Danish wheelbarrows: above, east Denmark; below, western Jutland

the western part of Jutland the manure-barrow was low and heavy, the side planks of the body frame were continued and tapered to form the handles, and instead of legs it had a cross-bar beneath the body which acted as a fulcrum for swinging up the wheel and front of the barrow by pressing down the handles. With this balanced barrow one could raise the wheel back to the trundle board in the midden when it had slipped off. The explanation of this type of barrow may be that from the eighteenth century at least it was the custom in the Jutland heath region to augment the manure with heather turf. As the dunghills grew very large and high, the cattleman had to carry the manure far in his barrow, and there was increased likelihood that the barrow might slip off the trundle board.

However, adaptation is rarely complete. Most problems cannot be explained by functional aspects alone, and a great many should be attacked by other methods.

At the second conference for research on ploughing implements, in Sweden in 1966, Professor B. Bratanić stated that linguists may make valuable contributions to understanding implements and their constituent parts.[19]

> If we follow the spatial distribution of such terms, we are doing no specific linguistic work—every ethnologist can handle them just like any other ethnological element. In such a way Haudricourt[20] could show that the Indo-European term *yoke* is found in a number of quite different Asian languages (Caucasian, Turkish) in an uninterrupted range as far as to the Chinese. Similarly, the word *hames* (for horse harness) is known in English as well as in German, in all Slavonic languages, to Turkish, to Mongolian, to Tunguz. . . . The local interpretation of such phenomena is often quite misleading, especially if attempts are made to explain distributional or historical facts by purely functional causes. . . . A proper typology is indispensable . . . [but] for what purpose? We could well make functional typologies for various practical purposes, or we could attempt . . . to establish a historical (genetic) one which is something quite different and very difficult to produce. Both kinds are explicative. But it is a heuristic typology that we need now and by which we may gain new knowledge. In such typology, quite secondary, and from an agrotechnical point of view, quite useless qualities of a ploughing implement can be most important because they tell us about historical happenings.

Bratanić has developed a classification of ploughing implements from the basic forms of the construction of the frame (combinations of particular formal qualities or syndromes of constructional qualities) based on a formal, or heuristic, typology. He has worked for many years on his objective typology which will be published in *Tools and Tillage*.[21] František Šach published another classification system in 1966 based on a combination of function and form,[22] and this has appeared in a slightly revised form in *Tools and Tillage*. However, a problem arises in connection with such formal classifications of tools. It may not be possible to produce an exact system of description which will apply to all tools. A formal typology would have to be more than an arbitrary classification of curves, but would have to be based on exact measurement defined by a system of co-ordinates.

Many years ago when I had to describe a great number of crescentic flint sickles, I reasoned that the important part of the tool was the cutting edge, an obvious starting point.[23] I classified these as symmetrical or asymmetrical, straight or concave, and I further divided them according to the radius of their curve (1–10 cm., 21–30 cm., and 31–40 cm.). However, the curve radius is not a very satisfactory measure, especially for asymmetrical sickles, and as the edge determined the functioning, a finer classification should be based on the measurement of the edge. This description should include the length of the edge (convex and straight), and so I had to find a unit applicable to both symmetrical and asymmetrical types. The edge of a symmetrical sickle describes the segment of a circle, but the projected edge of an asymmetrical sickle is a straight line. I therefore drew a template, one side of which consisted of concentric arcs, the other of straight lines which were projections of the arcs. All the flint sickles fitted well into this template at some point unique to individual sickles. A common unit of measurement for the curve and the straight line was devised. This was a tenth of the radius of the curve. By this measure two sickle edges of the same drape receive in the same descriptive formula the same numerical value regardless of the curve radius and the length. For the asymmetrical sickle the formula is $(a+b)r = x$, where a is the straight part measured in units of curve radius, b is its curved part measured in the same way, and r is the curve radius measured in centimetres. The formula for the symmetrical sickle is $b \times r = x$. The edges can now be placed in a two co-ordinate system and classified (Fig. 3). Applying this method of classification it could be demonstrated that the most curved sickles were concentrated in North Jutland in Denmark and Bohūlan in Sweden, where agriculture must have reached a developed stage already in the late Neolithic. Sickle edges were also more asymmetrical in these areas than in Upper Scandinavia.[24] In my opinion this attempt to combine an exact description with a functional idea shows that relevant information can be drawn from such a classification system. Furthermore it illustrates how a heuristic, or formal, typology may be arrived at in a mathematical sense, and possibly it will be neces-

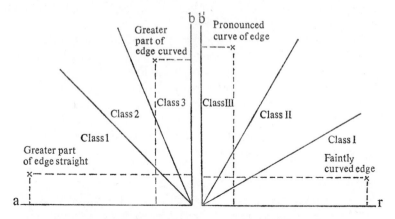

Figure 3   Co-ordinates for classifying the curve of sickles

sary also to classify ploughing implements by the aid of mathematical formulae in the future instead of inexact descriptions of curves.[25] But until now many scholars have been in the habit of combining functional and formal aspects when they classify groups of tools, as in Fritz L. Kramer's book on hoes and digging-sticks.[26]

The dating of tools

The dates of tools were rarely carved or painted on the wooden parts or inscribed on the iron mountings until the last 200 or 300 years. Craftsmen's tools, especially, will be dated in such a way in this period. Another means of determining the date is from printed sources. In books on husbandry, often with illustrations of the familiar agricultural implements, one may find when new types are introduced, and early newspapers and periodicals often published new ideas and inventions. Also ancient factory catalogues and price lists may provide useful information. Another important source of information is notation in old registers and manuscripts of different kinds. A well-known example is Theophilus' work on the various arts in the third book of which he describes a number of tools, from hammers, files and rasps to polishing-stones and a gold-smith's outfit.[27] Even more famous are the classical Roman authors' works, Chinese and Japanese works of a similar kind and the early printed books of Europe.

However, in most cases dating must be by other means. Linguistic datings are especially important. Often phonetic changes can be fixed within a century, and in countries like Finland and in the Slavonic and German border regions of Europe, it is possible to fix the date of adoption of a great many foreign terms, including some concerning tools and implements. For example, Professor Kustaa Vilkuna of Helsinki has written a number of papers in which he uses linguistic datings for sickles, ploughing implements, etc., with impressive scholarship.[28]

Of course the weakness of this method is that there may in some cases be uncertainty as to what a particular term really covers. It must be remembered how many variations terms of the same class could have—one has only to look at terms like *molendinum* in the new international dictionary of medieval Latin—and that normally very few of these senses have survived till modern times. Also the same term may sometimes cover different tools, such as the word *marr*, which in central Iraq is a shovel, but in Djeble on the Syrian coast is a spade with a tread bar; whereas such a spade in central Iraq is called *misha*, of the same derivative as Syrian *mishiyya*, which means a traction spade. *Marr* is a derivative of Sumerian *marru*, and cognate to Egyptian *m-r*, a hoe, and Roman *marra*, which Columella describes as a toothed implement, a kind of hoe.[29] From this example it appears that one can only be sure of the kind of tool mentioned in ancient manuscripts if this or that local term is accompanied by a short explanation in a standard language like Latin.

Archaeological datings may often be unreliable, and pollen analysis has proved to be not good enough to stand alone. When in the 1930s Professor Knud Jessen dated the Tømmerby Plough from Jutland to *c.* 400 B.C. most archaeologists believed in this method, but very soon the palynologists themselves found that local conditions had influenced the development of vegetation and so robbed the method of its authenticity. However, the pollen method gives good information when connected with the Carbon-14 method, and a number of prehistoric and medieval ploughs ranging in age from the early Bronze Age to *c.* A.D. 1500 have been dated by the Carbon-14 method in the last few years in Denmark and Germany.[30]

Man and his tools

An armchair philosopher who has hardly been familiar with tools other than a razor, scissors and a knife will never learn how intimate the relations are between a craftsman and his tools. A tool must be well balanced and perfectly fitted to the person who is to use it. Therefore, a butcher will make his choice of a knife at the ironmonger's shop only after he has thoroughly examined and tested it for weight and balance. In former times joiners and carpenters often made the wooden parts of their tools, and the blacksmith could produce them entirely with his own hands. Farmers were clever in some countries and could renew or repair their own implements. Of course every person had his own tools, which were never lent to others; they could be treated in a wrong way and damaged. Young persons were at first equipped with tools that were either quite new and not adjusted or with old ones that had been set aside. In the hay harvest it could be very exhausting for a young man to keep up with the trained mowers until he learned to adjust his scythe in the right way and keep the edge sharp. Grinding and polishing edge-tools has always been an initiate stage of learning by the exponents of ancient crafts.

It is obvious that men and women, adults and children did not always use the same kind of tools, nor did they use the same tool in the same manner. It may be well known that women handled a threshing flail in a different way from men. Often children were furnished with their own tools as a sort of toy. I have seen boys not yet started school handling their own small flails alongside their elder brothers, and also scythes were sometimes produced for children. In Iran, as mentioned above, I saw adult men harvesting with large sickles (*mangal*) where there was space enough for them, while in the same field women and old men were cutting grain with small sickles of another shape. They could not handle the heavy *mangal* and therefore they had to cut the stalks that were left between thorny bushes and in other irregular places. In museums we often find tools from the same area broadly intended for the same work but of different shapes, with no explanation. Every tool will bear the owner's imprint in one way or another. Young girls may have their rake or their wooden milk-pail carved in a special way. Every man recognizes his hoe or his fork among numerous others, maybe by apparently unimportant details, which on closer examination prove to be significant. Nobody knows an implement until he has handled it for some days, and even then he may not become accustomed to the balance if different from his own. That is also an important reason why new inventions are accepted with reluctance.

When the complicated and heavy old wheel-plough in the early nineteenth century was challenged by the lighter and simpler swing plough the peasants were suspicious because the new implement seemed to be very unstable. The wheel plough forced its way without much care from the driver. If he wanted it to make a broader furrow he only pressed against the landside, and if he wished to deepen the furrow a little he pressed down on the plough-handle. The swing plough behaved in just the opposite way: if he pressed down on its handles the share jumped out of the soil and did not make a furrow, and if he pressed against the landside the plough went into the previous furrow and no soil was turned over. The most irritating feature was its irregular motion to which he and his boys at first had difficulty in adjusting.

Peasants have been accused of conservatism, but the main reason was an unwillingness to learn new movements and adjust their muscles to new tools. A farmer in one district of Norway, I was told, had hired a new boy. One day when they started to scatter manure in a field the boy came with a modern dungfork made of iron whilst the farmer himself brought a wooden fork which was the normal type in this area. At first he threatened his boy and asked him not to use such a modern invention here, but on his way home he observed over his shoulder that the boy continued to work with his steel fork. The farmer was offended, but when he found that the new tool worked much more quickly he changed his mind, went out to the boy and said that he wished to be the first in this neighbourhood to introduce the steel fork.

Very few special investigations have been made on the connection between man and his tools, but in the 1950s two scholars, Edit Fél and Tamás Hofer, studied a large Hungarian village, Atány in komitat Heves. They registered thoroughly the working tools and their uses in all respects in a lengthy manuscript. This important investigation will be published in a slightly shortened form by co-operation between the Hungarian and the Royal Danish

Academies. It is to be hoped that such studies on man and tools will be continued in other countries before ancient traditions have been extinguished.

Notes

1. F. C. J. Spurrell, 'Notes on Early Sickles', *Archaeological Journal*, 49 (1892), 53 Hdl.; 'A. Steensberg, *Ancient Harvesting Implements*, Copenhagen, 1943, 2 f. and 128.

2. A. Steensberg, 'North West European plough-types of prehistoric time and the Middle Ages', *Acta Archaeologica* 7 (1937), 258.

3. P. V. Glob, *Ard og Plov i Nordens Oltid*, Aarhus, 1951, 62 ff.

4. B. A. Šramko, 'Drevnij derevjanyi plug iz sergeevskogde torfanika', *Sovetskaja Archeologija* 4 (1964), 84 ff.

5. A. Steensberg, 'A Bronze Age ard type from Hama', *Berytus* 15 (1964), 111 ff.

6. H. Schwabedissen, 'Die Ausgrabungen im Satruper Moor', *Offa* 16 (1957–8), 5 ff., Fig. 8.

7. A. Scheibe, 'Die Landbauverhältnisse in Nuristan', *Deutsche im Hindukusch*, Berlin, 1937, 104 ff. and 119 ff.; cf. G. S. Robertson, *The Káfirs of the Hindu-Kush*, London, 1896, 548: A. Gailey and A. Fenton (eds), 'The spade in northern and Atlantic Europe', *Belfast 1970*, p. 207, Fig. 6.

8. A. Fenton, 'Material culture as an aid to local history studies in Scotland', *J. of the Folklore Inst.* 2, iii (1965), p. 334.

9. A. Steensberg, *Ancient Harvesting Implements*, 209.

10. Mongez, 'Mémoire sur les instruments d'agriculture des anciens. Premier mémoire: sur les charrues', *Mémoires de l'institut royal de France, classe d'histoire et de littérature ancienne*, Paris, 1815, 2, 616 ff.

11. K. H. Rau, *Geschichte des Pfluges*, Heidelberg, 1845.

12. F. Nopcsa, 'Zur Genese der primitiven Pflugtypen', *Zeitschrift für Ethnologie* (1919), 234 ff.

13. A. Steensberg, 'Trilleploven', *Sprog og Kultur* 5 (1936–7), 1 ff.; *idem*, 'Den nordvestjyske Hjulplov', *Sprog og Kultur* 7 (1938), 113 ff.; *idem*, 'En Muldfjaelsplov fra førromersk Jeralder', *Aar bøger for nordisk Oldkyndighed og Historie* (1936), 130 ff.; *idem*, 'North West European ploughtypes of prehistoric time and the Middle Ages', *loc. cit.*

14. A. Steensberg, 'A Bronze Age ard type from Hama', 120 ff.

15. A. Fenton, 'Early and traditional cultivating implements in Scotland', *Proc. Soc. Antiq. Scotland* 96 (1962–3), 315.

16. H. Kothe, 'Völkerkundliches zur der neolithischen Anbauformen', *Ethnographisch-Archäologische Forschungen* 1 (1953), 58; *idem*, 'Das Hirsemesser im Furchenstockbau', *Opuscula Ethnologica Memoriae Luduvici Bíró Sacra* (1959), 338.

17. J. Kramaʼík, 'Některé otázky studia ʼeskych oradel', *Československá Ethnografie* 6 (1958), 113 ff.

18. E. Frankowski, *Sochy, Radla, Płużyce i Plugi w Polsce*, Poznan, 1929, 12.

19. B. Bratanić, *Newsletter no. 18 from the International Secretariat for research on the history of ploughing implements*, Copenhagen, 1967, 6 f.

20. A. G. Haudricourt and M. Jean-Brunhes Delamarle, *L'Homme et la charrue*, Paris, 1955, 164 ff.

21. Cf. B. Bratanić [a paper will presumably be printed in *Tools and Tillage* (1971)]; cf. *idem*, 'Plug i ralo', *Slovenski Etnograf* 5 (1952), 226; *idem*, *Research on Ploughing Implements*, Copenhagen, 1956, 45 ff.; *idem*, 'The One-Sided Plough in Europe', *Laos* 2 (1952), 51 ff.

22. F. Šach, 'Proposal for the classification of pre-industrial implements', *Prameny Historie Zěmědelstvi a Lesnictvi, no. 1, Zěmědelske Muzeum,* Praha, 1966; *idem*, identical title, slightly altered text in *Tools and Tillage* 1, i (1968), 3 ff.

23. A. Steensberg, *Ancient Harvesting Implements, loc. cit.,* 28 ff.

24. *Ibid.*, 139 ff. and plates 4–5.

25. Y. E. Novikov presented an attempt of such a mathematical description in 'la Mécanique l'outils de labourage les conditions écologiques et les traits ethniques spécifiques', to the VII International Congress of Anthropological and Ethnological Sciences in Moscow 1964. But the formulae, which were mimeographed in the French translation, must have been misprinted, because some of them were without meaning.

26. F. L. Kramer, 'Breaking Ground', *Sacramento Anthropol. Soc.* paper 5 (1966).

27. C. R. Dodwell (ed.), *Theophilus de diversis artibus*, London, 1961.

28. K. Vilkuna, 'Zur Geschichte der finnischen Sicheln', *Finska Fornminnesföreningens Tidskrift* 40 (1934); *idem*, 'Die Pfluggeräte Finlands', *Vortrag auf dem II Finnougristenkongress in Helsinki* (1965) [mimeographed].

29. A. Steensberg, 'A Bronze Age ard type from Hama', 136 ff; K. D. White, *Agricultural Implements of the Roman World*, Cambridge, 1967, 40.

30. A list of such datings will be published from time to time in: A. Steensberg, A. Fenton and G. Lerche (eds), *Tools and Tillage* (Copenhagen). The first one has appeared in Vol. I (1968), 56 ff.

5
Society, man and environment

John Mogey

Ever since I went as an undergraduate apprentice with Estyn Evans into the hills and byeways of Ulster, digging in the horned cairns of prehistoric settlers, or looking at the ruins of recently deserted huts and cottages, the problems of the interaction between the physical environment and human society have been with me. I have them still as intellectually unfinished business and in this paper I will try to untangle one of the sociological strands of these puzzles. The argument that the environment controls or directly affects man is, at its simplest, geographical determinism and like all simple causal explanations for human behaviour fails to stand up to testing. Yet the belief that some influences on human affairs come directly from the physical environment is so persistent that the intellectual exploration of these problems remains attractive. Although our society has now acquired tremendous capacities to alter the landscape, some explanation of the impact of the physical environment as a complex variable on social life is important.

Adaptation to environment

Geographers talk of 'man', sociologists of 'human behaviour' and 'society'. Many other disciplines use the term 'human being', in the sense of a creature functioning as a single biological entity in an environment. Some even talk of the 'real' world as distinct from the world of thought and ideas. In this sense the 'real' world in its effect on mankind means, so far as I can judge, the direct, unmediated influence of climate, soil, latitude, germs, etc., on the biological functioning of the individual. So we have studies of the effects of altitude on the oxygen levels of the atmosphere and the consequences of these levels either for the performance of athletes or on the lung capacity of Andean peasants.[1] The correlations so established are statistically meaningful and the results reported are interesting. None the less something important is missing in these equations. They overlook the fact that human behaviour is social and therefore has to be learned. We never react merely as biological pawns buffeted by external forces. All human life is social life. We cannot really talk meaningfully of man and society. Man is society. He is created by his society and in one sense creates the society anew every generation. Continuity and order in societies come about through the overlap of the generations or, in other words, through socialization. By means of language the repetition of accumulated and transmitted knowledge is easier than an entirely new creation of the human social fabric.

Every society has as one aspect of its social matrix its means of adaptation to its environment: these means represent one part of its solution to the problems of survival. They consist of techniques and desired objectives and both are learned. Even the capacity to learn has to be learned. Harlow has shown that Rhesus monkeys given adequate food, shelter, and comforting from a mechanical mother develop biologically but do not develop the capacity to interact sexually or socially with other Rhesus monkeys.[2] Studies of autistic children reveal that biological, sociological and psychological capacities develop in different ways: it is now suspected that most accounts of feral children are really folk tales to explain the appearance of autism in the midst of otherwise normally socialized children.[3] If we wished to study the interaction of biology and environment in a culture-free group, these unfortunates might be the only possible subjects.

The existence of societies as the primary matrix for human living complicates enormously the problems of understanding the adaptive processes. By these I mean the attitudes, values and techniques held by members of a society towards the external world. Societies are variable and rarely stable. They affect each other in complex ways and adapt to the physical or biological world with many distinctively different solutions to common problems.

It is this variability from place to place, coupled with the liability of societies to change, that makes arguments from the environment to man, or human behaviour, so treacherous. It is easy to demonstrate that most specific social changes at the present time are not accompanied by, and therefore not to be explained by, changes in any environmental conditions. Natural disasters, earthquakes, tornadoes, floods, if rare, do not necessarily lead to changes in social life: if they are frequent and expected, the society has adapted to their recurrence and continues without any basic change. Consider two simple biological facts to which all societies have to adapt: (a) that only women bear children, and (b) that only sexual intercourse with a male makes conception possible. The variety of socially approved arrangements for impregnating the females of the world gives us some first idea of the complexities of the social problems of adaptation.[4] In addition, every society knows of several unapproved conditions for achieving pregnancy.

These considerations lead to the basic theme of this essay—that the problems of adaptation are social problems. In consequence, it follows that explanations about variations in adaptive processes and about adaptive innovations—which is an isomorphic statement —are to be looked for in variations of other elements of sociological systems, and not in changes of either ecological or biological systems.[5]

Studies of the acceptance of new seeds, fertilizers, tools and methods of husbandry by rural sociologists illustrate the social nature of innovations. These studies prove over and over again that the acceptance of efficient and profitable new ideas in agriculture is a slow and complex social process.[6] To the rural sociologist, an innovation has been accepted only when a majority of a community practise it without outside encouragement.

The almost universal social rule against incest points to the next step in this argument. Since parent–child and sibling incest are universally taboo, the basic social structural unit of society cannot be the family, any more than it can be the isolated individual.[7] The existence of this taboo means that for continuity beyond one generation a minimum of two families, which exchange children as mates, must exist.[8] Such a unit, existing in a territory and meeting all its problems of survival and continuity, is a community. These statements hold good even though the incest taboo is often broken;

its existence as a universal rule of society means that the community must also exist as a universal social group. The work of Murdock has established this empirically.[9]

The community has as important a role in socialization as in survival, for no family ever completely socializes a child. Simple communities are marked by closed boundaries, although the closure is never so complete that all external influences are excluded. Such communities are endogamous and may appear like extended kinship groups. The existence of work teams, religious practices and educational processes within all communities marks them as functioning units of all societies. To the geographer the community appears as a settlement pattern, and the geographical classification of types of villages and open-country, single-family houses is a body of fact much neglected by sociologists.

The role of community in adaptation

We reach at this point the first proposition in the sociological analysis of adaptation: the community is the structural unit of society through which the adaptive processes work. If this is accepted then we have to abandon the simple deterministic type of statement such as that water is essential to settlement. Rather the reverse is more plausible: a water supply becomes significant only because of settlement. In the Irish countryside I was amazed at the number of farmhouses that had no domestic water supply. One abandoned farmhouse we used as headquarters for a field project on Inishmore, Co. Fermanagh, was more than half a mile from the nearest source of drinking water. This spring was not beside any other house. Considering that any shallow well in Ireland will fill with drinkable water, this fact might be explained by a preference for spring water with a consequent neglect to dig a well for every farmhouse. The point being made here is that adaptive patterns as the dependent variable are explained by the community as the independent variable. The community factor isolated in this example is the meaning or value assigned to spring water.

The variety of meanings that can be assigned to any single adaptive process is great: however, it is presumably not infinitely great. One illustration of such variety comes from studies in New Mexico. Living in the same physical and climatic area, a geographical tableland occupying a corner of the high plateau, are two irrigation agriculture communities, one of Pueblo Indians and one of Mormons, two ranching communities, one Spanish–American and one Navajo Indian, and a specialist dry-zone bean farming group of Texan Presbyterians. That is to say, there are five distinctive communities in a single geographical area. The desires of the members of these communities, their ways of co-operating to reach their desired objectives, the obligations they feel towards their spouses, children and kinsmen, their religious beliefs, and their technology all differ.[10] A second illustration from the Old World is afforded by Israel. Over the past 40 years there has been a substitution of Israeli Jews for Arab Palestinians; here we have two different communities living side by side in the same environment.

These community differences are so striking that we could say, justifiably, that members of each community looked at, and therefore lived in, different physical environments. All the physical and ecological variables, the climate and the territory, are similar for all five communities in New Mexico and the two in Israel. From the viewpoint of the inhabitants, each community behaves differently in the face of the environment. Perhaps we could say that the society creates the environment as a system of meanings in the same way as it may be said to create the individual. At this point, however, we seem to have substituted a sociological determinism for the earlier geographical determinism. The parallel is more apparent than actual. The earlier argument was that variables in the physical environment affected human behaviour directly. The present argument is that the definition of desires and the availability of techniques determine what effect the physical environment can have on community. Both of these arguments are over simple. We must look more closely both at the structural elements and social processes of the community, and also at the environment as a matrix of possibilities, given certain levels of technology.

Major environmental areas

Taking the environment first, some areas of the world are evidently more suited to human life than others. Geographers have for a long time recognized natural ecological regions of the world such as 'areas of increase', where a small effort will bring a lot of return in subsistence, or 'areas of difficulty', where great effort is needed to reach a bare subsistence level. A recent attempt at a more precise classification recognizes four environmental types:

Type 1 Areas of no agricultural potential including tundra, desert, tropical savanna, swamps and mountain ranges.

Type 2 Areas of limited agricultural potential such as the tropical forest of South America.

Type 3 Areas of improvable agricultural potential including temperate forest lands of Europe and the U.S.A. as well as irrigation areas like parts of California, Iran, Iraq, or Utah.

Type 4 Areas of unlimited agricultural potential where climate, soil, terrain and fertility are for all practical purposes inexhaustible. These areas include the seats of all Old World and New World civilizations.

The recognition of agriculture as a cultural technique in the development of communities and societies is implicit in this classification.[11] It is the response of the environment to the adoption of a new way of living by the community that is important.

This is but one aspect of adaptation. The appearance of agriculture is not more crucial than the emergence of groups of full-time craft specialists, the urban revolution, or the rise of complex local societies in the emergence of civilizations. Consequently to associate in a direct fashion the agricultural responsiveness of the environment and the rise of a complex civilization is to overlook a major sociological fact: that adaptation is not a simple stimulus–response process but exists as a complex of causes and a complex of consequences.

Earlier we mentioned the small intermarrying community as one polar type of human settlement: one form of this is often called a 'closed corporate peasant community'.[12] These communities have very clear boundaries but are never closed in any absolute sense. Even the pre-Neolithic fishers of Ireland imported some goods: in the next archaeological period Irish Neolithic tombs already show objects of jade from Brittany, amber from the Baltic and glass from Portugal or the Mediterranean. In spite of this, we may assume that ideas and techniques were accepted slowly. Modern examples of

closed corporate peasant communities abound as villages of subsistence farmers in all continents. One important sociological
characteristic of these communities is the lack of a leadership
structure. Although reports of village headmen are common, most
groups resemble the Skara Brae prehistoric community where every
hut was the same size and had the same equipment, showing a
minimal degree of status differentiation. Each had only one fireplace: this was interpreted to mean a single family or at any rate
one wife per hut.[13] Rights in lands were often redistributed at
intervals, in the manner of the infield–outfield economy of the
proto-historic Scots and Irish clachan settlements, so that families
had equal shares. A study of a modern Tennessee corporate community showed that this redistribution was managed by an outside
auctioneer who apparently reached decisions through a formal public
bidding, but in reality all decisions were in accordance with prior
discussions with the community.[14] There is a parallel here to the
classification of farms in Northern Ireland as either Protestant or
Catholic when they are put up for auction. Such corporate groups
are often communities of equals, where every adult member takes
responsibility for the affairs of the community. The Amish of the
United States are a typical example of such a group.[15] In such
communities the goal of equality of life chances has been reached:
fraternity, too, is an ideal characteristic, thanks to inter-marriage.
The preferred marriage partners in Tennessee in 1965 were double
first cousins. If within the community all are of equal status, this
can only be maintained from generation to generation by some
mechanism such as the redistribution of basic resources, and by
strict attention to boundary maintenance to keep traditional ways
strong and the strangers who carry new ideas, such as achievement
or individual betterment, out. Dozens of examples from India to
Ireland are available to illustrate this ideal system of adaptation.
The community adapts by applying its traditional skills to its own
environment and by distributing the resources produced by these
skills to maintain its own status system.

If the community is the group that controls the adaptive processes
in any society, then it follows that different community types will
follow differing adaptive processes. This means that there may be
no one explanatory theory in a strict sense that can cover all the
varieties of adaptation. In this essay the adaptive processes are

G

considered one part of solutions to complex problems of community survival. Survival, however, is a wider concept than simply the adaptation of a community to its environment. It encompasses internal processes of change as well as the relationship of one community to other external social systems which are part of its environments.

Types of Communities

No adequate typology of communities exists for our purpose. Most classify communities by the state of technology into: (a) simple hunters, fishers or gatherers, (b) horticultural, using the hoe, (c) agricultural, using the plough, (d) mercantile, and (e) industrial. Many variants on this scheme exist.[16] The levels of technology represent the major innovations of human societies as they seek to provide resources such as food, shelter and safety for their members. The innovations of domesticated animals, crop husbandry, urban settlement and industrial organization are the adaptations that are to be explained by any theory of adaptation. But if our arguments are correct, for the study of adaptation the classification criteria must include not only techniques but also community values. Therefore an alternative classification of communities based on their value systems must now be constructed. Two complex variables may be used: first, the pattern of status in the community which may be either 'egalitarian' or 'hierarchical'; second, the way by which status is acquired which may be either by birth or caste ('ascriptive') or by merit or performance ('achievement'). The first unit of a classificatory scheme drawn up on this basis has been introduced as the closed corporate community. The value system of such a community is 'ascriptive egalitarianism'. Using the structural variables of ascription and achievement together with egalitarianism or its opposite—status differentiation or a hierarchy of social ranks —we can arrive at the following typology:

TABLE I

Value system	Ideal community type	Example
Ascriptive equalitarian	closed corporate	Tennessee
Ascriptive hierarchy	feudal	Japan
Achievement equalitarian	utopian	Israeli kibbutz
Achievement hierarchy	modern industrial	U.S.A.

Explanations for the appearance of major new innovations in any community have been advanced by many theorists. The diffusion theory placed all major social, technological, religious and political innovations in one regional area and explained their appearance elsewhere by export procedures. This was hardly satisfactory.[17] An alternative explanation is the environmental challenge and response theory: there appears to be better grounds for this theory, since it allows for multiple centres of innovation.[18] Moreover, the desire to reach new goals, or to use new techniques to reach existing goals, is not adequately accounted for by environmental challenges. Another widely accepted theory of innovations is that they are the contribution of Great Men, uniquely gifted individuals. Adaptive innovations represent major changes in both goals (values) and techniques. While Great Men have made their contribution at intervals, the fact of change is constant, though its rate may vary.[19] Lacking any good, well-tested hypotheses, the assumption that innovations are always present and that many small innovations may on occasion be combined into a major adaptive change seems justified as a quantitative approach to the problem.[20]

Recent work in comparative culture gives, through the analysis of newly collected data, some common value configurations or patterns. Most of these reports use the nation or some combination of nations as a spatial aspect of the analysis. One study of 2,500 cultural measures of sixteen California Indian tribal groups finds two distinct patterns: (a) a 'wealth oriented, competitive, individualistic, sedentary' one, characteristic of ten of the tribes and (b) a 'more co-operative, outgoing, nomadic' one, characteristic of six of the tribes.[21]

Studies based upon data from the responses of samples of population in modern nation states are more difficult to interpret, partly because of sampling problems, partly because of methodological differences, and partly because of the variety of instruments used. Some use multivariate analysis, some simpler correlation techniques, and, while some report empirical factors arising out of clusters of responses in the data, others assume *a priori* clusters of values and therefore can only report simple frequencies. However, all find common or invariant values to report. Amongst the values two seem to have common aspects that are relevant to the theme of adaptation. These are variously phrased as A(I) vigorous order versus unadapted rigidity; A(II) act and enjoy life through group participation; B(I) cultural pressure and complexity versus direct expression of energy; B(II) constantly master changing situations.[22]

These research efforts, yielding empirical values as illustrated above and testing *a priori* normative values as in the New Mexico research, are building a body of knowledge that can in the future enrich the potentiality of the theory of adaptation. The classification of communities mentioned earlier used two complex variables as if they were dichotomous: in reality, each is, in all probability, multidimensional. The basic attitude of each of these community types towards the twin elements that affect the adaptive process, values and techniques can also be treated as if they were dichotomous: they may resist innovations (−) or they may accept them (+). Using this approach, we get the table below:

TABLE 2

| Community type | Changes in | |
	Values	Techniques
Ascriptive equalitarian	−	−
Ascriptive hierarchy	−	+
Achievement equalitarian	+	−
Achievement hierarchy	+	+

The Ascriptive Equalitarian community is small in size, traditional in culture, closed as to marriage, and almost always archaic in its technology. Ascriptive hierarchies, the community base of feudal empires, while traditional in their value system, are still innovative in their approach to technology. This is a structural consequence of the existence of a hierarchy that includes an *élite*. Even under ascriptive rules, any *élite* position is not secure: these types of upper status positions require the use of power to maintain their claim to the majority of the surplus produced by the community. Even though the holders of these positions use religious leaders to support their privileged position, the continuity of *élites* over several generations is always problematical.[23] The exercise of power requires constant watchfulness coupled with eagerness to adopt new techniques such as cross-bow, armour, gunpowder or fortifications to maintain a superior position.

Communities based both on equalitarian access to the resources they produce and achievement are so rare in the natural history of communities we may simply note that they run the continuous risk of becoming ascriptive equalitarian communities after the founding generation has died. This process may explain in part the failure of many utopian communities, though not all utopian communities aim at equality.

Achievement hierarchies represent a major social innovation—the bureaucratic organization. Bureaucracies are hierarchies of specialist roles directed specifically at problem solving as their normal task. A bureaucracy, therefore, by its structure and recruitment, is an instrument of innovation. It functions to solve problems of adaptation.

In this sense, the bureaucracy is almost as old as human civilization. The organization of specialists into a single social structure goes back to the first urban centres: early priest-kings operated through this form of social organization. Although the recruitment pattern may not have been based on tests for merit, early documents show the controls that were placed on officials to be efficient, timely and industrious.

There is no explicit or implicit order to the statement of these types of communities: no evolutionary sequence or stages of development are intended. If there is any quantitative change through time, it refers only to the rate of increase in the search for, and acceptance of, adaptive innovations. Neither is the typology complete, for bureaucratically organized achievement hierarchies have their own internal rigidities which can lead to ritual performance rather than creative problem solving.

Some of the theoretical ideas in this paper may be tested later with data taken from the Ethnographic Atlas. The lack of data from two points in time that relate to a variety of community types makes possible only a rough test. As data banks about the contemporary world are established, more extensive tests can be carried out.[24] One small-scale field test is reported for the Philippines. In it the degree of receptivity to community development innovations was sought to be explained. Out of twenty-three variables that had some relationship to receptivity of innovations, three are more important than others: (a) highest grade (of education) completed; (b) preference for democratic-type leadership in job tasks; (c) rating of house and grounds for good order. Both (a) education and (b) leadership seem from the text to refer directly to achievement values and hierarchal position based on capacity or performance rather than inheritance. The third probably refers to family co-operation between husband and wife. Other variables such as 'size of farm' and 'size of largest field' are statistically less strong and are weaker than 'clique popularity' and 'having held a local office'. Within the small-scale local peasant community this report shows that achievement and acceptance by peers are both strongly related to the acceptance of innovations.[25]

To take the analysis further the interrelations between other orders of values than those appropriate to status would have to be examined. The goals of the community or the society in the areas of political, religious, economic and familial values would have to be added to the simplified matrix presented in this essay. That task is much beyond its scope. In it we have argued that the existence of leaders as a consequence of a status hierarchy is not, by itself, enough to account for either the emergence or acceptance of adaptive innovations. Consequently the Great Man theory of social change does not explain the acceptance of adaptive innovations. The environment as a static and relatively unchanging element to which community social systems have to adapt if they are to survive cannot in itself account for the fact of change. Change is a universal social fact: adaptation to the environment is one element of social change. In explaining the process of innovation and acceptance of adaptive changes, this paper has looked at two structural elements of community social systems: (a) the patterned arrangement of the roles they provide in family, work team, religious group and political system; and (b) the value system that underlies the community rules whereby individuals may legitimately occupy these roles.

The basic propositions advanced in this essay are:

1. The community is the unit of social structure through which environments affect human behaviour. This process is called adaption or adaptation.
2. Any adaptive innovation requires modification both of the value system and also of the techniques of the community if it is to be acceptable.

3. In equalitarian communities rates for the appearance of adaptive innovations will be low.

4. The mere presence of a status system which supports a set of leaders does not guarantee the ready acceptance of innovations.

5. Adaptive innovations are frequent and acceptable in communities with bureaucratic organizations because they have values based on achievement and a status hierarchy that demands performance.

6. Bureaucratic organizational systems have their own internal rigidities which may impede their performance in the process of adaptation. More work on the interrelations of value systems and techniques in political, religious and family systems is clearly essential.

This essay claims only to be an exploration of one sociological strand in the study of adaptation: it is offered in the hope that others may consider it a constructive beginning, worthy of being extended and tested with appropriate data.

Notes

1. C. Monge, 'Biological basis of human behaviour', in A. L. Kroeber (ed.), *Anthropology Today*, Chicago, 1953.

2. H. F. Harlow, 'The nature of love', *American Psych.* 13 (1958), 673–85.

3. B. Bettelheim, 'Feral children and autistic children', *American J. Sociol.* 64 (1959), 455–67.
   W. F. Ogburn, 'The wolf boy of Agra', *American J. Sociol.* 64 (1959), 449–54.

4. M. Levy *et al.*, *Aspects of the Analysis of Family Structure*, Princeton, 1965. Marriage rules in different societies approve child marriage, grandparent–grandchild marriage, monogamy, polygyny, polyandry, the existence of wives and mistresses, concubinage, cicisbeism and so on. Levy points out that in spite of the extreme variety of these rules actual behaviour in marriage is much less variable.

5. An early statement of this purposive and sociological approach is given by the concept of 'telesis' in L. F. Ward, *Pure Sociology*, New York, 1903, 457–576.

6. E. A. Wilkening, 'Joint decision making in farm families as a function of status and role', *American Sociol. Rev.* 23 (1958), 187–92; E. M. Rogers, *Social Change in Rural Society*, New York, 1960.

7. R. Middleton, 'Brother–sister and father–daughter incest in ancient

Egypt', *American Sociol. Rev.* 27 (1962), 602–11; gives an opposite point of view.

8. T. Parsons, 'The incest taboo in relation to social structure and the socialization of the child', *British J. Sociol.* 5 (1954), 101–17.

9. G. P. Murdock, 'Statistical relations among community characteristics' in P. F. Lazarsfeld and M. Rosenberg (eds), *The Language of Social Research*, Chicago, 1955, 305–11.

10. F. R. Kluckholn and F. L. Strodtbeck, *Variations in Value Orientations*, Evanston, Illinois, 1961.

11. B. J. Meggers, 'Environmental limitations to the development of culture', *American Anthrop.* 56 (1954), 801–24. Quoted from J. B. Bresler (ed.), *Environments of Man*, Boston, 1968.

12. E. Wolf, 'Closed corporate peasant communities', *Southwestern J. Anthrop.* 13 (1957), 1–13.

13. V. G. Childe, *Scotland before the Scots*, London, 1946.

14. E. M. Mathews, *Neighbor and Kin*, Nashville, Tenn., 1965, 14–20.

15. S. A. Freed, 'Suggested type societies in acculturation studies', *American Anthrop.* 59 (1957), 55–68.

16. G. Lenski, *Power and Privilege, a Theory of Social Stratification*, New York, 1966.

17. W. J. Perry, *The Children of the Sun*, New York, 1923.

18. A. J. Toynbee, *A Study of History*, London, 12 vols, 1934–1959.

19. S. Hook, *The Hero in History: a Study in Limitation and Possibility*, Boston, 1955.

20. W. Moore, *Social Change*, New York, 1965.

21. K. F. Schuessler and H. E. Driver, 'Factor analysis of sixteen primitive societies', *American Sociol. Rev.* 21 (1956), 393–9. Quoted from R. M. Marsh, *Comparative Sociology*, New York: Harcourt, Brace & World, 1967, 220–2.

22. R. M. Marsh, *op. cit.*, 221–7.

23. S. Keller, *Beyond the Ruling Class*, New York, 1963.

24. R. B. Textor, *A Cross Cultural Summary*, New Haven, 1967, pp. 208 with 2,000 pp. tables; A. D. Coult and R. Habenstein, *Cross Tabulations of the World Ethnographic Sample*, Columbia, Mo., 1965.

25. F. C. Madigan, 'Predicting receptivity to community development innovations', *Current Anthropology* 3, ii (1962), 207–8.

6
Fields and field systems

Harald Uhlig

Fields and field systems are interrelated but, while the former are morphological features in the landscape, the latter are primarily functional. For example, the shape of fields may be determined by property boundaries, both permanent and temporary; they may also appear as cultivation plots, although these are usually temporary subdivisions of larger units. Field systems, however, are derived from the spatial arrangement of the arable crops, reflecting the prevailing methods of rotation both on common land and on individual holdings, and from the traditional organization of fields favoured by the community.

Over many years, research has revealed much of the regional variety and differing historical evolution of fields and field systems, their complexity being reflected in the terminology developed by many scholars, working in different regions and speaking a variety of national languages. Indeed, variation in the terminology used has increased the difficulties of interpretation and comparison, for certain terms have often been associated with specific hypotheses, or perhaps with certain ethnic or economic criteria. This is unfortunate, particularly in a subject which deals with many variables, for the terms used for individual elements and features must be clearly understood before one can compare, say, the factors involved in the evolution of field systems in different regions.

The need for a clear terminology
In these circumstances it might be useful to discuss possible new

ways of approaching the study of fields and field systems through a clearly defined terminology. The need for this is indicated by the current reappraisal of theories on the evolution of field systems in continental Europe. This concerns especially the *Gewannfluren*, which were once thought to represent the original form of land distribution among early peasant village communities.[1] Their scattered open strips were grouped into furlongs (*Gewanne*), several of which formed areas of common rotation (*Zelgen*) of winter-crops, spring-crops and common harvest, common pasture on fallow and equality of shares according to difference in soils, micro-climate and accessibility.

An entirely different system seemed to be represented in the block-shaped (*Blockfluren*, *Weilerfluren*), associated with hamlets and single farmsteads and developed through medieval forest clearance in the hill regions of south Germany. In western Europe, however, including parts of north-west Germany, similar block-shaped fields and single farmsteads were associated with Meitzen's hypothesis of the Celtic *Einzelhöfe*.[2] This involved ideas which were developed later by H. L. Gray in England,[3] where he con-trasted 'Celtic' with 'Anglo-Saxon' field systems; in France a similar dichotomy arose between *bocage* and *champs ouverts*.[4] It has been shown, of course, that these field systems do not belong exclusively to specific ethnic groups.[5] Indeed, the so-called 'Celtic' field system is better expressed as 'infield–outfield', while the descriptive term *Kammerfluren*, suggested by K. Scharlau and meaning literally 'chambered fields', or the *oltidsagre* of G. Hatt, may be substituted for 'Celtic fields'.[6]

Early research suggested that block fields and loosely grouped hamlets were so closely interrelated in origin and function that the term *Weilerflur* was invented for them. The same happened with re-spect to the large nucleated villages (Haufendörfer), which were thought to be so inseparably connected with fragmented strip-hold-ings, based on a common three-field rotation that the terms *Gewannflur* and *Gewanndorf* became established. But further work has shown con-siderable variation in the history and functional organization of these types, so great indeed that certain terms developed in earlier periods of research should now be discarded because their conceptual associations are outmoded.

For example, recent research has shown that the rotation of three or more common fields (*Zelgen*) was invented only in late medieval times, resulting from the reorganization of many arable areas to meet the demands of a rising population for higher grain production. The *Gewannfluren* also varied considerably in arrangement: for example, some lay parallel, others were laid crosswise; similarly there were variations in width, length, shape, size and degree of regularity.[7] They could also originate in different ways. Some developed from former infield–outfield nuclei through the conversion of the long, block-shaped outfields into additional bundles of strips which resembled the long, open strips of the infield itself (*Langstreifenkernflur, Eschkern*).[8] Elsewhere, former block fields were simply divided into *Gewanne* to form *Block-Gewannfluren*[9] or mixed *Block-Streifenfluren*, while, in parts of central and eastern Germany, medieval colonists favoured extremely regular arrangements of common fields.[10] This was the case in the colonization of the upper Rhine lands by the earlier Frankish state.[11] Yet other origins have emerged through detailed research on early land registers in Hesse and Franconia, where a fairly regular pattern of *Hufen*-like, broad, parallel strips underlay a more fragmented and scattered strip pattern. This showed that many *Gewannfluren* were derived from the subdivision of former *Breitstreifen* (i.e. one or more broad, compact strips of land belonging to a single farm) and others from former block-parcels, following the introduction of common field rotations.[12] Elsewhere, gavelkind inheritance accentuated fragmentation. In summary, it is clear that many evolutionary sequences might be involved in the development of a field pattern that can be called *Gewannfluren* only in very general terms, the various types assuming a similar form mainly through the superimposition of new systems of common field rotations (*Verzelgung*).

Further investigations into the origin of *Langstreifenfluren* have been stimulated by Swedish work which has shown that simple methods of land measurement may be as significant as ploughing techniques in the general process of strip-division; further evidence for late and post-medieval strip-arrangements of fields was discovered for several regions of Europe and the Near East.[13] In Westphalia, for example, it has been shown that *Langstreifenfluren* gradually emerged from the subdivision of very old block-parcels. This stresses the parallels to Scottish run-rig practices,[14] and to Irish rundale, whose study owes much to the pioneer work under-

taken by Estyn Evans and his students in Belfast;[15] P. Flatrès described the enclosure-patterns of the Atlantic fringe, which sometimes preserve former strip-divisions. Even for regions where there
is early evidence of common field systems, it can be shown that these
developed from earlier shifting schemes of cultivation from late
Merovingian times onward. The change to common three-field
systems occurred mainly after the Carolingian era, especially with
the forest clearance of the medieval period.[16]

These examples indicate something of the complexity of field
patterns and field systems on a European scale, regardless of the
variety that can exist within quite small regions or even the fields
of one village, caused by gradual extensions, changes or reorganiza-
tions of property or land use. As research has developed at regional
level, many scholars have become convinced of the need to devise
a new terminology for the subject, unhampered by existing pre-
conceptions. One such framework is discussed in this essay.[17]
Field patterns and systems are examined in their formal aspects,
for this provides uniform data on which valid comparisons can be
made. Genetic and functional associations should be included
through individual descriptions, or may be achieved at a later stage
in the attempts to establish an agreed classification. With these
reservations, all existing field patterns can be defined by a restricted
number of unequivocal criteria, and grouped into an hierarchy which
reflects the different possibilities of the lay-out of the farmland
in any community.

Field patterns

The smallest geographical unit of any field pattern is the parcel
or plot, which usually appears in two basic shapes: the strip or the
block. A '*block*' is a parcel of either regular (if it has at least two
parallel sides) or irregular shape; a ratio of approximately 1:2·5
between width and length distinguishes rectangular blocks from
strips. Furthermore, a distinction can be made between large and
small blocks, depending on the average size within the region under
consideration.

A '*strip*' is an elongated parcel, with more or less parallel sides,
which may be straight or curved. They can be differentiated into
short or long (over 250–300 m.), narrow (less than 30–40 m.) and
wide strips.

The arrangement of parcels is also significant. Those belonging to one farmer may be intermingled with those of his neighbours to form a *pattern of fragmented holdings* (*Gemengelage*), or they may form a *pattern of compact holdings* (*Einödlage*). This term may be used whether or not there is *direct access to the farmstead* (*Hofanschluss*), but the term *Gemengelage* does not apply to isolated patches of cultivated land such as single intakes in moor, forest or common; for these the term is *Streulage*, literally '*scattered plots*'.

In most cases, the total improved land of a community (*Flur*) does not consist simply of a number of undivided, individual parcels. Usually parcels are arranged in smaller units, representing, for example, different periods of land clearance, or derivations from other field systems and methods of land use. The *Gewann* is a typical arrangement of such strip-parcels although, as has been noted, it has been defined and translated in several ways, for example as 'shott' or 'furlong'. To overcome this difficulty it is suggested that the basic grouping of strips or blocks may be termed *Parzellenverbände*, when these *bundles of strips* are of similar shape and arranged side by side; and *Parzellenkomplexe*, when the bundles combine to form topographically recognizable subdivisions of a *Flur*.

Usually several *Parzellenkomplexe* constitute the total improved land of a community, but there are cases in which a *Flur* consists of only one *Parzellenverband*, and in a few extreme examples, only one large parcel. Besides the *Flur*, the total land of a community may include both common grazing and forest, as well as streams and roads, the whole unit being known as *Gemarkung*, literally 'townland'.

In the same way, the categories designated above may be applied to the basic term, *parcel*. Thus one may speak of a '*bundle of strips*' (*Streifenverbände*), the word 'bundle' (*Verband*) meaning a grouping of adjacent, uniform parcels as in a *Gewann*, and a 'complex (of bundles) of strips' (*Streifenkomplex*). Likewise one can refer to a '*bundle of blocks*' and a '*complex of blocks*'. If the total improved land of a community consists of a uniform block pattern, the term *Blockflur* may be used in the original sense; but quite frequently the entire *Flur*, or portions of it, may consist of a mixture of blocks and strips, known in German as *Blockstreifen*, *-verband*, *-komplex* or *-flur*. If shape is distinguished as well as arrangement, then one can include '*a bundle of strips with a pattern of fragmented holdings*' (*Streifengemengeverband*) and '*a bundle of blocks with a pattern of compact holdings*' (*Blockeinödverband*), although the shape of the latter does not really correspond to a bundle.

These terms for the basic features of parcels and their combinations are sufficient to cover almost all existing field patterns; they should enable any particular case to be easily identified and placed in the context of its relevant prototype. Admittedly these categories are based only on formal appearance, but in the study of field patterns this seems to be the only criterion capable of uniform definition and universal application. Other variables such as functional relationships and/or genetic origins cannot be uniformly defined or classified in worldwide standard terms, as similar forms may result from quite different historical processes or develop from contrasting field systems.

The chief advantage of this classification is that any field pattern may be placed in an appropriate, systematic context and recognized by a specific definition. Its shape will be the outcome of certain functional and ecological factors which will affect others of similar shape, though not necessarily in the same way. These may be included in the explanation following the standard definition of ground plan, as may various historical, ethnic or economic situations which may influence form but cannot be included in any uniform scheme.

To illustrate these points one can cite the example of the *Waldhufenflur*, first recognized in the mountains of central Europe where it is associated with late medieval clearances. Similar field patterns have been described subsequently in many other areas, for example the 'ladder farms' first described by Estyn Evans in Ireland;[18] the lay-out of croft settlements in Scotland;[19] the *Marschhufen*, *Hagenhufen* and *Moorhufen* of north-west Germany and the Dutch heathlands, the 'fish-bone' villages of Normandy which may have influenced the settlements of Canada;[20] the *Flusshufen* of the Mississippi delta;[21] the *Huza* of Ghana;[22] and even various settlement schemes in the forests of Latin-America.[23] The first examples were usually labelled *Waldhufen*-like, a description which is correct in certain formal and functional aspects but which covers fields and settlements of quite different historical origin, some linked by diffusion, others apparently only by convergence. In the suggested terminology all of these would be defined as: 'parallel broad strips within a pattern of compact holdings, with direct farmstead access'. Besides a similar formal appearance, this definition would imply many common functions: compact farmsteads and individual choice in land use; rational organization of land and easy access to its constituent parts; and the functional organization of a village community in contrast to the looser links normally associated with scattered, isolated farmsteads. Individual features within this type may be explained by differences in historical background and evolution which may affect the colonization of forest and moorland or concepts of social organization and inheritance.

Field systems

Apart from earlier works such as H. L. Gray's *English Field Systems*, W. Müller-Wille was the first to develop a classification for the study of field systems within the context of north-west Germany.[24] His concepts have been the basis for the following draft which aims at universal application on lines similar to those already suggested for field patterns (Table 1). Strictly speaking, the field systems represent one section of the wider context of *land-use systems* only. Regarding certain transitional phenomena (e.g. the shifting systems, interchanging arable and grassland or moving over forest land, or the combinations with permanent tree-crops (e.g. *cultura mista*), plantation agriculture, etc), it might still be considered whether the term *arable land-use systems* might be more adequate. The entire draft is aimed as a challenge for further discussion, not yet as a final version.

Two main categories of field systems may be distinguished: *shifting systems (Flächenwechselsysteme)* and *permanent arable systems (Dauer(acker)-Systeme)*, both of which may be applied to the total improved land (*Flur*) of a community, or to certain complexes within the field pattern. Not infrequently, land use and field patterns combine both systems, as in the infield–outfield system, so that a third category may be added. Individual units in this category of *combined field systems (Kombinierte Feldsysteme)* may be defined in terms of either of the above systems, but their combination, now or in the past, may become so characteristic as to warrant separate definition.

TABLE I.   *A provisional classification of field systems*

(*arable land-use systems*)

A. Shifting systems

1. Field–forest systems
   (a) tropical shifting cultivation
   (b) non-tropical partial systems
2. Shifting systems on unimproved land
3. Field–grass systems

B. Permanent arable systems

1. Unregulated grain systems
2. Common field systems
3. Unregulated (individual) crop rotations

C. Combined field systems

1. Infield–outfield systems
2. Combined wet and dry field systems
3. Combinations of various seasonal systems

A. SHIFTING SYSTEMS

In this the cultivated parcels are moved after one or more years, returning to the same plot after an intervening period of fallow, unless the site has been completely abandoned. This may be caused, for example, by soil impoverishment or because the secondary vegetation growth is difficult to clear. Other factors of importance are the rhythms of change, the intensity and type of land use, and the role of shifting cultivation in the total land use of the community. For example, distinctions can be made according to whether the system is fully integrated with the economy and culture, is a supplement to permanent cultivation (as in the combined field systems category above) or is simply a provisional stage during forest clearance which will be replaced finally by permanent systems. Bearing these factors in mind, the most important sub-systems in the shifting category seem to be: the *field–forest systems* (*Feld-Wald-Wechselsysteme*), *shifting systems on unimproved land* (*Feld-Wildland-Wechselsysteme*), and *field–grass systems* (*Feld-Gras Systeme*).

1. Field–forest systems

Field–forest systems may be further divided according to whether they are tropical or non-tropical. Of these the tropical is the most important; it supports millions of people, and is the most varied in terms of crops, rotations and in its associated economic and social organizations. Within its subdivisions a major distinction can be drawn between true *shifting cultivation* which includes frequent movement of the settlements (*Wanderfeldbau*), and that which is restricted to the shifting of the cultivation plots only (*Landwechsel-wirtschaft*).[25] Frequently it includes outlying clearings with temporary huts.

In contrast to tropical shifting cultivation, the *non-tropical field–forest systems* are only partial shifting systems, for these include pioneer clearings made by fire, most of which are gradually brought into more permanent use. Two sub-systems may be distinguished according to forest management. The first is the *field–coppice system* (*Feld-Niederwaldsystem*), which allows fairly regular intercropping since coppice may be cut after 10–17 years' growth. Formerly this was quite widely practised, as in the well-known *Haubergswirtschaft* of the Siegerland, in which the stems of oak trees were cut every 15–17 years to provide bark for tanning; the scrub was then burnt and one or two crops of rye taken from the ground during the regrowth of the trees from the remaining stumps.[26] This system was last practised during the period of food shortage after the Second World War, but there were other regional variations (*Reutberg-* or *Rottwirtschaft*), especially in the widespread coppices of the Rhenish massif,[27] in southern Germany and Switzerland.[28]

A different system, known in Germany as *Feld-Mittelwald* and *Feld-Hochwald* systems, involved the cultivation of one or more grain crops between forest clearance and replanting. *Mittelwald* refers to forests which have developed from former coppice, while *Hochwald* is a mature forest of individually planted trees. In the Odenwald, this cultivation practice was termed *Röderland-wirtschaft*, and in Bavaria *Birkenberge*.

In addition to these traditional peasant uses, a similar practice, involving the sowing of between one and three grain crops before replanting with timber, was introduced into professional forestry

H

in the early nineteenth century by H. v. Cotta, and was known as *Baumfeldwirtschaft*. This European practice was introduced into tropical forest management, for example by D. Brandis who came from Bonn to India in 1855 at the invitation of the British Government to devise methods for the reafforestation of teak on clearings made by Karen tribes in Burma, while practising shifting cultivation. Hence the Karen term *taungya* has been used for this type of regulated shifting cultivation–afforestation which has also been practised in Africa and may well have an important future in the economic development of tropical countries.[29]

2. *Shifting systems on unimproved land*

A variety of terms may be used to describe this practice in German. *Feld-Wildland* is perhaps the most appropriate, since this means unimproved land such as heath or moor which is grazed extensively and cropped periodically. Alternative terms are *Feld-Ödland-* or *Feld-Hutung-System*, which means unimproved pasture used for herded livestock.[30] Such systems have been found in the past in many different regions where marginal land is abundant, varying from temperate heaths and mountain pasture to the steppes. Their common characteristic is the periodic or intermittent cultivation of plots of unimproved land (usually extensive common grazing) which has been burnt before tillage and cropped for one or two seasons. The practice may lead to the gradual enclosure of 'intakes', but usually the land reverts to rough pasture until the next cultivation cycle.

In Germany the best known example of this system is the *Schiffelwirtschaft* of the Eifel,[31] but it was also practised in the High Sauerland (*Torfen*)[32] and in the Rhön Mountains (*Rauchfelder* or *Wechselgüter*).[33] The 'paring and burning' or 'denshiring' of outfields prior to cultivation has been described by Estyn Evans[34] for regions in the Atlantic fringe from Ireland to Galicia and Asturia, and in the uplands of France.[35] Similar systems are known in other climatic zones, in the ephemeral fields sometimes cultivated by nomads at the desert's edge, or the burning of the *páramo* on the cordillera in Colombia, which is ploughed for one crop of potatoes after 7–10 years. Another variant in the north Colombian lowlands is a system termed *rozas* in which grazing land, overgrown by secondary scrub, is reclaimed by leasing the land to small tenant-farmers for one or two years. They burn the scrub, crop according to the length of their lease, and then hand the land back to the owner, sown in grass. Normally the term *roza* is used in forest colonization, and is thus to be grouped with the field–forest systems, either in true shifting cultivation (*milpa*) or in the incipient stages of clearing by fire prior to permanent use. A number of transitional types are caused by cases of shifting cultivation in which the secondary growth does not become jungle before re-use, but consists of poor savanna and similar wasteland, as in the *guatales* of Central America.[36]

Finally, special sub-types may be included in this category, for example *field–bog cultivation* which may precede permanent colonization, and the periodic use of empty fish-ponds for the tilling of a crop of oats (*Teichwechselwirtschaft*), a practice still found in a few districts of Bresse and Dombes in France.

3. *Field–grass systems*

These are still important in many regions, unlike some of the previous categories, and may be subdivided according to whether all or only a part of the improved land is based on a field–grass economy. In the former, ploughed parcels are shifted in a fixed cycle over the *Flur*, the remainder of which is in grass, whereas the latter is confined mainly to an outfield. The total field–grass system is usually found in areas with high precipitation, for example in the *Egartenwirtschaft* of parts of the eastern Alps, or the ley-farming of western and northern Europe. A further distinction may be made between improved field–grass systems, in which grass or clover is seeded following a period in tillage, and unimproved systems where grass growth is spontaneous. Rotation-grass, sown as part of certain arable rotations—about 1–3 years—represents a transition to permanent systems; its inclusion in this category may be justified only if the years in which a parcel is in arable exceed those in which it is under grass.

A further problem arises in cases where unimproved grass leys are reverting to common grazing after cropping, and the arable plots or shares are allotted before reploughing. Functionally these types might be included with unimproved systems because of the long period in which the land remains as common pasture. But the improvement resulting from several years repeated cultivation, the stricter regulation of the arable pasture rotations, and the presence of fixed boundaries on strip parcels—even where these are periodically redistributed through run-rig lot—all point towards inclusion in the field–grass system. Examples may be found in *Machairs* of the Hebrides[37] which are similar in structure and function to the former *Vöden* of Westphalia.[38] In some instances the latter, divided into long open strips, were gradually converted into permanent *Langstreifen* infields,[39] a point which stresses the significance of this type for research on the development of field systems.

Similar periodical redistributions (*Umteilungen*) of communal pasture into individual ploughing-strips exist(ed) as well in Cumberland as in the former Russian *Mir*-system, the *Muscha'a* of the Near and Middle East, Persia and north-west India,[40] connected with rural societies with strong communal or tribal links and emphasis on livestock-economy. As the width of narrow strips was the most obvious unit of simple land-measurement, bundles of strips prevailed, many of them merged finally into a permanent strip pattern.

B. PERMANENT ARABLE SYSTEMS

Permanent arable systems exist when the period in which the land is cultivated exceeds or at least equals the time it lies fallow. This means that arable production is achieved by crop rotation instead of land rotation; hence crop rotation becomes a major criterion in the recognition of field systems, though only where the cultivation is continuous as in early common field farming systems.

1. *Unregulated grain systems* (*Ungeregelte Getreide-Systeme*)

These practise a simple monoculture using the same fields for the exclusive cultivation of only a few cereals. Cultivation is usually continuous, but a fallow may be introduced after a long sequence of cropping. Three sub-categories may be recognized:

(a) *One-field systems* (*Einfeldersysteme*) These were common in several European regions where population densities were high yet conditions of climate and soil limited the area of arable land, creating considerable pressure on available land resources especially before the introduction of new crops and fertilizers. An extreme example were the *lazy-beds* used on marginal land in Scotland and Ireland, which were cropped in oats before the introduction of the potato led to an almost exclusive concentration on this more prolific crop. Similarly, on the sandy heathlands of north-west Germany, continuous cropping of up to 40 years in rye (*Ewiger Roggenbau*) is recorded in the mid-nineteenth century although in more recent times the practice was modified.[41] For example, in Westphalia winter rye accounted for about 80 per cent of the crop, and might be grown in one of three ways: for 20 or more years, 5–10 years or 3–4 years. After these periods the land was left in fallow for 1 or 2 years, or cropped with oats or buckwheat. Barley or buckwheat, which mature quickly, are grown in a one-field system in higher mountain areas, as well as winter rye in some of the dry, steep valleys of the western Alps.[42]

Under one-field systems, soils are quickly impoverished, and need heavy manuring, using not only animal dung but seaweed, calcareous sands and the rotten, nitrate-rich thatch taken off the 'blackhouses' of the Atlantic fringe, or the *Plaggen* of north-west Germany.[43] The latter were divots cut from the heaths, placed in byres over the winter to be impregnated with dung. They formed the most important source of fertilizer for the *Eschfluren*, their application over many centuries creating artificial *Plaggen* soils on areas of permanent cultivation. These stand out as highly fertile 'islands' in the poor heathlands from which the divots were cut, and which have been improved only recently with modern farm techniques and fertilizers.[44]

Similar practices are recorded by McCourt and Leister in nineteenth-century Ireland,[45] while in Spain maize was cropped continuously in such provinces as Asturia and Galicia.[46] Continuous cultivation is also recorded in isolated dolines in the mountains of south-east Europe, in northern Finland and Sweden where it was mainly based on the potato, and in the humid parts of the eastern Alps and the high German Mittelgebirge. Many of these modern examples, which are found under marginal farm conditions, represent recent developments in farm practice, especially following the abandonment of subsistence grain growing in favour of cattle raising. Usually potatoes now form the main crop, grown in a one-field rotation, for it is cheaper to grow locally than to transport from elsewhere. But elsewhere, as in north-west Germany, the one-field system was abandoned following the introduction of new techniques of arable farming.

(b) *Unregulated perpetual grain systems (Freie Körnerfolgen)* The main difference between this and the previous category is that different grains may be introduced in the cropping course, for example, a change from winter to spring cereals, or between rye, barley, oats or buckwheat *(Körnerfolgen)*.[47] Fallow was introduced in the cropping sequence only at irregular intervals *(Körnerbrachsysteme)*, until it was finally replaced by root crops and clover—the so-called 'improved perpetual grain cultivation' *(Verbesserte Körnersysteme)*. This system is distinguished from regulated rotations chiefly because the rotation of grains and fallow is not communally regulated—indeed each individual has access to his parcel, even within a fragmented pattern of strip-holdings on an *Esch*, and thus new crops may be introduced quite easily.

(c) *Irrigated one-field systems* These systems are extremely widespread, and include both 'wet' tropical crops and the irrigated crops of drier regions. Many of their essential features are similar to those described above, although here the replacement of soil nutrients is provided by water. The exclusive and continuous cropping of wet rice represents a major prototype, similar to the unimproved one-field systems when the crop is raised once a year after direct seasonal flooding, as in the back-marshes behind the levees of monsoon river valleys.[48] The installation of artificial irrigation and the extension of crop rotation corresponds with the improvements made by artificial fertilizers and new crops under European cropping systems. Many variations are possible in this type of improved one-field system; for example, two or three rice crops may be achieved per year under favourable conditions of water and soil and with more elaborate agricultural techniques. But when regular seasonal changes are introduced between wet rice and crops such as wheat, tobacco or sweet potatoes, this must be considered a different system.[49] In addition to rice, this category includes other tropical crops such as wet taro, jute and sugar-cane which may be cropped continuously without rotation, and also grains and root-crops which may be cropped with irrigation under steppe, semi-desert and oasis conditions.

One-field systems of crops that are normally unirrigated may also be found in restricted localities of dry climate, for example, as a result of the late introduction of some root-crops to the local economy. This applies to such crops as the potato, so important in the dry, inner valleys of the Swiss and French Alps where the restricted food-base of the traditional, dry, cultivated grains (wheat, barley) required the addition of irrigated fields solely for potato production.[50] Less common are examples of irrigated, unregulated continuous cultivation, for irrigation to be applied to more varied rotations.

2. Common field systems (Zelgensysteme und Felderfolgen)

The truly systematic element in field systems is most apparent where fragmented holdings, comprising separate bundles or complexes of parcels, are organized in regulated rotations[51] and originally include such features as common fallow and pasture on stubble, and rights of way across neighbouring parcels (Flurzwang). Under these conditions the individual fields were unenclosed, held mainly in strips, or sometimes in blocks or intermixed strip and block patterns. Sometimes, however, a temporary, common fence (Zelge) was erected around the cropped area to protect it from grazing cattle;[52] alternatively, the cattle might be herded on stubble.[53] In some regions the Zelge was complemented by another fence (Etter) placed around nucleated settlements to prevent cattle straying in, like the gates formerly placed around village greens in England. It was this type of fence which led Huttenlocher to support the term Etterdorf for those Haufendörfer which were connected with the Gewannfluren of former Zelgen systems.[54]

The regional or historical contrast of these open fields with those of enclosed areas (Bocage, Heckenlandschaft) suggested a connection between the pattern of fragmented, open-strip parcels and the practice of a common three-field rotation which has caused so much confusion in the use of the term 'open-field system'. In reality there were many open-field systems, and still more patterns of unenclosed fields.[55]

Open—i.e. unenclosed—fields may appear in strips as well as in blocks; in a pattern of fragmented as well as of compact holdings. They may be cropped in common systems, but likewise in un-regulated, individual systems. Apart from differences in their physiognomic character, enclosed fields differ from open fields in function, for they are designed entirely for the application of individual systems; this function, of course, comprises various economic and ecological, legal and social reasons.

One problem centres on the double meaning of 'field', which could be either a single parcel (*Feld*, *champ*) or a bundle or complex of strips, cropped and fallowed in common as one of the three constituent parts (*Zelgen*) of a classical open-field system. In certain German dialects *Feld* has this dual meaning (other regional terms as *Ösch*, *Schlag*, *Arten*, *Fluren*); but in scientific usage the term *Zelgen* has been accepted, the corresponding term in French being *sole* and the system itself *assolement*.

Earlier theories on the original lay-out of open-field systems have been discussed above, but one important feature of the gradual super-imposition of common field regulations was the better control of cattle grazing which helped to rationalize the system. Thus the organization of common arable fields into *Zelgen*-systems was most noticeable where most of the agricultural land was in tillage, whereas *Zelgen* were less common in districts with extensive forests or moorlands for cattle grazing. Thus in the Harz-foreland area *Zelgen* were found in the strong arable communities situated on loess soils, but not in villages at the edge of the Harz mountains where there was extensive forest grazing (*Waldweide*).[56] This point also explains the distinction between *Zelgen* regions and those which originally had an infield–outfield system with ample grazing lands. Müller-Wille, for example, considered the rational pasturing of fallow an important factor in the introduction of *Zelgen* in former infield–outfield areas.[57] The extension of *Zelgen* is also thought to be responsible for the intensification of grain production which led to the desertion of many settlements in late medieval times and their concentration in larger, compact villages.[58] This process also seems to have affected some former infield–outfield areas, causing the former outfield blocks to be divided into bundles of permanently tilled strip fields, and regrouping former infield into three *Zelgen*.[59]

In the old world, common field systems predominate over a broad area, lying between the field–grass systems of northern and western Europe with their damper climates and the cooler Alpine mountain zone, and the mainly one-field system of tropical wet-rice cultivation. Within this area there were exceptions, sometimes for ecological reasons, sometimes because of peculiar economic and social developments like the enclosure movement in the British Isles or the highly individualistic *cultura mista* of Upper Italy, associated with *mezzadria* tenants. But the prevalence of the system may be explained by the available types of grain, and the possibilities for alternating spring and winter crops with fallow. Mostly, traditional practices have been discarded through the effects of the Agricultural Revolution but frequently crops like potatoes, turnips and clover have simply taken the place of the former fallow and become 'improved' two- or three-field systems.

Common fields still survive as the preferred system in certain parts of Europe, though greatly improved in their husbandry and less rigorous in their organization. Generally climate, and certain economic restraints, are responsible for their survival in such mountain districts as the Hunsrück, Taunus, Spessart and Franconia in Germany, and in Switzerland, where the climate is too cool for extensive cultivation of lucerne and beets and where there is insufficient precipitation to switch to a grass-economy.[60] The need for fallow to compensate for long growing-seasons and/or dry local climates, together with economic weaknesses, have helped to preserve fine examples of the system in the high western Alps[61] and the Pyrenees;[62] in Yugoslavia, Bulgaria and Greece; and further south, from the mountains of north Africa to Ethiopia and the Hindu-Kush.[63]

Nor are common rotations of crops restricted to European grains. Recently H. J. Nitz published examples from the Kumaon Himalayas, where *Zelgen*-systems are adjusted to the south Asian season in a 2-year rotation with four crops. Similar types exist, for example, in Kulu, Nepal, Sikkim. In the first year millet is grown during the monsoon and the land left fallow in winter; in the second year dry upland-rice is the monsoon crop, followed by winter wheat. In the adjacent foothills he found *Zelgen* with a partial irrigation for wet rice, together with certain recent adjustments following the introduction of sugar-cane.[64]

Meanwhile, intensified grain growing among former nomadic

economies has led to the evolution of new common field patterns. Examples have been recorded in the Near East, by de Planhol and Hütteroth,[65] and in Bolivia[66] and Senegal.[67] In the latter, outfields, which complemented permanently cultivated infields, were divided into three fenced areas, cropped extensively in common with millets and groundnuts and with common pasture of the fallow. As Juillard and Meynier have noted, this apparent similarity to European three-field systems does not imply a direct causal link, but rather represents a convergence of similar techniques, applied under different ecological and ethno-sociological conditions. Their example is an admirable illustration of the prime aim of this essay: to establish a framework of agreed terms as an aid to classification, and also to explain the individual features of regional cases. Once this has been achieved it should be possible to compare similar types on a world scale, both to extend our regional knowledge and to develop an understanding of functional and historical relationships.

(a) *Two-field systems* This system, which involves 1 year grain, 1 year fallow, is fairly widespread in relatively warm areas with dry climates, where evaporation overcomes leaching and quickly restores soil nutrients during fallow. It is found, often in partly improved state, in the Mediterranean and the Near East, often associated with terraced fields in hilly districts; and in the dry valleys of the western Alps.[68] It has disappeared from certain small districts of southern France and central Europe, including parts of the Upper Rhine plain; and from its former locations in Britain, Denmark and Sweden.[69] In its improved form, the system usually includes rotations of several varieties of winter or spring grains with potatoes or maize. Under extremely dry conditions, fallow—with extensive pasture—may be extended to 2 years, alternating with 1 year of grain, as on the *cultivo al tercio* practised on some *campo secano* in central Spain. Niemeier classified this as a type of field–wasteland system, since the years of fallow exceed those of a crop.[70] Certainly it represents the transition between permanent arable and field–grass systems or even shifting systems on unimproved land; but since the land is reploughed regularly every third year it seems reasonable to include this extended two-field system as a sub-type of the latter. Lauer, for example, has indicated the links between the ancient

Mediterranean two-field system and modern techniques of dry-farming, the latter differing from the former mainly through its special treatment of fallow to help retain moisture.[71]

(b) *The common three-field systems* (*Dreizelgen-Systeme*) So many variations of this system are known that the model rotation of winter crop, spring crop and fallow must be regarded as something of a myth.[72] Nor can the system and its related types be regarded as specifically Anglo-Saxon; it is found widely distributed in Asia, as well as in Europe, where it was probably introduced some centuries after the Anglo-Saxon invasion of England.[73] The standard winter-spring–fallow rotations, known as the common three-field system, was later modified after the advent of roots and clover which replaced the fallow year; this is known as the improved three-field system (*Verbessertes Dreizelgen-System*).

(c) *Extended common field systems* (*Erweiterte Zelgen-Systeme*) With the introduction of modern agricultural practices, common field systems were either abandoned in favour of individual rotations, or the number and type of rotations was developed into what may be called 'the extended common field systems'. Sometimes potatoes were added, as in the western Alps where the new four-field rotation was: fallow, winter-grain, spring-grain and potatoes.[74] Elsewhere the *Zelgen* became four-, five- or six-field rotations, while the most extreme form, a seven-field rotation, was described by Tichy in the Odenwald, south of the river Neckar.[75] Here in 1954 examples of seven-field *Zelgen* were found to have evolved in three phases: the basic improved three-field system first of roots, replacing fallow; second, winter grain and third, spring grain (oats). Following the reorganization or enlargement of the bundles, or complexes of fragmented strip-holdings, there was added a two-fold, intensive crop rotation of, fourth, potatoes, and, fifth, winter-grain (rye) and finally a further, more extensive rotation of clover and a second year of clover or a second spring-grain (oats, barley or maize).

Further sub-classes may be added to this group, based on the distinction between the four-field fallow system (*Vierzelgenbrach-system*) and the improved four-field system (*Verbessertes Vierzelgen-system*); the same applies to examples which use irrigation.

(d) *Regulated crop rotations* (*Geregelte Felderfolgen*) In a few areas, for example in north-western Germany, regulated rotations of grain and fallow were practised on individual holdings, but there was no organization of common fields. In addition to this case, Müller-Wille suggested[76] the inclusion in this category of the many *Zelgen* systems, whose abolition was not strictly enforced and which still adhere loosely to the older system. However, these are clearly related to the *Zelgen* systems to which they belong, noting that they have undergone improvement in individual cases. Those which have lost their traditional connections, or which were never related to the *Zelgen* systems, should be included in the next category below.

3. *Unregulated (individual) crop rotations (Freie Fruchfolgesysteme)*

In many regions, the patterns of fragmented holdings were preserved despite the abolition of the *Flurzwang*. Such areas did need some consolidation to ensure access to each parcel by field-lanes, but this was often achieved without a radical change in the basic field pattern. Through these processes, change proceeded as far as was necessary to allow individual rotation, perhaps through enclosure by erecting a compact pattern of blocks or broad strip-holdings at the beginning of clearing or colonization, or even with fragmented but open and individually worked block-patterns. It is difficult to describe these unregulated rotations as real field systems; instead they are better expressed as crop sequences which constitute parts of a prevailing land-use system (*Bodennutzungssystem*). In northern, western and central Europe, the rotation of grains in traditional practice was easily adapted to the regulated field systems, although their classification is complicated by the later additions of root and foliage crops, and additional catch crops. Hence the term 'unregulated crop rotations' includes the complex crop rotations of a modern, scientifically based husbandry, like the Norfolk rotation, worked out by individual farmers.

Even more difficult to systematize are the varied crops of agriculture in warmer climates, a point which justified making a distinction between '*grain system*' (*Getreidesystem*) and the more general '*crop-rotation systems*' (*Fruchwechselsystem*). In the latter, the degree of communal organization is generally lessened. Nevertheless, in any region geographical conditions usually provide the basis for a certain uniformity in farming practice, resulting in a distinctive agricultural landscape even where there is a great variety in crop rotations. This is a notable feature even in a complex *cultura mista* or of Chinese market gardening, or the vast uniform wheat regions of the Ukraine or Canada. Finally, this category, which includes all types in which there is no obvious regulated or common sequence of a few crops, may be refined at a later date.

One sub-class may be noted—the variable rotations which are based on irrigation and which are not organized in common fields. Some originated by the addition of secondary crops such as maize, tobacco or sweet potatoes to former rice one-field systems. A distinction here may be made between rotations that are permanently irrigated, and those which resemble *Zelgen* types with a regular and common change of one irrigated crop, for example, rice cropped during the monsoon, and an irrigated winter crop like wheat.

Tillage under trees and special cultivations Tillage under orchards is difficult to classify statistically in the land-use ratios of most regions,[77] but this is a less serious problem in dealing with combinations of arable and trees such as olive, vine, mulberry, coco, date and sugar. In principle the existence of trees may be noted and the fields classified according to their relevant system, as in a two-field system of winter wheat and fallow under olive trees which is so widespread in Mediterranean agriculture. Tree and arable combinations may also appear in unregulated crop rotations, as with *cultura mista*. Special crops like hemp, tobacco, asparagus and jute, grown for commercial purposes (*Sonderkulturen*), may be included under unregulated crop rotations if they are grown within arable fields.

C. COMBINED FIELD SYSTEMS

In the categories discussed so far, the term 'field system' was applied to the regulation and distribution of crops and rotations of uniform fields. Frequently, this one system covers the entire arable land of one community.

In other cases, however, the economy is based on a combination of units of two or more of these systems, and in some types, this combination is of such an integral character, that it is traditionally also called 'a field system' although in reality it is a combination of parts of different systems.

1. *The infield–outfield system*

This is known in many parts of the world, including west and north-west Europe where infields are restricted to patches of better soils, often better drained. These are usually in permanent cultivation, either in one-field continuous grain rotation, but also in free grain rotation (heavily manured), both with individual access to the strips.[78] There are, however, some cases of common three-field systems. Both were supplemented by field–grass outfields. Originally H. L. Gray considered these to be Celtic in origin, but H. C. Darby has suggested that this system was a device for utilizing poor soils.[79] Finberg, however, noted its association with a superabundance of rough pasture, which made it unnecessary to have a large proportion of ploughland under grass each year.[80] Usually the field–grass systems of the outfields are found with block-parcels, but they may also occur in fragmented patterns of strips. In Brittany and north-west Germany, for example, the outfields consist of units with a fairly regular, or even improved field–grass system, often enclosed and with additional shifting systems on the adjacent unimproved heathland. But the infield–outfield need not necessarily combine such markedly different systems. Sometimes it is distinguished simply by the intensity of improvement, signified by greater application of dung, more frequent tillage, greater value of crop, care in soil selection, irrigation or proximity to the settlement. Such a differentiation may even be applied to infield–outfield worked under various common field systems. For example, this type was fairly widespread in Germany, as in the Nahe valley where some villages in the 1950s still used an infield on good soil next to the settlements in what was an improved common field system (winter wheat, spring barley, roots). The outfields were on poorer soils, some distance uphill from the settlement, and farmed in an extensive five-field rotation of rye, oats, potatoes, clover and some fallow. Both complexes consisted of similar bundles of narrow, short strips in a fragmented pattern of holdings. In the neighbouring district of Birkenfeld, Müller-Wille likewise showed how different zones of intensity within the *Flur* were created by the time required for transporting dung and harvesting crops, an illustration of von Thünen's intensity zones. In 1936, this district had various common field *Zelgen* in the infields as well as in the outfields, with additional *Wildland* shifting systems.[81]

2. *Combined wet and dry field systems*

Parallels to the intensively worked infield, and extensively used outfields, are to be found in regions where the farming communities combine the tillage of irrigated and dry land. This applies to the Mediterranean combination of *campo regadio* and *campo secano*, where usually the former is worked in an intensive unregulated crop rotation (grain—including maize, beans, cabbages, vegetables, lucerne and melons), partly combined with tree cultivation; while the latter is tilled for grain, frequently under olive-trees either in common two-field systems, or the *al tercio* type of one-year spring wheat, two years of pastured fallow. This last closely resembles outfield. Another typical example is the Kashmir basin, which combines irrigated, intensively worked rice-fields, in a one-field system with only some oilseeds during the fallow months; and on dry sites, such as river terraces or levees, includes additional dry fields, tilled for wheat, barley and pulses in winter, and in summer grows maize and millets with extensive fallows.

The scarcity of land capable of irrigation is mainly responsible for this combination,[82] as in a case studied by the author in Thailand, where older practices, based on an irrigated one-field system which was developed in old-settled intermontane basins, were extended into pioneer settlements, but had to be complemented there by additional shifting cultivation of dry upland rice. The reverse development took place among certain hill tribes of north Thailand and Burma, who had formerly only planted dry upland rice as the core of a fully integrated shifting cultivation. Recently they took over some permanent wet-rice fields on plots quite distant from the main villages. These may remain as an addition to the economy, or they may result in the development of an entire new infield with changes from shifting to permanent homesteads, as in the example of Dusun groups in north Borneo.

Thus in south-east Asia, there are various combinations of wet rice on permanently irrigated fields, and dry upland rice grown in shifting cultivation on surrounding hill slopes. They show striking parallels to European infield–outfield, with an intensively worked and permanently irrigated infield, combined with a shifting cultivation where the field–grass system is replaced by the tropical field–forest system.

3. *Combinations with additional seasonal systems*

Specific variations of the infield–outfield (or wet and dry field) combinations appear notably in high mountains, where the ecological differences between arable sites belonging to a community, caused mainly by differences in micro-climate, may result in several combinations of tilled land in various systems. Frequently the vertical and/or horizontal distances from the main settlement are so considerable that these fields are equipped with temporary settlements, as is also the case in shifting cultivation. Various local terms, like *Sommerdörfer* in the Alps, are used to describe fields and huts at high elevations which are restricted to one short growing-season.

The distant fields need not necessarily be of inferior or extensive outfield character; sometimes they may have greater ecological potential than certain permanent fields near the main settlements. These may lie on lower and warmer or better irrigable sites, but are used only seasonally for reasons of security, or because of malaria infection. A striking example is provided by the Jaunsari of the Garhwal Himalayas, who combine in one community the cultivation of wet rice in an irrigated one-field system in the low-lying hot valleys quite distant from the village, with an infield of dry crops, maize, millets, or spices, grown during the monsoon; and wheat, barley and pulses in the winter season. Here the infield is situated on hill slopes near the main village. In addition, they practise a high-level cultivation of potatoes, again in a one-field system; formerly there was some extra shifting cultivation, but the land used for this is now left to grazing, since the cash-income of the potatoes released the pressure for producing more grain for home consumption.[83]

Similar examples, though rather less complex, can be found in hill settlements of different mountain regions in the Alps, southeast Europe, and Nepal. But in this category are included only those villages which work part of their arable cultivation in field complexes used at different seasons, and with or without temporary settlements. The inclusion of shielings, variously known as *Almwirtschaft*, *alpage*, *saeter*, is relevant in this category only where significant amounts of tillage are combined with the summer grazing which forms the core to this type of land use. The typical *Alm* was used only for grazing and dairying, but some former Scottish shielings were apparently used for additional crops, for example, some shielings in Assynt were recorded as 'in corn' in Home's Survey of 1774. These must have combined the normal outfield usage with that of a shieling situated near the main settlement; indeed they might be better classified with the infield–outfield system.[84]

In the Alps, depopulation of higher ground has led to the transformation of quite a number of former permanent settlements into low-lying shielings (*Aston, Maiensässe*), some with continued, although restricted, arable cultivation. Others were transformed into full 'summer-villages', used by the entire population of the lower main villages after ploughing and seeding of the 'home' fields. During a temporary stay, they cultivated a spring crop—barley or sometimes buckwheat, rye or potatoes—and made hay, applying a field–grass or an improved two-field system, as in a few surviving examples in the Lechtaler Alps.

This situation arose in converse examples too, for example, in the former *Kalyvia* settlement of Greece. Here the population retreated from the plains controlled by the Turks, into hill villages with only extensive arable systems, originally serving for summer pasture, whilst after that retreat they stayed there and descended temporarily to the original fields in the plains, which they worked from the *Kalyvia* huts.[85]

In conclusion, it may be stressed again that this essay presents only a tentative classification of field systems, based on selected examples. It is hoped that it will stimulate further attempts to achieve a comprehensive classification and definitive terminology which will prove an indispensable aid for the international exchange of research experience, so vital in geographical studies.

Notes

1. R. Gradmann, 'Markgenossenschaft und Gewanndorf', *Berichte zur deutschen Landeskunde* 5 (1948), 108–14. This paper gave a retrospective summary of the development of the thoughts of himself, V. Ernst, A. Meitzen *et al.* at the end of the nineteenth and during the early twentieth centuries.

2. G. Niemeier, 'Streusiedlungsursprung und Keltenfrage', *Geographischer Anzeiger* (1935), 193–7.

3. H. L. Gray, *English Field Systems*, Cambridge, Mass., 1915 (reprint 1959).

I

4. E. Juillard, A. Meynier, X. de Planhol, and G. Sautter, 'Structures agraires et paysages ruraux', *Annales de l'Est*, Nancy (1957).

5. A. H. R. Baker, 'Howard Levi Gray and English field systems: an evaluation', *Agricultural History Review*, 39, ii (1965).

6. G. Hatt, *Oltidsagre*, Copenhagen, 1949.

K. Scharlau, 'Kammerfluren (Celtic fields, oldtidsagre) und Streifenfluren in westdeutschen Mittelgebirgen', *Zeitschrift für Agrargeschichte und Agrarsoziologie* (1957).

7. G. Niemeier, 'Gewannfluren und Eschkerntheorie', *Petermanns Geogr. Mitteilungen* (1944).

8. G. Niemeier, *ibid*.

E. Obst and H. Spreitzer, 'Wege und Ergebnisse der Flurforschung im Gebiet der großen Haufendörfer', *Petermanns Geogr. Mitteilungen* (1939).

K. Scharlau, 'Flurrelikte und Flurformengenese in West-Deutschland', *Geogr. Annaler* 43 (1961), 264–76.

9. F. Steinbach, 'Gewanndorf und Einzelhof', *Festschrift Aloys Schultze zum 70. Geburtstage*, Düsseldorf (1927).

10. W. Ebert, *Ländliche Siedelformen im deutschen Osten*, Berlin, 1936.

R. Kötzschke, *Ländliche Siedlung und Agrarwesen in Sachsen*, Forschungen zur deutschen Landeskunde, 77, Remagen, 1953.

A. Krenzlin, *Historische und wirtschaftliche Züge im Siedlungsformenbild des westlichen Ostdeutschland*, Frankfurter Geographische Hefte, 1955.

11. H. J. Nitz, 'Regelmäßige Langstreifenfluren und Fränkische Staatskolonisation', *Geographische Rundschau* (1961), 350–66.

12. A. Krenzlin and L. Reusch, *Die Entstehung der Gewannflur nach Untersuchungen im nördlichen Unterfranken*, Frankfurter Geographische Hefte (1961).

13. D. Hannerberg, 'Solskifte and older methods of partitioning arable land in Central Sweden during the Middle Ages', *Annales de l'Est*, 21 (1959), 245–59.

S. Helmfrid, 'The storskifte, enskifte and lagaskifte in Sweden—General features', *Geogr. Annaler* 43 (1961), 114–29.

S. Dahl, 'Strip Fields and Enclosure in Sweden', *Scandinavian Economic History Review* 9 (1961).

S. Göransson, 'Regular open-field pattern in England and Scandinavian solskifte', *Geogr. Annaler*, 43 (1961), 80–104.

S. Gissel, 'Die Dreifelderwirtschaft auf Seeland bis 1700', *Beiträge zur Genese der Siedlungs- und Agrarlandschaft in Europa*, Beihefte, Geographische Zeitschrift 18 (1968), 44–9.

S. Ilešič, 'Die jüngeren Gewannfluren in Nordwestjugoslawien', *Geogr. Annaler* (1961), 130–7.

W. D. Hütteroth, 'Die Bedeutung kollektiver und individueller Landnahme für die Ausbildung von Streifen- und Blockfluren im Nahen Osten', *Beiträge zur Genese der Siedlungs- und Agrarlandschaft in Europa*, Beihefte, Geographische Zeitschrift 18 (1968), 85–93.

A. Verhulst, 'L'évolution du paysage rural en Flandre au moyen âge', *Beiträge zur Genese der Siedlungs-und Agrarlandschaft in Europa*, Beihefte, Geographische Zeitschrift 18 (1968), 174–5.

14. H. Uhlig, 'Langstreifenfluren in Nordengland, Wales und Schottland', *Deutscher Geographentag Würzburg 1957*, Tagungsbericht und wissenschaftliche Abhandlungen, Wiesbaden, 1959.

H. Uhlig, 'Die ländliche Kulturlandschaft der Hebriden und der westschottischen Hochlande', *Erdkunde* (1959), 22–46.

H. Uhlig, 'Typen kleinbäuerlicher Siedlungen auf den Hebriden', *Erdkunde* (1959), 98–124.

H. Uhlig, 'Old Hamlets with Infield and Outfield Systems in Western and Central Europe', *Geogr. Annaler* 43 (1961), 285–312.

15. E. E. Evans, 'Some survivals of the Irish openfield system', *Geography* 24 (1939).

E. E. Evans, *Mourne Country*, Dundalk, 1951.

E. E. Evans, 'The Ecology of Peasant Life in Western Europe', W. L. Thomas, Jr. (ed.), *Man's Rôle in Changing the Face of the Earth*, Chicago, 1956.

E. E. Evans, 'Rural Settlement in Ireland and Western Britain: Introduction', *Advancement of Science*, 55 (1959).

R. H. Buchanan, 'Rural Change in an Irish Townland, 1890–1955, *Advancement of Science* 56 (1958).

J. H. Johnson, 'The development of the Rural Settlement Pattern of Ireland', *Geogr. Annaler* 43 (1961), 165–73.

D. McCourt, 'Infield and Outfield in Ireland', *Economic History Review* (1955), 369–76.

V. B. Proudfoot, 'Ancient Irish Field System', *Advancement of Science* (1958), 369–71.

V. B. Proudfoot, 'Clachans in Ireland', *Gwerin* 2 (1959), 110–22.

P. Flatrès, 'La structure agraire ancienne du Devon et du Cornwall', *Chronique géogr. des pays celtiques* (1949), 4–14.

P. Flatrès, *Géographie rurale de quatre contrées celtiques: Irlande, Galles, Cornwall, et Man*, Rennes (1957).

P. Flatrès, 'Les structures rurales de la frange atlantique de l'Europe', *Annales de l'Est*, 21 (1959), 193–202.

16. W. A. Boelcke, 'Die frühmittelalterlichen Wurzeln der süd-westdeutschen Gewannflur', *Zeitschrift für Agrargeschichte und Agrarsoziologie* (1964), 131.

17. H. Uhlig, 'Probleme und Aufgaben der internationalen Arbeitsgruppe für die Terminologie der Agrarlandschaft', *Beiträge zur Genese der Siedlungs- und Agrarlandschaft in Europa*, Beihefte, Geographische Zeitschrift 18 (1968), 176–87.

H. Uhlig and C. Lienau (eds), *Types of Field Patterns* (Flur und Flurformen; Le Finage agricole et sa structure parcellaire), *Basic Material for the Terminology of the Agricultural Landscape*, I, Giessen (1967).

C. Lienau, 'Die Flur und ihr Besitz- und Nutzflächengefüge', *ibid.*, 71–190.

18. E. E. Evans, *op. cit.* (1939).

19. H. Uhlig, *op. cit.* (1959).

20. P. Deffontaines, 'Le rang, type de peuplement rural du Canada français', *Cahiers de géogr. de l'Université Laval* (1953).

M. Derruau, 'A l'origine du "rang" canadien', *Cahiers de géogr. de Quebec* 1 (1956).

E. Juillard, A. Meynier, X. de Planhol and G. Sautter, *op. cit.* (1957), 21.

21. H. Blume, 'Die Entwicklung der Kulturlandschaft des Mississippideltas in kolonialer Zeit', *Schriften des Geographischen Institutes der Universität Kiel* (1956).

22. W. Manshard, 'Afrikanische Waldhufen und Waldstreifenfluren', *Die Erde* (1961), 246-58.

23. P. Monbeig, 'Les structures agraires dans la frange pionnière de São-Paulo', *Cahiers d'Outre-Mer* (1951), 1-22.

L. Waibel, 'Die europäische Kolonisation Südbrasiliens (bearbeitet von G. Pfeifer)', *Colloquium Geographicum* (1955).

R. Eidt, 'Japanese agricultural colonization: a new attempt at land opening in Argentina', *Economic Geography* 44 (1968), 9.

24. W. Müller-Wille, 'Der Feldbau in Westfalen im 19. Jahrhundert', *Westfälische Forschungen* 1 (1938), 302-25.

W. Müller-Wille, 'Zur Systematik und Bezeichnung der Feld systeme in Nordwestdeutschland', *Zeitschrift für Erdkunde* 9 (1941), 40-2.

25. W. Manshard, 'Wanderfeldbau und Landwechselwirtschaft in den Tropen', Heidelberger Geographische Arbeiten, 15, *Pfeifer Festschrift* (1966), 245-64.

J. E. Spencer, *Shifting Cultivation in Southeastern Asia*, University of California. Publ. in Geography, 19, Berkeley, Los Angeles, 1966.

K. J. Pelzer, *Pioneer Settlement in the Asiatic Tropics*, New York, 1948.

P. Gourou, *Les Pays tropicaux*, Paris, 1947.

R. F. Watters, 'Some Forms of Shifting Cultivation in the South-West Pacific', *Journal of Trop. Geography* (1960), 35-50.

H. C. Conklin, *Hanunóo Agriculture*, a Report on an Integral System of Shifting Cultivation in the Philippines. FAO Forestry Development Paper, 12, Rome (1957).

H. Uhlig, 'Hill-tribes and rice-farmers in the Himalayas and south-east Asia', *Transactions and Papers of the I.B.G.* 47 (1969).

26. Th. Kraus, 'Das Siegerland', *Forschungen zur deutschen Landeskunde* 28, i (1931).

P. Fickeler, 'Das Siegerland als Beispiel wirtschafts geschichtlicher und wirtschaftsgeographischer Harmonie', *Erdkunde* (1954).

27. J. Schmithüsen, *Der Niederwald des linksrheinischen Schiefergebirges*, Beiträge zur Landeskunde der Rheinlande, 2, iv (1934).

W. Müller-Wille, *Die Ackerfluren im Landesteil Birkenfeld und ihre Wandlung seit dem 17. und 18. Jahrhundert*, Beiträge zur Landeskunde der Rheinlande, 2, v (1936).

28. H. Schmitthenner, 'Die Reutbergwirtschaft in Deutschland', *Geographische Zeitschrift* (1923), 115-27.

29. H. Hesmer, *Der kombinierte land- und fortswirtschaftliche Anbau*, I, *Tropisch Afrika*, Stuttgart, 1966, 61.

30. K. H. Paffen, *Heidevegetation und Ödlandwirtschaft der Eifel*, Beiträge zur Landeskunde der Rheinlande, 3, iii (1940).

G. Niemeier, 'Die kulturgeographische Analyse', *Homenaje a Don Luis de Hoyos Sainz*, Madrid, 1949.

31. K. H. Paffen (1940).

32. K. Engelhard, *Die Entwicklung der Kulturlandschaft des nördlichen Waldeck seit dem späten Mittel alter*, Giessener Geographische Schriften, 10 (1967).

33. W. Röll, *Die kulturlandschaftliche Entwicklung des Fuldaer Landes in der Frühneuzeit*, Giessener Geographische Schriften, 9 (1966).

34. E. E. Evans, *op. cit.* (1956), 229.

35. M. Bloch, *Les caractères originaux de l'histoire rurale française*, Instituttet für sammenlignende kulturforskning, Serie B, 19 (1931).

36. L. Waibel, 'Die Sierra Madre de Chiapas', *Mitt. d. Geogr. Ges. Hamburg*, 43 (1933).

37. H. A. Moisley, 'Some Hebridean Field Systems', *Gwerin* (1960), 22–35.

H. Uhlig, *op. cit.* (1959, 1961).

38. W. Müller-Wille, *op. cit.* (1938), 314.

G. Niemeier, 'Vöden. Kulturgeographische Studie über eine Sonderform der gemeinen Mark', *Festschrift für L. Mecking* (1949), 185–200.

39. W. Müller-Wille, 'Blöcke, Streifen und Hufen', *Berichte zur deutschen Landeskunde* 29 (1962), 296–306.

H. Hambloch, 'Langstreifenfluren im nordwestlichen Alt-Niederdeutschland', *Geographische Rundschau* (1962), 345–56.

G. Mertins, *Die Kulturlandschaft des westlichen Ruhrgebietes*, Giessener Geographische Schriften, 4 (1964).

40. G. G. Elliott, 'The system of cultivation and evidence of enclosure in the Cumberland open fields in the sixteenth century', *Actes du Coll. Int. Géogr. et Histoire Agraires*, Nancy (1957) (*Annales de l'Est*, 1959).

G. Schwarz, *Allgemeine Siedlungsgeographie* (3rd ed.), Berlin, 1966, 221–6.

H. Bobek, 'Soziale Raumbildungen am Beispiel des Vorderen Orients', *Deutscher Geographentag München 1948* (Vorträge und Abhandlungen), Landshut (1950/51), 193–206.

B. H. Baden-Powell, *The Indian Village Community*, London–New York–Bombay, 1896, 225.

J. Despois, *Le Hodna*, Publications de la Faculté des Lettres d'Alger, Paris (1953).

A. Latron, *La Vie rurale en Syrie et au Liban*, Mémoires de l'Institut Français Damas, Beirut, 1936.

J. Weulersse, *Paysans de Syrie et du Proche Orient*, Paris, 1946.

P. Birot and J. Dresch, *La Méditerranée et le Moyen Orient*, 2 vols, Paris, 1953, 1956.

B. Fautz, *Sozialstruktur und Bodennutzung in der Kulturlandschaft des Swat (NW Himalaya)*, Giessener Geogr. Schriften 3 (1963).

W. D. Hütteroth, *op. cit.* (1968), 86.

41. W. Müller-Wille, *op. cit.* (1938), 318.

W. Müller-Wille, *op. cit.* (1941), 41.

H. Pohlendt, 'Die Feldsysteme des Herzogtums Braunschweig im 18.

Jahrhundert', *Mortensen Festschrift* (Akademie für Raumforschung und Landesplanung, 28) (1954), 179–95.

42. F. Monheim, *Agrargeographie der westlichen Hochalpen*, Ergänzungsheft zu Petermanns Geographischen Mitteilungen nr, 252, Gotha (1954), 74.

43. H. Uhlig, *op. cit.* (1957, 1959, 1961).

44. G. Niemeier, 'Die Altersbestimmung der Plaggenböden als kulturgeographisches Problem', *Geographischer Anzeiger* (1939), 237–45.

G. Niemeier, 'Carbon-14' Datierungen der Kulturlandschaftsgeschichte Nordwestdeutschlands', *Abhandlungen der Braunschweigischen Wissenschaftlichen Gesellschaft*, 11 (1959), 87–120.

W. Müller-Wille, *op. cit.* (1938).

W. Müller-Wille, 'Langstreifenflur und Drubbel. Ein Beitrag zur Siedlungsgeographie Westgermaniens', *Deutsches Archiv für Landes- und Volksforschung* (1944), 9–44.

E. Bertelsmeier, *Bäuerliche Siedlung und Wirtschaft im Delbrücker Land*, Arbeiten der Geographischen Kommission im Provinzial-Institut für westfälische Landes- und Volkskunde, 7 (1942).

45. D. McCourt, *op. cit.* (1955), 370.

I. Leister, *Das Werden der Agrarlandschaft in der Grafschaft Tipperary (Ireland)*, Marburger Geographische Schriften, 18 (1963).

46. G. Niemeier, *op. cit.* (1949), 252.

47. W. Müller-Wille, *op. cit.* (1941), 41.

Korn (pl. *Körner*) means in German the regionally prevailing grain for bread (mainly rye); the traditional name for continuous grain-systems, scientifically used by J. N. v. Schwerz, 1816, was *Erzkörnerbau*.

48. J. Delvert, *Le Paysan Cambodgien*, Paris, 1961.

C. A. Fisher, *Southeast Asia*, London, 1964.

H. Uhlig, 'Typen der Bergbauern und Wanderhirten in Kaschmir und Jaunsar-Bawar', *Deutscher Geographentag Köln*, 1961, Tagungsberichte und wissenschaftliche Abhandlungen (1962).

H. Uhlig, *op. cit.* (1969).

49. R. D. Hill and H. Uhlig, 'Draft of a terminological framework for the geographical types and terminology of rice-cultivation', *Malaysian Inter-Congress* 1969, Pacific Science Association, Standing Committee on Geography Tokyo (1970).

50. F. Monheim, *op. cit.* (1954), 77.

51. G. Pfeifer, 'The Quality of Peasant Life in Central Europe', in W. L. Thomas, Jr. (ed.), *Man's Rôle in Changing the Face of the Earth*, Chicago, 1956.

R. Butlin, 'Some terms used in agrarian history: a glossary', *Agricultural History Review* 9 (1961), 100–1.

J. Thirsk, 'The common fields', *Past and Present* 29 (1964), 3–25.

J. Thirsk, 'The origin of the common fields', *Past and Present* 33 (1966), 142–7.

52. W. Müller-Wille, *op. cit.* (1938), 317.

53. H. Pohlendt, *op. cit.* (1954), 193.

G. Oberbeck, *Die mittelalterliche Kulturlandschaft des Gebietes um*

Gifhorn, Schriften der Wirtschaftswissenschaftlichen Gesellschaft Niedersachsens, N. F. 66, Bremen (1957).

54. F. Huttenlocher, *Versuche kulturlandschaftlicher Gliederung am Beispiel von Württemberg*, Forschungen zur deutschen Landeskunde, 47, Stuttgart (1949).

55. J. A. Sheppard, 'Pre-Enclosure Field and Settlement Patterns in an English Township', *Geogr. Annaler* (1966), 59–77.

A. R. H. Baker, 'Howard Levi Gray and English Field Systems: An Evaluation', *Agricultural History* 39 (1965), 87.

A. R. H. Baker, 'Some Fields and Farms in Medieval Kent', *Beiträge zur Genese der Siedlungs- und Agrarlandschaft in Europa* (Ergänzungsheft 18, Geographische Zeitschrift), Wiesbaden (1968).

A. R. H. Baker, 'Some Terminological Problems in Studies of British Field Systems', *Agricultural History Review* 17 (1969), 136–40.

J. Thirsk, *op. cit.* (1964).

H. Uhlig, *op. cit.* (1961), 306.

56. H. Pohlendt, *op. cit.* (1954).

57. W. Müller-Wille, 'Das Rheinische Schiefergebirge und seine kulturgeographische Struktur und Stellung', *Deutsches Archiv für Landes- und Volksforschung* (1942), 563.

58. H. Mortensen, 'Fragen der nordwestdeutschen Siedlungund Flurforschung im Lichte der Ostforschung', *Nachrichten der Akademie der Wissenschaften, Göttingen*, phil.-hist. Klasse (1946/47).

K. Scharlau, 'Die Bedeutung der Wüstungskartierung für die Flurformenforschung', *Berichte zur deutschen Landeskunde*, 29 (1962), 215–34.

A. Krenzlin, 'Blockflur, Langstreifenflur und Gewannflur als Funktion agrarischer Nutzungssysteme in Deutschland', *Berichte zur deutschen Landeskunde* 20 (1958), 256.

H. Jäger, *Entwicklungsperioden agrarer Siedlungsgebiete im mittleren Westdeutschland seit dem frühen 13. Jahrhundert*, Würzburger Geographische Arbeiten, 6 (1958).

59. H. Uhlig, *Die Kulturlandschaft—Methoden der Forschung und das BeispielNordostengland*, Kölner Geographische Arbeiten 9/10 (1956).

A. E. Smailes, *North England*, London and Edinburgh, 1960.

R. A. Butlin, 'Northumberland field systems', *Agricultural History Review* 12 (1964), 99–120.

60. L. Aario, 'Die Kulturlandschaft und bäuerliche Wirtschaft beiderseits des Rheintales bei St. Goar', *Acta Geographica* 9, Helsinki (1945).

J. Schmithüsen, *Das Luxemburger Land*, Forschungen zur deutschen Landes- und Volkskunde, 34, Leipzig (1940).

W. Müller-Wille, *op. cit.* (1936).

H. Bobek, *Südwestdeutsche Studien*, Forschungen zur deutschen Landeskunde, 62, Remagen (1952).

W. Kuls, *Wirtschaftsflächen und Feldsysteme im westlichen Hintertaunus*, Rhein-Mainische Forschungen, 30 (1951).

H. Carol, 'Die letzten Dreizelgenwirtschaften der Schweiz: Merishausen und Salvenach', *Geographica Helvetica* 11 (1956).

H. Boesch and M. Bronhofer, 'The decline of the "Three-Zelgen-System" in Northeastern Switzerland', *Geographica Helvetica* (1960).

A. Herold, *Der zelgengebundene Anbau im Randgebeit des fränkischen Gäulandes und seine besondere Stellung innerhalb der südwestdeutschen Agrarlandschaften*, Würzburger Geographische Arbeiten, 15 (1965).

61. F. Monheim, *op. cit.* (1954).

62. D. Faucher, 'Polyculture ancienne et assolement biennal dans la France méridionale', *Révue géographique des Pyrénées et du Sud-Ouest* (1934), 241–55.

63. H. Wilhelmy, *Hochbulgarien, I: Die Ländlichen Siedlungen und die bäuerliche Wirtschaft*, Schriften des Geographischen Institutes der Universität Kiel, IV (1935).

A. Beuermann, 'Studien zur griechischen Agrarlandschaft', *Deutscher Geographentag Würzburg*, 1957, Tagungsbericht und wissenschaftliche Abhandlungen, Wiesbaden (1958).

J. Célérier, 'Le paysage rural au Maroc', *Hesperis* (1943).

W. Klaer, *Eine Landnutzungskarte von Libanon*, Heidelberger Geographische Arbeiten, 10 (1962).

W. Kuls, *Bevölkerung, Siedlung und Landwirtschaft im Hochland von Godjam (Nordäthiopien)*, Frankfurter Geographische Hefte, 39 (1963).

J. Hövermann, 'Bauerntum und bäuerliche Siedlung in Äthiopien', *Die Erde* (1958).

E. Grötzbach, 'Kulturgeographische Beobachtungen im Farkhar Tal (Afghanischer Hindukusch)', *Die Erde*, Berlin (1965), 291.

64. H. J. Nitz, 'Formen der Zelgenwirtschaft im Kumaon-Himalaya und seinem Vorland (NW-Indien)', *Zeitschrift für Agrargeschichte und Agrarsoziologie* (1966), 83–9.

S. D. Pant, *The Social Economy of the Himalayans*, London, 1935.

W. Haffner, 'Ostnepal—Grundzüge des vertikalen Landschaftsaufbaus', *Khumbu Himal*. Ergebnisse des Forschungsunternehmens Nepal Himalaya, 1, Berlin–Heidelberg–New York (1967), 389–426.

H. Uhlig, 'Agrarlandschaften in westlichen Himalaya, Kulu, Mandi, Kangrar (Himachal Pradesh)', *Festschrift für K. Kayser*, Köln, 1970.

65. X. de Planhol, *De la Plaine pamphylienne aux lacs pisidiens*. Etude de géographie humaine, Paris (1958).

W. D. Hütteroth, *op. cit.* (1968).

66. C. Troll, 'Die tropischen Andenländer', *Handbuch der Geographischen Wissenschaft* (ed. F. Klute), Potsdam, 1930.

F. Monheim, 'Studien zur Haziendawirtschaft des Titicacabeckens', *Heidelberger Studien zur Kulturgeographie* (Pfeifer Festschrift), Wiesbaden (1966).

67. P. Pélissier, 'Les paysans Sérères. Essaie sur la formation d'un terroir au Sénégal', *Cahiers d'Outre-Mer* (1953), 105–27.

E. Juillard and A. Meynier (trans. W. Hartke), *Die Agrarlandschaft in Frankreich*, Münchener Geographische Hefte, 9 (1955), 23.

68. F. Monheim, *op. cit.* (1954).

69. D. Faucher, *op. cit.* (1934).

F. Monheim, 'Die Anbauverhältnisse auf dem Neckarschwemmkegel im

Jahre 1669. Ein Beitrag zur historischen Agrargeographie', *Berichte zur deutschen Landeskunde* 7 (1951), 87–101.

E. Juillard, 'L'assolement biennal dans l'agriculture septentrionale. Le cas particulier de la Basse-Alsace', *Annales de Géographie* 61 (1952).

W. Boelcke, *op. cit.* (1964).

G. Schröder-Lembke, 'Wesen und Verbreitung der Zweifelderwirtschaft im Rheingebiet', *Zeitschrift für Agrargeschichte und Agrarsoziologie* 7 (1959), 14.

G. Schröder-Lembke, Römische Dreifelderwirtschaft, *Zeitschrift für Agrargeschichte und Agrarsoziologie* 11 (1963), 25.

G. Schröder-Lembke, *Wandlungen in der Flureinteilung und Fruchtolge des Rhein–Main–Gebietes im späten Mittelalter*, Mainz, 1957.

S. Dahl, *op. cit.* (1961).

S. Gissel, *op. cit.* (1968).

J. Thirsk, *op. cit.* (1964).

A. R. H. Baker, *op. cit.* (1965).

70. G. Niemeier, *op. cit.* (1949), 253.

71. W. Lauer, *Formen des Feldbaus im semiariden Spanien*, Schriften des Geographischen Instituts der Universität Kiel, 15, i (1954).

72. A. Krenzlin, *op. cit.* (1955).

73. A. R. H. Baker, *op. cit.* (1965).

74. F. Monheim, *op. cit.* (1954).

75. F. Tichy, *Die Land- und Waldwirtschaftsformationen des kleinen Odenwaldes*, Heidelberger Geographische Arbeiten, 3 (1958).

76. W. Müller-Wille, *op. cit.* (1941), 42.

77. J. T. Coppock, *An Agricultural Atlas of England and Wales*, London, 1964.

78. H. Uhlig, *op. cit.* (1959; 1961).

79. H. C. Darby, 'An Historical Geography of England: twenty years after', *Geographical Journal* 126 (1960), 147–59.

80. H. P. R. Finberg, 'The Open Field in Devon', W. G. Hoskins and Finberg: *Devonshire Studies*, London, 1952, 265–88.

A. R. H. Baker, *op. cit.* (1965), 5.

81. W. Müller-Wille, *op. cit.* (1936).

82. H. Uhlig, *op. cit.* (1962; 1969).

83. *Ibid.*

84. R. Miller, 'Land Use by Summer Shielings', *Scottish Studies* 11 (1967), 200.

A. Simms, *Die Kulturlandschaft eines 'Keltischen Reliktgebietes' im nordwestschottischen Hochland. Aufgezeigt am Beispiel von Assynt*, Giessener Geographische Schriften, 16 (1969).

85. A. Beuermann, 'Kalyviendörfer im Peloponnes', *Mortensen Festschrift*, Veröffentlichungen der Akademie für Raumforschung und Landesplanung, 28, Bremen, 1954.

7
The dynamic quality
of Irish rural settlement

Desmond McCourt

In the study of European settlement patterns there have been two outstanding landmarks since Meitzen's pioneer work in 1895,[1] both organized under the auspices of the International Geographical Union: the Commission on Types of Rural Settlement of 1928 and the symposium held at Vadstena during the nineteenth International Geographical Congress in 1960. Each produced a synthesis of views on the settlement problems then current,[2] and the progress that had been made in the period between them is exemplified by their respective findings in regard to Ireland. The first stressed the predominance there of isolated dwellings set in enclosed farms which were regarded by Demangeon as long-standing developments of an agrarian system geared to stock raising.[3] In the second report, by contrast, the former importance in Ireland of infield–outfield, with hamlet, schemes is recognized and their place within a wider western and central European context appreciated, notably by H. Uhlig.[4]

The key to the progress achieved in the interval between these two landmarks was Estyn Evans's pioneer and penetrating essay of 1939.[5] Before this the different elements in Irish rural settlement had only been partially recognized and their structure, as well as the processes in their development, imperfectly understood. In Seebohm's work, for example, the evidence is conflicting: on the one hand, he was aware of nineteenth-century traces of rundale and 'village' settlement in Ireland which he linked in origin with a tribal stage of agrarian and social development; on the other hand, he described the settlement pattern under this tribal organization as one of 'homesteads scattered over the country' though grouped into 'artificial' or 'numerical' clusters for purpose of tribute or legal jurisdiction.[6] Meitzen, who relied heavily on Seebohm and on the evidence of the 6-inch plans of Irish townlands, drawn in the mid-nineteenth century, emphasized the *Einzelhöf* pattern, which he regarded as a long-standing Celtic feature going back at least to the seventh century, almost to the exclusion of clustered settlement with its associated open-field system. He was not unaware of the existence of the latter, but he does not seem to have appreciated its significance as part of a complex and flexible duality of settlement and field patterns.[7]

Of all the earlier writers H. L. Gray probably came nearest to achieving this understanding, chiefly through his knowledge of the internal structure of Irish open-field communities and thereby of the flexible processes involved in their development.[8] But his findings have only recently received the recognition they deserve,[9] possibly because of his insistence on the label 'Celtic' for field systems of the infield–outfield type in west Britain. His work, like that of the earlier writers generally, also lacked the field-work basis that would have given a functional view of such systems in their ecological setting. In this respect Evans's 1939 study, by combining field investigation in part of west Donegal with archaeological and documentary evidence, was on firmer ground. In essence he saw that the scattered dwellings and compact farm units in many parts of Ireland were a late development evolving from more communal schemes of open-field with clustered settlement. He considered that both *Einzelhöf* and clustered patterns co-existed in Ireland from the Iron Age and that under certain conditions there was the possibility of the former at any time evolving into or emerging from the latter.[10] Not surprisingly, these broad tenets— though based at the time on limited local study—have stood up to later analyses on a national scale.[11] One of these, by the present author, laid emphasis on the dynamic aspects of Irish settlement, recognizing the need to understand the evolutionary processes behind the waxing and waning of house clusters and the space-time changes in their distribution relative to that of *Einzelhöfe*.[12] The present essay is a summary of this earlier work reviewed in the light of material derived from recent regional settlement studies in Ireland.[13]

Clustered and dispersed settlements

Settlement is merely one component of a rural landscape complex which, because it is an expression of man's economic and social relations with his physical and biotic environment, varies in space and is liable to changes through time. For this reason the settlement pattern in any region at a given moment contains elements of diverse origin, some contemporary, others survivals of former ecological adjustments. Failure to recognize the significance of this dynamic element in settlement history led Meitzen to conclude that Ireland's predominantly dispersed pattern was Celtic in origin. In taking this view he exaggerated the degree to which the pattern in his day may have portrayed conditions as they had been in the remote past. It may well be that in certain parts of the late-settled drumlin belt of south Ulster, for example, there had been no pattern other than the dispersed one since Celtic times, but over much of the country the origins of dispersal are extremely diffuse. In many areas the so-called 'Celtic' farmstead is clearly a relatively recent feature, the result of certain economic and social developments in the late eighteenth and early nineteenth centuries. In other areas dispersal was the pattern developed by alien planters in the seventeenth century, especially by English settlers, as, for example, in the lowland corridor reaching along the Lagan valley through north Armagh into east Tyrone. In yet other localities—like Monaghan and Cavan—the even spread of small-holders was largely a product of the resettlement of the native population following the Ulster plantations.[14]

These diverse origins of the *Einzelhöf* may also explain why dispersal does not form a homogeneous pattern in Ireland. On the dissected drumlin country of Cavan, Monaghan and mid-Armagh, or on the hummocky dead-ice topography of east Tyrone, where small-holdings predominate, the farmhouses are scattered in an even film because each kame or drumlin mound provides a separate dry-point settlement site. Alternatively, the pattern created by landlords and their agents in marginal areas in the early nineteenth century consists of hillside and bogside alignments resulting from the placing of the new homesteads near the junction of arable and pasture land on the redesigned striped holdings. Professor Hughes speaks of other linear patterns of cottier houses around the margins of the grazier estates of Leinster.[15]

Dispersed settlement, though now predominant in Ireland, is not entirely ubiquitous, for here and there in the remoter parts of the north and west are vestigial traces of another settlement form—small clusters of farmsteads. Both Seebohm and Meitzen had noticed these in the nineteenth century without fully appreciating their historical significance, for even in their day they were anachronistic features. Ulster geographers after Evans call these settlements 'clachans', a word derived from Scottish Gaelic and still used locally in this sense in Donegal, north Antrim and north Derry, and in the early nineteenth century among people of Scottish descent in south Armagh.[16] The Irish word *baile* was also used for such settlements, but a source of some confusion is the fact that it was also the name for the associated unit of land—the townland—and could be applied to all types of settlement whether scattered or clustered. An alternative name is 'town', from 'ton', the Old English equivalent for *baile*.

But though 'ton', meaning a village in the English sense, was equated with *baile* in medieval documents from the twelfth to the fourteenth century, it must have been recognized at the time that there was no more than a passing resemblance between the two settlement forms. The English agricultural village, cast in its manorial shell and within the territorial framework of the parish, belonged to a feudal-manorial order; the Irish clachan was an outgrowth of tribal society and functioned within a framework of minute territorial divisions and an agrarian–tenurial system different from that of contemporary England. It is only by studying the clachan as an integral and functioning part of this socio-economic complex that one can hope to understand its evolutionary character. But this complex is difficult to analyse because it is an accretion of elements of varying age and diverse origin which have experienced change at varying rates and have undergone modifications in response to locally varied environmental conditions. Consequently field evidence and documentary sources of the last three centuries reveal not an established, uniform synthesis but various combinations of elements changing both temporally and areally. The one common factor was economic—an agrarian system which had many facets, the particular blend in any area depending on the physical setting and the different categories of land use available for exploitation. In response to environmental and cultural factors there was a strong bias towards stock raising, using the extensive areas of hill pasture, grazed in common in summer, to supplement the grazing found within the township. Cultivation was a subsidiary activity, but varied somewhat in importance with locality, being more developed in the south-east than in the north and west because of ecological and historical factors. Its intensity, too, was variable, depending on soil fertility, size of population relative to the amount of land suitable for conversion to arable, the availability of fertilizers, and regional agricultural practice. Geographers in the north of Ireland, working in an area noted for its historical connections with Scotland, have perhaps unduly stressed the distinction so strongly marked in Scottish usage, and to some extent in that of Ulster too, between shifting outfield cultivation and continually tilled infield, one invariably complementing the other.[17] But this duality was less apparent in the rest of Ireland where eighteenth- and nineteenth-century evidence invariably indicates purely movable outfield schemes whose intensity varied locally according to soil fertility and whether or not manure was applied to the crop.[18] These evolved at times and in certain areas, such as the congested west, where supplementary sources of fertilizer were available and where there was increasing population pressure on the decreasing areas of waste land, into schemes of more continuous cultivation—'running the land to heart' was the usual description[19]—and culminated in true infield usage in exceptional instances, as on one Kilkenny farm where ninety successive crops had been taken without fallow or ley intervening.[20]

The conversion of rough pasture or ley grass to crop gave opportunity for a redistribution of the arable portions of holdings; and this flexibility was maintained, where the land was more continuously cultivated, by means of periodic reallotments at intervals of from 1 to 3 years, though by the middle of the nineteenth century permanent occupation of particular holdings had become fairly widespread. To these recurrent allocations of land were added the less regular redivisions that took place among the coheirs of a deceased person in accordance with the custom of partible inheritance. The aim of these periodic land adjustments was to equalize shares over a period of time in relation to the changing state of population. To attain this they were not merely given the same area; their constituent portions of land were scattered over soils having a similar range of quality, situation and exposure. The resulting landscape was normally one of open fields of intermixed strips and plots whose length, breadth and shape depended on locally varying factors such as soil consistency, topography and technology. But throughout the west, especially in south Connemara, holdings though fragmented had a different field pattern of small, oval-shaped, wall-enclosed patches evolved largely in response to spade cultivation on rocky surfaces and dissected topography, though also possibly reflecting the persistence of ancient agrarian usage.

The effect on this landscape of successive subdivisions among coheirs was progressive fragmentation of intermixed holdings in each succeeding generation. There are cases on record of single compact farms in the late seventeenth century becoming small rundale holdings by the middle of the nineteenth century.[21] Frequently this process was carried to extremes in the congested western areas where population had increased rapidly since 1800 on the limited areas of good land, giving rise to townlands where twenty or thirty holdings might be fragmented in 300 to 400 inter-mixed parcels.[22] In the few instances where the rundale system has survived in the north of Ireland some of the individual holdings are dispersed in twenty or more pieces, and generally these holdings can be traced in origin to a compact farm in the eighteenth century.[23] Even when it is evident that fragmentation had occurred through the subdivision of an original group of two, three or more contiguous farms, these in the beginning were also often held in severalty.[24] Nonetheless, many instances were also documented in the nineteenth century of complex rundale schemes having evolved from farm groups that were in partnership, or held jointly, from the beginning, with commingling of the arable and meadow portions of holdings. Indeed this process, by which either single farms or small jointly-held farms might grow in time into a complex open-field system, was endemic in Irish rural society and is well authenticated in estate maps of the seventeenth and eighteenth centuries. In either eventuality, whether the original holdings were in severalty and compact or in common and commingled, inheritance and subsequent subdivisions took place only within the confines of each ancestral holding and among the kindred descended from each of the original holders. Accordingly, even where an open-field complex has evolved from an original joint-farm group, the pattern of fragmentation will betray the location of the original holdings.[25]

The progressive subdivision of ancestral holdings, which was often the basis of rundale developments, was connected with the expansion of the founding families to form larger and wider kindred associations whose members grouped their houses around the original single family farmsteads to form clachans. This tendency to live in family clusters instead of isolated farmsteads was largely a response to the high degree of mutual dependence made necessary in Irish agrarian–tenurial practice. This was manifest in the regulation of common grazings, co-operative ploughing, the frequent redistributions of cultivated and meadow land, and other communal obligations, and also in the scattered pattern of land holding. It was in keeping, too, with the familistic basis of Irish society according to which the kin-group (*fine*), containing all the relations in the male line of descent for several generations,[26] was the normal unit for owning and inheriting property. Frequently the patronymic name was incorporated in the name of the clachan, usually following the prefix 'bally' or followed by the suffix 'town'. But this causal link between social organization, field system and settlement pattern was apparently not a constant, for in Wales the existence of the kin-group (*gwely*) as the basic unit of social organization, and of fragmented ancestral holdings laid out in bundles of strips, did not in certain areas prevent the dispersal of settlement in scattered homesteads (*tyddynod*) belonging to free tribesmen.[27]

Clustered settlement could, and on occasion did, exist in certain parts of Ireland independently of open-field cultivation. Buchanan has shown, for example, that many clachans arose during the eighteenth century in parts of south-east County Down after rundale had given way to single tenancies, and frequently among descendants of seventeenth-century 'planters'.[28] Similar developments have been attested south-west of Lough Neagh on the former lands of the Brownlow family. A sequence of estate maps of the mid-eighteenth century and mid-nineteenth century shows clachans growing both from the subdivision of single tenancies and from small settlement groups which, in townlands occupied by the Irish, were associated with partnership tenancy from the beginning and in 'planter' townlands with holdings in severalty. Subdivision in the Irish areas resulted in fragmented rundale holdings, and in the English areas in an increased number of small compact farms.[29] Uhlig would hesitate to designate clusters without rundale developments as clachans, preferring instead to call them hamlets.[30] In the south-west Lough Neagh region these hamlet settlements have been adopted by the immigrant planters in imitation of native practice because they suited a fenland environment where arable holdings and habitations became concentrated on the dry-point sites afforded by the occasional drumlin.

The process by which single families spilled over to form clachan communities continued to operate especially in those parts of northern and western Ireland where native institutions were still strongly entrenched in the mid-nineteenth century; this was noted by both travellers and by those sitting on the various royal commissions of the period. For example, a witness of the 1845 Devon Commission stated that in the south-west of the country 'upon every townland there was a village which had accumulated during the time of the lease, the original lessee subdividing and resubdividing till at length the village was created'.[31] It was the sporadic way in which such settlements grew that explains their haphazard layout, a notable contrast to the more regular plan of most English manorial villages.

Though it is often the single farm that emerges when we are able to trace clachans to their origin, not every clachan developed as a kin-group from an original single farmstead. It is clear from a comparison of estate maps of different periods that often the oldest nucleations were found where joint-leasing by small partnership groups was permitted. To begin with these were not kin-groups, the founding partners being unrelated. But in time, through population increase and subdivision of the ancestral holdings, separate agnatic associations tended to develop and on occasions to form distinct family groups within the main nucleus. Leasing to partnership groups became common in the eighteenth and nineteenth centuries, especially in the western counties of Mayo, Roscommon, Donegal and Galway, where it was only by combining their labour and equipment that the increasing number of small tenants found it possible to take up leases of land.

Thus in the Irish, and to some extent also the Scottish, settled areas, where rundale agrarian–tenurial arrangements were tradi-

K

tional, there was no sharp distinction between isolated farmstead and clachan from the seventeenth century on. Both were part of a single flexible scheme of settlement and land holding within which nucleation and dispersal, joint and individual ownership, were alternative and often co-existing developments. In some instances holding was exclusively by partnership, in others the single farm was locally predominant; but more often both forms existed together harmoniously in the same townlands, the predominance of either at a given time depending on changing social and economic factors. Moreover, as there was an endemic tendency for one form to develop into another, settlement in Irish townlands was constantly in a state of flux. Where estate maps give a continuous picture back to the seventeenth century, the pattern emerging at a particular time is invariably the mixed one of *Einzelhöfe* and clachans with groups of varying size between these extremes.[32]

The obvious weakness of such flexibility was the tendency inherent in rundale practice to extreme fragmentation of property. However, as long as a rough balance was maintained between the size of population and the amount of cultivable land available to colonists from groups that were becoming overcrowded, there was no danger of subdivision becoming excessive. Even where this might have happened locally it would seem there were built-in checks to prevent it getting out of hand. For example, one of the functions of the *derbfine*—the kin-group within which the inheritance of land was normally confined—was to put a brake on the fragmentation of joint-family property by limiting inheritance to those descended from a common great-grandfather.[33] Ó Buachalla, in his researches on ancient Irish law, was also of the opinion that 'village' clusters were once confined by blood relationship to certain degrees of kindred only.[34] There is no hint in the laws as to how those outside the *derbfine* acquired land; one may speculate that pressure on the parent joint-family farm was relieved by the formation of secondary settlements on not too distant pockets of suitable land where, in time, new and distinctive *derbfine* kin-groups evolved. Though customary regulations of this kind seem to have been set aside by the time detailed documentary evidence became available in the eighteenth and early nineteenth centuries, landlords who were resident and interested in estate improvement were able to keep subdivision within bounds because of the frequency of tenancy-at-will and the prevalence of short-term leases (generally for not more than 31 years) which allowed them to rearrange holdings periodically on their lands. On Tory Island where this *clann* system of inheritance continues unrestrained by institutional sanctions, holdings are kept relatively stable by self-imposed customary checks such as the tacit abandoning of claims on the part of those marrying into land.[35]

Generally the growth in the size of kin-groups was gradual, and their clustered settlements remained fairly small till towards the end of the eighteenth century. There were several reasons for this: checks to the subdivision of holdings, the smallness of Celtic territorial units, more extensive and shifting schemes of cultivation, the preeminence of stock raising and the existence of extensive areas of uncolonized waste land capable of absorbing a population which, though it was slowly increasing, was still small following the social and political disruptions of the sixteenth and seventeenth centuries. For example, of 150 clachans recorded by the author from estate maps covering parts of counties Derry, Antrim and Down around 1780, the biggest contained eleven houses, only fifteen had six or more houses, and the average size was 3·5 houses. But during the agricultural prosperity of the later eighteenth century and the first quarter of the nineteenth century cultivable land became increasingly scarce as population grew rapidly and encroached on the former waste. This restricted the hiving-off of new farmsteads or joint-family groups and thereby caused a continual expansion in the size of existing nuclei and the progressive subdivision of their arable and meadow portions until the whole system was undermined and the landlords had to intervene, carrying out sweeping rearrangements of holdings and settlement. The evolutionary trend in Claggan townland, near Limavady in north Derry, where a group of two houses in 1698 doubled in size by 1782 and eventually grew to a clachan of eighteen dwellings in 1832, illustrates the essentially dynamic character of Irish settlement in this period.[36]

But it was the rapidity of such developments between the late eighteenth century and the first reliable census of 1841, during which the Irish population increased by over 100 per cent,[37] that is really striking. In such circumstances, with clachans growing in the course of two generations, the former checks to subdivision associated with the four-generation *derbfine* group would no longer have been effective even if they had continued to exist. For example, the townland of Dreenan, County Derry, which was leased as one compact farm in 1734, was found to contain a group of twenty-five families all descended from the original lessee when leases were renewed in 1861;[38] in County Clare the entire 'village' of Liscanor, containing 200 houses, developed on a virgin site between 1775 and 1841.[39] But the reverse process—the replacement of clachans by dispersed farmsteads, following the break-up of rundale by landlords and the rearrangement of the fragmented holdings into compact, enclosed farm units—was equally endemic and especially rapid after the mid-nineteenth century. This waxing and waning process was aptly illustrated in the townland of Upper Beltany, County Donegal, where a single dwelling on a compact farm of 205 acres in the late eighteenth century evolved by the 1840s into a clachan of twenty-nine households with holdings fragmented into 422 intermixed lots. After landlord intervention it reverted just as quickly to a pattern of scattered dwellings each placed on a ladder-shaped farm.[40]

The distribution of settlement types

It is clear from the way clachans with fragmented rundale holdings evolved from single farms and dispersed just as fortuitously again, that the relative distributions of the two settlement types were liable to fluctuations from one period to another according to changing social and economic conditions.

The present pattern is clearly predominantly dispersed, with clachans that have survived the wholesale clearances and land rearrangements of the nineteenth century forming an anachronistic and residual element around the seaboard and hill margins of the north, west and south. But traced back to the 1840s when population in Ireland was at its peak, these clustered farm groups increase in number and their distribution becomes more extensive. Figure 4, based on the 6-inch plans of the first edition of the Ordnance Survey published between 1832 and 1840, shows the main areas of dispersal and clachans at this period and provides a useful vantage point for assessing the various factors behind their respective distributions. The distinction between the eastern area of dispersal and the crescent of clachan concentration in the north, west and south-west is strikingly sharp and seems to be the product of centuries of social and cultural change rather than of marked physical differences; in fact both patterns extend over wide areas with little reference to environmental conditions.

The predominance of the *Einzelhöf* over the Central Plain from the Ulster corridor to east Munster and Leinster is related to several factors. Firstly it is linked with the prevalence there (in what physically is the most favoured part of the country) of compact farms in severalty, larger than the subsistence holdings along the western margins. Most of these eastern farms were created by the colonial landlord class which, from the Anglo-Norman period onward, and especially following the plantation schemes of the seventeenth century, succeeded in wresting much of the land of Ireland from the native owners, many of whom were shifted to harsher habitats in the west. As Professor Hughes has shown, it was in these eastern counties that the grip of the landlords was tightest when the system of the landed estate was at its height in the eighteenth and early nineteenth centuries.[41] Here lived the sponsors of the new agrarian ideas and techniques promulgated by contemporary literature, and here their modifications of landscape and rural society were most marked and complete, fragmented rundale holding especially being rigorously opposed.

The dispersal of settlement in south Ulster from Armagh to Cavan, with an extension into Leitrim, is distinctive. Here it was a concomitant of the pattern of small compact farms that emerged in this dissected drumlin region from the land redistribution schemes of the seventeenth-century 'plantations'. Some of these farms represented grants made to the new alien settlers though possibly perpetuating originally small native holdings; others were the product of allocations to natives displaced from the northern parts of Ulster.[42] Their size was further reduced by subsequent subdivision aggravated during the eighteenth and nineteenth centuries by the growth of rural population and the practice of combining agriculture with the domestic manufacture of linen so that by 1841 at least eight-tenths of holdings were less than 15 acres in size.[43]

Secondly, the dispersed settlement pattern in the eastern half of Ireland was related to the more individualistic and commercial type of agriculture that developed there from 1750 onwards. This trend owed much to the high prices for livestock and corn in Britain

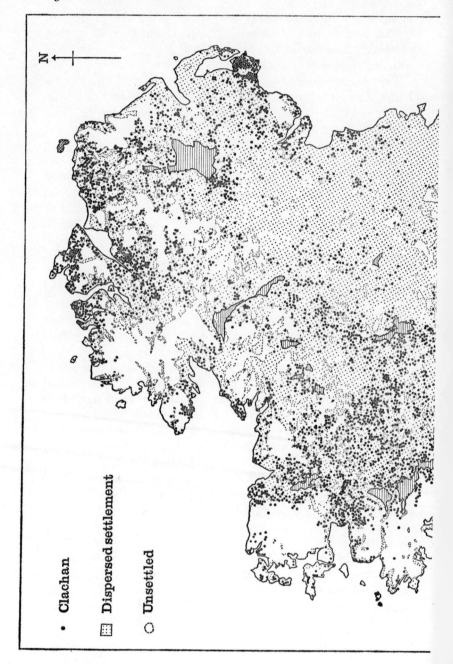

N ←——

• Clachan

⊞ Dispersed settlement

○ Unsettled

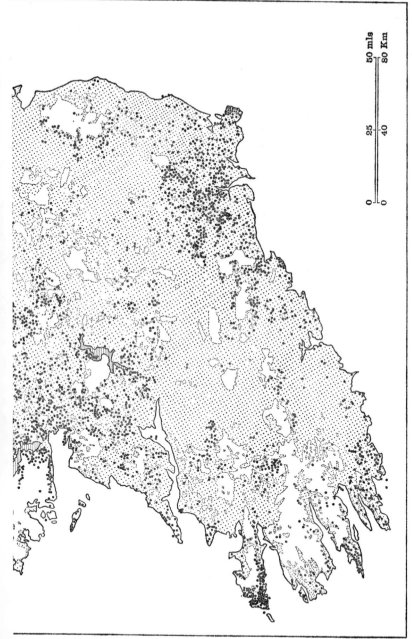

Figure 4   Rural settlement patterns, 1832–40

during the French wars, to increased demand for food by the rapidly growing home population and to the stimulus of the landlords who in the same period were not only showing interest in estate improvement but also, less altruistically, in the higher rents to be expected from individual tenancy and commercial farming. Tillage especially expanded in response to these stimuli, mainly in the counties south-east of a line from east Down to Clare, and particularly in the area from south Kildare to Waterford and Wexford where there had been a continuous tradition of intensive arable farming from Anglo-Norman times.[44] In contrast, stock-raising interests were paramount over the midlands from east Connacht to west Munster, the wealthiest Irish farmers of the period probably being the graziers of Limerick, Tipperary, north Roscommon, south-east Galway, Longford, east Clare and parts of Sligo. Here a tradition of stock-rearing dated back possibly to the Celtic colonization, for these counties have the greatest surviving concentration of raths, the remains of the farmsteads of Celtic cattlemen.

Thirdly, it was the lowlands of eastern Ireland, open to the Irish Sea, that were most exposed to both cultural innovation and the influx of colonist settlers from Britain from Anglo-Norman times onward. Consequently it became a zone of acculturation in which the customs and agrarian practices of the more dominant colonial element in time replaced those of the native society.

The clachan on the other hand was the main form of settlement, within an essentially mixed and flexible pattern, in the north, west and south. This peripheral distribution reflects its residual nature, for though the mid-nineteenth century undoubtedly witnessed a maximum development of clustered groups in areas where communal schemes of land use were still functioning and possibly evolving, the clachan was also a relic in many localities where rundale was already abolished.

The marked concentration of clachans within this marginal crescentic belt of receding native culture is to be explained by several factors. Firstly, the constant westerly dislocation of native people, especially of the landowning freeholders, that followed the land confiscations of the sixteenth and seventeenth centuries, greatly enlarged the already considerable numbers of the same classes in the territory west of the Shannon and led to rapid fragmentation of the existing small properties.[45] This tendency continued in the eighteenth century when the increased emphasis on grazing, begun in the seventeenth century, encouraged the engrossing of small farm units into large grazier ranches, not only in west Leinster but in parts of east Connacht as well. This caused further displacement of population westward.[46] As a consequence, many freeholders who formerly had sufficient land to live off, mainly by cattle raising, were increasingly degraded to the occupation and rank of cultivator. In fact it has been calculated that, from the sixteenth century onward, the non-landowning classes increased in proportion to landowners in the ratio of 4:1[47] so that by the seventeenth century it could be recorded that 'the inferior rank of husbandmen, called *scullogues*, herded together in villages and cultivated the land everywhere'.[48] This suppression of the native freehold classes and their submergence in the mass of lowly cultivators, who had probably been the bond element in medieval Celtic society, continued during the period of the penal laws which for much of the eighteenth century deprived Roman Catholics of the right to buy land or take leases for longer than 31 years. As a result, by about 1780 scarcely 5 per cent of Irish land remained in the hands of native landowners.[49] In this way small peasant holders became preponderant in rural society in the west of Ireland generally.[50] During the late eighteenth and first half of the nineteenth century their numbers increased, partly through subletting by middlemen to hordes of cultivating under-tenants, all competing for land, partly through natural increase in population which reached a peak of over 8 million just before the famine years of 1845–7 and which in the congested west was accommodated by rundale subdivision of holdings that were already unduly small.

A second reason for the high density of clachans in this peripheral area was that this was a refuge area, far distant from the eastern area of innovation. A marginal land in environment and economy, its closed peasant communities existed on small subsistence holdings of the infield–outfield type, retaining an archaic technology and culture generally, and strongly resisting change. Consequently, though these communities also operated within a framework of large landlord estates, the rearrangement of holdings and agrarian improvements, that had wrought such changes in the east, had scarcely begun to touch the landscape of the west by the mid-nineteenth century.

It is apparent from Figure 4 that, within the broad peripheral zone of clachans, there were marked concentrations in certain habitats because they still possessed types of land conducive to exploitation by the communal methods of rundale.

Firstly, distribution was dense in mountain glen and on hill margin: in Antrim, the Sperrins, the west Wicklow mountains, the Mournes, the Knockmealdown and Comeragh ranges of east Cork and Waterford, and on the highland fringes of west Cork and Kerry. In all these clachan survival was due not only to isolation, which delayed agricultural improvements, but also to the presence of marginal land—rough mountain and blanket bog mostly—whose exploitation for turbary, common grazing and outfield intakes helped to prolong traditional agricultural practices and types of settlement.

Secondly, concentration was also marked on the gravel terraces overlooking rivers and lakes where the proximity of fen and seasonal land, flooded in winter and overgrown with natural meadow grass in summer, encouraged communal use of land even after the infield patches had been rearranged and enclosed. This was especially the case around the lakes of Galway (Corrib and Mask), of Mayo (Conn and Cullen) and of the Shannon country (Derg and Ree) as well as northern lakes like Lough Neagh and Beg. The other concentrations close to the flood plains of the rivers Bann, Main and Shannon, the estuary reaches of the Boyne and Foyle and the lower courses of south-eastern rivers like the Nore, Barrow and Suir, are equally marked.

The remaining clachans were densely clustered on nearly all the peninsulas and islands of Ulster, Connacht and Munster, especially the southern tip of the Ards and in Lecale, County Down, as well as the coastal margins of the western and southern counties from Donegal to Wexford. In all of these remoteness from the main currents of social change in the eighteenth and nineteenth centuries was an important factor in allowing old settlement forms to persist. But equally important was the fact that here were to be found special resources like fishing, seaweed and shell beds for providing lime for the infield, all of which not only attracted a dense population and therefore indirectly encouraged fragmentation of holdings, but were also conducive to communal use.

The concentrations of clachans in the northern parts of Ulster appear unusual in view of the systematic plantation of the area in the seventeenth century. They can be explained firstly by the fact that most of the new settlers were Scots who came in great numbers following the Cromwellian and Williamite campaigns of the second half of the seventeenth century and who were already familiar in their own country with runrig practices scarcely different from those of Irish rundale. However, contrary to the terms of the plantation, many of the Irish were permitted to remain in the northern escheated counties, and the open-field communities they evolved, which were interspersed with those of the Scots, were not finally abolished until the middle years of the nineteenth century.

The great numbers of clachans in south Leinster, especially in Waterford, Wexford, Kilkenny and south Carlow, and also in south-east Down, notably in Lecale and south Ards, are in one respect puzzling. These areas were part of the wider manorial territory of eastern Ireland reaching from County Wexford to Down in much of which there were few clachans in the mid-nineteenth century. While there is no certain evidence that clachans were part of the medieval landscape, estate records of the period indicate the presence of septs of servile tenants who were of Irish origin and cultivated the land probably by the native system.[51] These betaghs (Ir. *biatach*), or 'nativi', had been the unfree element of Gaelic society for whom the Norman conquest merely meant a change of overlords.[52] They appear to have lived in kin-groups and it may have been these settlements that survived into the nineteenth century as clachans. Their confinement at that time to certain localities within the former manorial territory may be explained by the fact that the lands they cultivated in common lay in groups of townlands which were quite separate from those of the rest of the agrarian community; moreover they were not an element of all Norman manors.[53] They were probably already strongly localized in the pre-Norman period in areas that had long been traditionally associated with tillage, and the Normans clearly must have regarded them as an asset—the equivalent probably of the cultivating villeins of the English village—and therefore made no attempt to dislodge them or their settlements. It is interesting that when plantation of the Ards region was being mooted in the late sixteenth century the same attitude prevailed, for it was con-sidered an advantage that there were 'great numbers of husbandmen which they call curls come to live under us and offer to farm our grounds'.[54] It may have been the labour potential of this class that influenced the location of the early manors in the areas in which they were concentrated. That some acculturation took place, however, is suggested by the prevalence in these localities of court-yard farm-types and their grouping around a central place or road crossing with a hint of formality that is in contrast to the amorphous character of the Irish clachan.

Thus the distributions of dispersed and clachan settlement shown in Figure 4 reflect one stage in a continuum that was still in motion at the period (1832-40) represented by the map; and the boundary between them indicates a momentary pause in a dynamic situation in which there was a flow of innovation from an expanding southern and eastern area to a receding northern and western one. The former was characterized by a hierarchical social organization dominated by a landlord *élite* who acted as catalysts in a society possessing a considerable alien element which was disposed to accept change and to resist assimilation into the Irish way of life; it also had physical conditions favourable to the diffusion of innovations. In the latter area, by contrast, still largely occupied by native Irish except in north Ulster where the Scots element was strong, society was egalitarian and traditional with an antipathy to change which was reinforced by isolation resulting from marginal location and difficult physiographic conditions. The importance of the Shannon as a cultural barrier is indicated by the sharpness of the boundary between clachan and *Einzelhöf* along its course.

Such a moving frontier between eastern and western elements applies not merely to settlement patterns; it recurs in many other Irish geographical and cultural distributions,[55] in all of which the Shannon divide stands out, emphasizing the consistent pattern of diffusion that runs through the country's cultural history and reflecting a regional dichotomy that is still relevant to the present-day geography and rural sociology of Ireland.

In order to account for changes through time in the location of this boundary between dispersed and clachan settlement one would need to reconstruct their respective distributions for different points in time, an impossible task because of the paucity of detailed data before the nineteenth century. However, it is possible to chart changes during the nineteenth century from the editions of the

6-inch Ordnance maps surveyed around the turn of the present century. These show (Fig. 5) that in the 50 years since the first Ordnance Survey the clachan had receded to the coastal margins of the north, west and south leaving a straggling line of remnants along the former Shannon contact zone. This residual distribution reflects especially the effects of the major social watershed in Irish nineteenth-century life—the famine years of 1845–9 and their aftermath—the wastage of clachans being particularly marked in the south-western peninsulas, Clare and east Connacht where population congestion and rundale had been concomitant features in the first half of the nineteenth century. The disappearance of the clachan from these areas is to be explained by several factors. The increasing substitution of commercial stock-farming for subsistence cultivation in the post-famine period encouraged landlords to consolidate and enlarge the size of farms. They did this in two ways: by amalgamating lands left vacant by rural depopulation, which was particularly heavy following the famine on the fragmented properties in the west; and by clearing them of congested rundale communities, as in the year 1855 when evictions numbered 175,000.[56] This trend towards larger stock farms continued in the 1860s, following the import of foreign grain and the decline in tillage, and in the 1880s as a result of increased emigration.[57] In addition the security of tenure that resulted from the break-up of the landed estates and their redistribution among the former tenants created the appropriate background for a departure from traditional rundale practice and the establishment of more efficient farming based on long rotations and improved grassland husbandry.

Pre-nineteenth-century changes

Fifty years before the first edition of the Ordnance Survey, a map of Irish settlement would probably have portrayed still different distributions from those shown on Figure 4, with perhaps clachans in areas where settlement had become dispersed by the mid-nineteenth century. The task of rediscovering these lost clachans is not easy for, whereas the English manorial village has left notice of its passing in statutes, law suits and parliamentary records, in Ireland no parliamentary authorization was required for the enclosure of open-field communities which, being smaller and milifastic in organization, have bequeathed few legal documents or

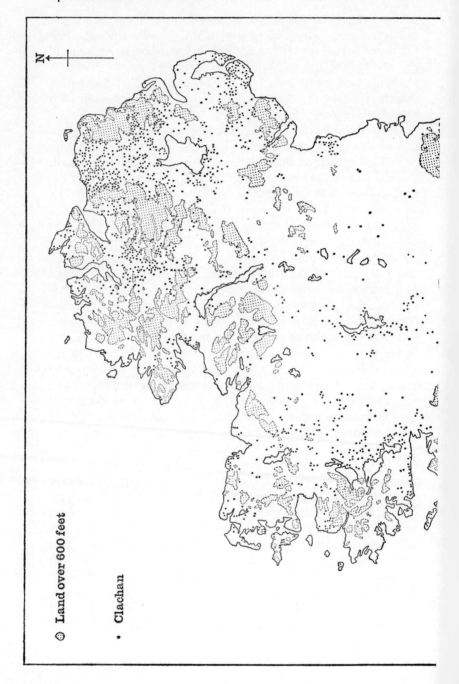

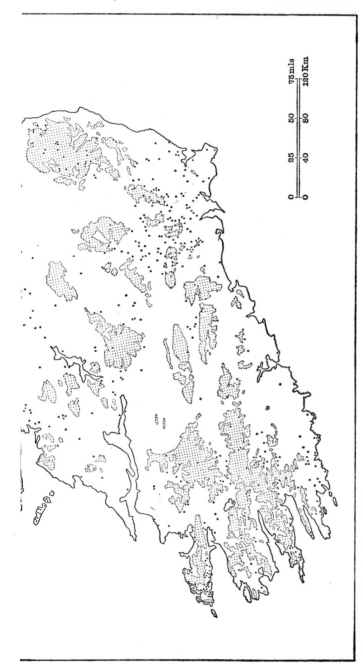

Figure 5   Distribution of clachans, *c.* 1900

even visible signs of their former existence. Consequently a systematic reconstruction of their distribution for earlier periods, which would be invaluable for the analysis of settlement changes in Ireland, does not seem practicable on a national scale, though the few intensive regional studies carried out in this connection show how rewarding an approach of this kind can be.

An alternative approach is to try to discover how widespread the concomitant infield–outfield practices were in the period just before the beginning of the nineteenth century. Statistical and travellers' accounts written at this time are important sources of such information although the evidence tends to be too qualitative to be mapped with any precision. However, they leave no doubt that rundale was practised formerly in many places where there was no sign of clachans on the Ordnance maps of the 1830s. A. Young, for example, referred in the 1770s to the partnership tillage system in east Limerick and over much of Tipperary, especially on the fringes of the Galtee mountains and in the Golden Vale;[58] yet there were scarcely any clachans in these districts some 50 years later. Rundale was also common in parts of Longford and Leitrim at the opening of the nineteenth century;[59] 30 years later there was hardly a kin-group left there. Again, there were no clachans in the vicinity of the Slieve Bloom mountains of Laois in the 1830s; yet Mason's *Parochial Survey* written 20 years previously tells of hamlets and cultivation right to the summits of these hills.[60]

Even when this rather general kind of information is supplemented by an exhaustive examination of all the sources of evidence on rundale for around 1800, the distribution that emerges reveals two facts: first, that this system was formerly practised in western areas like north Roscommon, south-east Galway, Longford and Leitrim where the competition of extensive grazing interests, following the decline in demand for grain at the end of the French wars in 1815, drove out the older subsistence partnership modes of agriculture and associated clachan settlements; second, the only part of the eastern innovative area in which rundale was still to be found in 1800 was in west Tipperary, east Limerick and parts of east Cork, all districts from which it disappeared in the next 50 years, in some areas by replacing subsistence with commercial farming and in other areas by consolidating holdings following the shift to grazing after 1815.

In tracing the history of Irish settlement patterns in the period before the late eighteenth century an important source is the rentals and estate maps that were being drawn up as an aid to estate management from the late seventeenth century onward. Most work of this kind has been concerned with the northern parts of Ireland where it has given a genetic picture of landscape developments during the eighteenth century. But these are areas in which colonization of waste land went on apace and traditional systems of land use and tenure, far from being vestigial, were extremely fluid and still evolving until the beginning of the nineteenth century. In them, too, clachans were still dominant landscape features in the mid-nineteenth century. Ideally, therefore, what is required is an extension of Dr Leister's work on the early documentation of estates in Tipperary[61] to the counties east of the Shannon where, because of the sweeping changes introduced by landlords, there is great difficulty in deciphering the nature of the pre-enclosure landscape and in determining to what extent Irish kin-groups holding land by co-partnership tenure were an important element in it.

Though this eastern region was one in which settlement was almost entirely dispersed in the nineteenth century, there is fragmentary evidence for the seventeenth century of 'villages' and intermixed holdings here, as well as single farms. In some instances these were unmistakably of the rundale–clachan type as, for example, the villages of servile cultivators (*scullogues*) described in Westmeath by Sir H. Piers in 1682.[62] Others are more difficult to define. In the Civil Survey (1654) of lands involved in the Cromwellian resettlement there are frequent references in the schedules of eastern counties like Dublin, Waterford, Limerick, Cork and especially Tipperary, to small nucleated settlements of which there is now scarcely a trace.[63] These are invariably described as 'village' or 'hamlet' but there seem to have been two distinct types. In one the arrangements resemble those of nineteenth-century infield–outfield communities; the number of 'thatcht cabbins' is listed, together with the names of the tenants in common, usually having the same Irish patronymic, and their lands described in terms like 'are soe intermingled by severall ridges amongst the severall proprietors and the pasture divided not that their meares and boundes can not be set forth'.[64] The other type is usually described as having 'a good little castle wanting repaire, with a good thatcht house and

L

bawne about it, some thatcht cabbins, a corne mill [and sometimes a church]'. Commonly, too, the arable holdings are intermixed though there is also frequent mention of 'inclosures with quicksetts'.[65] Settlements of this type may not have been of Irish origin, harking back instead, perhaps, to the villages and rural-boroughs established by Norman lords for their tenants in the eastern shires from Louth to Cork and the borders of Kerry.[66] Some of these were abandoned as a result of agricultural decline and the resurgence of Gaelic power in the fourteenth century, but many remained an important ingredient of the rural landscape with their associated open fields farmed in the two- and three-course rotations familiar in England. This was especially so in Leinster where such field systems survived into the eighteenth and early nineteenth centuries.[67]

Obviously the only way to make anything substantive of documentary evidence of this and similar kinds is to try by field survey and air photography to trace the sites of these deserted 'villages' and to excavate. Indeed this applies equally to the entire medieval period from the Norman expansion in the thirteenth century to the plantations of the seventeenth century—centuries for which documentary evidence is scant but which witnessed profound economic and social change wrought not only by the internal conflicts within a decaying Gaelic culture but also by the impact of planted cultures on the indigenous one.

Settlement origins

Medieval archaeology is unfortunately still in its infancy in Ireland, and those excavations that have been carried out have been too inconclusive to tell us to what extent clachans existed in the Middle Ages.[68] The alternative is to fall back on archaeological evidence of a different kind—the ring forts or raths whose circular earthen remains are marked on the Ordnance 6-inch maps from 1832 onwards and are still scattered by the thousand over the present Irish landscape. Excavation has established that they once enclosed isolated Celtic farmsteads occupied by single families of freehold status whose small, self-sufficient farms were based on mixed farming with a bias towards cattle raising. Their distribution (Fig. 6), taken from the various editions of the Ordnance Survey, suggests at first glance that this was the predominant form of settlement in Ireland during the first millennium A.D., the period in which most raths were probably built, though both Mahr[69] and Glasscock[70] believe they may have been occupied, especially in areas not strongly held by the English, until the end of the Middle Ages, bridging the gap between the Dark Ages and the plantations. They are especially widespread over the lowlands of Munster, Connacht and the adjoining fringes of Leinster, though not in the far reaches of Iar Connacht, largely unsettled until the seventeenth century, nor on the damp, boggy parts of the Central Plain and the Shannon country. But in Ulster, where they thin out rapidly in east Down and towards the north and west, and in south-east Leinster, where there is a striking decline in their numbers east of an arc from Louth through Meath and Laois to Kilkenny, they obviously do not give a complete picture of Irish settlement in this period, for there are extensive areas of good land in both provinces which are not accounted for and which must have been occupied, if not by raths, by some other form or forms of settlement.

The possibility that raths may not have housed the entire indigenous Dark Age–medieval population was first mooted by Dr E. Watson some 30 years ago while working on the prehistoric settlement of north-east Ulster. By plotting the church taxation values returned for the Tax of Pope Nicholas in 1306, which in a general way reflected the distribution of population about the end of the rath era, he was able to point to certain areas in south Antrim, notably the Six Mile Water valley and the shoreland from Carrickfergus to Larne and Islandmagee which had highly assessed churches but few raths, suggesting that a considerable population may have lived there in alternative forms of settlement. Working from distributional evidence he further believed that this population may have spread from the adjoining upland areas of older megalithic settlement.[71] This part of south Antrim had of course been penetrated by the Anglo-Normans which may have affected its church values; more likely it was the fact it was already well settled and cultivated that probably attracted the Normans there in the first place rather than to the pastoral rath areas further west. Proudfoot, using the same kind of evidence as Watson, reached similar conclusions in regard to County Down, showing that the thin scatter of raths in the fertile eastern parts of the county could hardly reflect the entire distribution of Dark Age population and that there must have been other types of settlement whose remains archaeologists have so far failed to locate.[72]

Watson thought these may have been huts which were perhaps attached to the souterrains that occur in such numbers, independently of raths, especially on the extensive sand and gravel spreads on the north side of the Six Mile Water valley.[73] Few souterrains have had their surrounding area examined systematically for structural remains but an unpublished excavation by the present writer of a souterrain (without rath) in similar sand and gravel terrain, at Coshquin, north of Londonderry, did in fact reveal the stone footings of a single small rectangular house built above ground about 4 feet from the stone-lined, underground storage place. Waterman discovered a similar unenclosed house while excavating a souterrain at Craig Hill near Bushmills, County Antrim.[74] As one writer estimated that the souterrains of this south Antrim area were 'as numerous as existing farms', a dispersed settlement pattern is indicated, though the discovery here of as many as five souterrains in one field equally suggests a tendency for houses to be loosely clustered.[75] Proudfoot likewise concluded that undefended house clusters, which he termed 'proto-clachans', may have co-existed with scattered rath settlements in the eastern part of County Down.[76]

There is some support from other fields of study for the view that Irish settlement during the first millennium A.D. had such a dual basis. The ancient law tracts, allowing for the defect that 'they ought not to be called law being bad custom',[77] codified from different periods and different parts of the country and compiled between the seventh and ninth centuries, are an important source in this respect. They tell of an ordered agrarian society broadly stratified into free and unfree elements, the former possessing private land and occupying single-family raths, the latter living on tribal common land, subject to periodic redistributions, and forming partnership groups ('comorbships') out of which Sullivan believed small 'villages' and rundale schemes arose.[78]

It has been suggested that these clusters of base tenants were located in areas long settled by early subject people who were for the most part permitted to remain on their lands under Celtic overlordship.[79] There is evidence in the laws that the unfree were grouped in distinctive *aithech tuatha*[80] (tribute-paying septs) occupying lands quite separate from those of the freemen whose raths perhaps indicate the full extent of Celtic colonization. This would lead one to look for the structural remains of bond clusters in areas complementary to those settled by raths. But, apart from sporadic traces in stoney upland areas of hut-with-field complexes, such as at Scrabo, County Down,[81] Cush, County Limerick,[82] or at Two Mile Stone,[83] County Donegal, which Duignan suggests was a crofter community of the middle of the first millennium A.D., dominated by landlords who inhabited the cashels associated with the lesser huts,[84] identifiable sites for excavation are lacking perhaps because, being undefended and built of wattle and timber or mud, they would have left no surface impression. Nor have any markings shown up, to date, from the air. This suggests an alternative possibility, which is really reviving a view put forward tentatively several years ago both by Evans and the present writer and which is in keeping with the continuity that runs through Irish pre-history and history:[85] that the servile cultivators of the laws (*bothaig* or *scullogues*) living in their clustered kin-groups have remained a constant element through centuries of change and conquest irrespective of changing overlordships. Descendants mostly of Neolithic farmers who were absorbed into the hierarchical social order introduced by the later Indo-European conquerors, they continued under the Norman yoke as the serf-like betaghs, *adscripti glebae*, though located on their traditional lands in clustered settlements which, like those that survived in the non-manorial parts of the country, came through the vicissitudes of the sixteenth and seventeenth centuries to be mapped by the Ordnance Surveyors in the middle of the nineteenth century.

If the nineteenth-century clachan is truly the successor of the proto-historic bond cluster, one might expect its distribution (Fig. 4) to be in some measure complementary with that of the rath (Fig. 6), assuming they were the settlements respectively of early and later colonists. Naturally there is limited value in comparing distributions which are neither contemporaneous nor complete and were liable to changes through time. That of the clachan was largely fashioned by the actions of planters and improving landlords of the seventeenth and eighteenth centuries and so cannot accurately portray conditions as they were in the medieval period or earlier. The rath map, encompassing at least 1,000 years in time, gives no

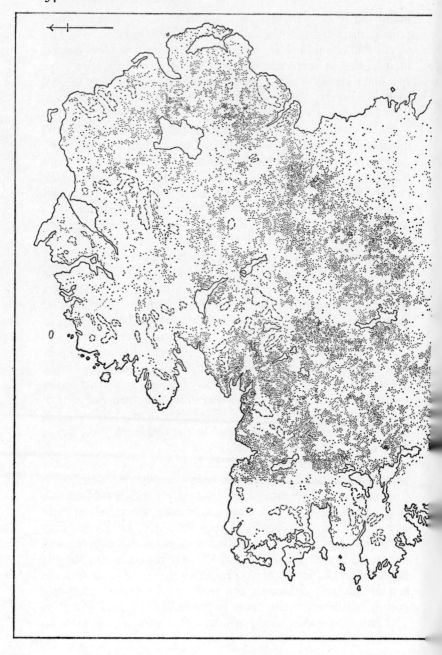

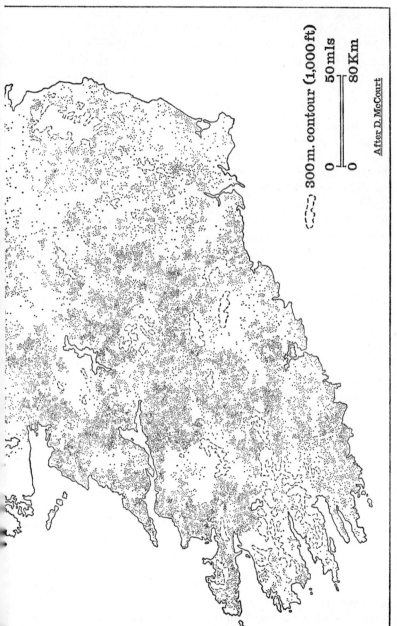

Figure 6   Distribution of raths: dot represents one rath

impression of distribution at a given moment within that span. Here and there, indeed, it may be purely relic.

Nevertheless, in certain areas, especially in Ulster, along the Shannon and in the river valleys of the south-east—all of them long settled—there are striking numbers of clachans in localities where raths are thin on the ground, a fact of distribution which may hark back to their different origins. Contrariwise, where raths are concentrated in much of Munster and in the western counties of the Central Plain, including Longford, Westmeath and Offaly, there are few clachans though this may not always have been so. The rareness of either type of settlement in the eastern counties may be due to the removal of one or other or both to make way for Anglo-Norman and later English colonists who seem to have introduced new settlement forms there. The one puzzling feature is the presence of unusual concentrations of both raths and clachans west of the Shannon in Connacht and Clare, areas not renowned for their fertility. The clachans mapped are of mid-nineteenth-century date, many of them in Iar Connacht, according to MacAodha, no earlier than the seventeenth century in origin;[86] the raths are at least 1,000 years earlier. One is therefore tempted to suggest that here an early pattern of raths evolved to a later one largely of clachans as a result, presumably, of increased population and fragmentation of ancestral rath farms. It has already been shown that such flexibility of settlement was endemic in areas of Irish occupation. Johnson, however, doubts if a people with a strong tradition of compact property would be prepared to make the grave break in habit involved in the subdivision of unified farms into smaller rundale holdings.[87] But this is precisely what happened in the west where a social revolution, arising from land-confiscation and dislocation of population in the seventeenth century, drove great numbers of the rath-owning freeholders into the menial ranks beneath them. In fact MacAodha has shown that the dichotomy between clustered and dispersed settlement in Iar Connacht was by no means rigid and that the majority of clachans there grew up around a single homestead or at most around a pair.[88]

Because of the discrepancy in time between the clachan and rath distributions it is not to be expected that they would accurately represent the areas occupied by each settlement type in the Dark Ages. Moreover, the nature of settlement in the east and south-east in which raths abruptly thin out is problematical. But there is evidence of another kind, admittedly speculative, which promises to throw light on the location of 'proto-clachans' in the period of the rath. Using the ancient glosses, the late Séan MacAirt suggested that the Irish word *baile* (whence English 'bally') may be of pre-Goidelic origin and that the occurrence of 'bally' in place names may indicate where the older peoples had been left undisturbed by the Goidelic expansion.[89] Proudfoot, pursuing this suggestion, found by mapping townlands in County Down containing the element 'bally' that they and raths tended to occupy complementary areas and therefore may have co-existed.[90] Glasscock thought this true for the country as a whole but the map he based his views on included townlands merely with the prefix 'bally'.[91] When townlands incorporating the element 'bally' generally are mapped (Fig. 7), their complementary relationship to raths while broadly apparent in Ulster is not so clear-cut in the rest of the country where indeed the distribution of 'ballys' is perplexing. They are numerous both in the clachan areas of the south-east and in the zone of rath concentration in Munster and east Connacht, but almost disappear in Monaghan and Cavan where raths are particularly thick on the ground. They are also, like raths, almost entirely lacking in Leitrim and Longford. But the two outstanding features of this 'bally' map are the almost empty spaces in the broad drumlin corridor from south Armagh and Monaghan to Mayo, Sligo and Roscommon, late settled and long a barrier between north and south, and in the eastern counties of Kildare, Dublin and Meath.

How is the lack of both raths and 'bally' townlands in these fertile and well-settled eastern counties to be explained? The clue perhaps lies in the fact that here the Irish *baile* was frequently rendered in medieval English as 'ton' and later as 'town'. When townland names containing the element 'ton' or 'town' are added to the 'bally' map, it is precisely in the east they are concentrated though also occurring sporadically in the south-east.

If MacAirt's hypothesis is correct, from the distributional evidence one would see the plebeian 'bally' settlements in the Dark Ages interspersed and perhaps closely associated with the rath in certain areas, while in other long-settled localities, perhaps untouched by Goidelic colonization, forming an almost exclusive and complementary pattern. If, as early sources such as Cormac's

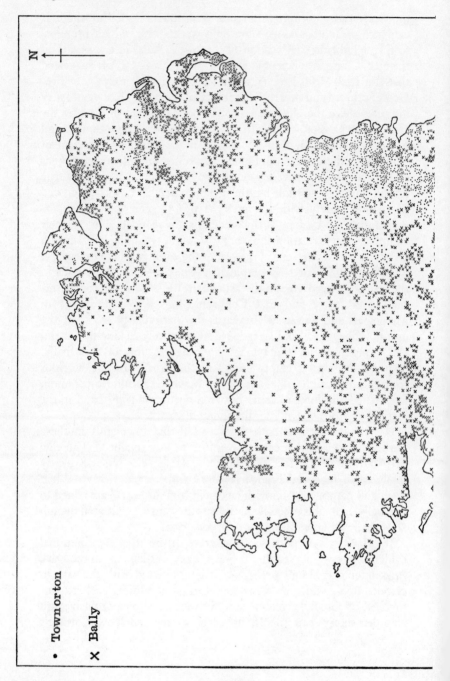

Townorton
Bally

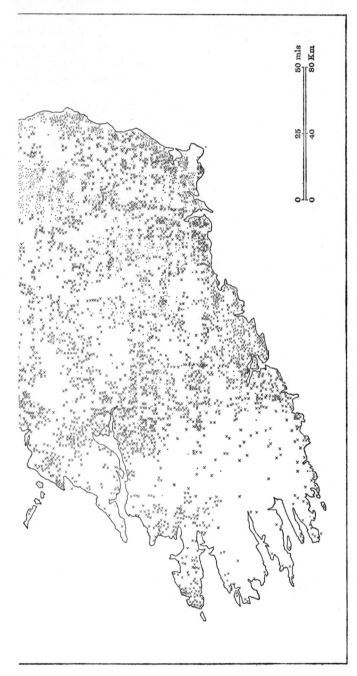

Figure 7   Distribution of place names containing the elements 'bally' and 'ton' or 'town'

Glossary (*c.* A.D. 900) suggest, *baile* was simply during a certain period an alternative for rath,[92] then the 'bally' distribution may merely broadly reflect the extent of Irish settlement on the eve of the Anglo-Norman conquest, for, as MacAirt admits, there is scarcely any evidence for the use of *baile* in place names before the eleventh or twelfth century.[93]

One thing is clear from this historical approach to the study of Irish settlement: single farms and kin-groups have been persistent forms from very early times and their respective distributions have fluctuated from one period to another according to changing social and cultural circumstances. It may be that prior to the medieval hiatus their distributions were more closely intermingled, allowing for some concentration of kin-groups in the areas of older, perhaps pre-Goidelic, settlement. But the dislocations and social upheaval arising from the various plantations and from the subsequent era of landlordism brought a sharp distinction between eastern areas of increasingly dispersed settlement and those in the west with a mixed and ever-changing pattern in which the clachan tended to become more and more the predominant element. The social catastrophe of the Famine and its aftermath sharply reversed this trend in western areas and out of it there emerged the present ubiquitous pattern of scattered farmsteads.

Notes

1. A. Meitzen, *Siedlung und Agrarwesen*, Berlin, 1895, 3 vols and atlas.

2. *Report of the Commission on Types of Rural Settlement: International Geographical Congress*, London and Cambridge, 1928.

S. Helmfrid (ed.), *Morphogensis of the Agrarian Cultural Landscape* [published as *Geografiska Annaler* 43 (1961)].

3. A. Demangeon, 'La géographie de l'habitat rural', *Geografiska Annaler* 43 (1961), 59.

4. H. Uhlig, 'Old hamlets with infield and outfield systems in Western and Central Europe', *Geografiska Annaler* 43 (1961), 285–312.

5. E. E. Evans, 'Some survivals of the Irish openfield system', *Geography* 24 (1939), 24–36.

6. F. Seebohm, *The English Village Community*, London, 2nd ed., 1883, 225–44.

7. A. Meitzen, *op. cit.*, I, 196–7, 207–17.

8. H. L. Gray, *English Field Systems*, Cambridge, Mass., 1915, 189–98.

9. A. R. H. Baker, 'Howard Levi Gray and English Field Systems: An Evaluation', *Agricultural History* 39 (1965), 86–91.

10. E. E. Evans, *op. cit.*, 28.

11. See especially P. Flatrès, *Géographie rurale de quatre contrées celtiques*, Rennes, 1957.

12. D. McCourt, 'The Rundale System in Ireland: a Study of its Geographical Distribution and Social Relations' (Ph.D. thesis, Queen's University, Belfast, 1950), 310–23.

13. T. J. Hughes, 'Landholding and settlement in the Cooley Peninsula of Louth', *Irish Geography* 4, 3 (1961), 149–74; 'Landlordism in the Mullet of Mayo', *Irish Geography* 4, 1 (1959), 16–34.

F. H. A. Aalen, 'Some historical aspects of landscape and rural life in Omeath, Co. Louth', *Irish Geography* 4, 4 (1962), 256–78.

J. Anderson, 'The decay and breakup of the rundale sytem in the barony of Tirhugh', *Donegal Annual* 6, 1 (1964), 1–42.

14. T. J. Hughes, 'Landholding and settlement in the Cooley Peninsula of Louth', *loc. cit.*, 151–4.

15. *Ibid.*, 160.

16. J. Donaldson, *A Historical and Statistical Account of the Barony of Upper Fews in the County of Armagh*, 1838 (reprint, 1923), 17.

17. D. McCourt, 'Infield and outfield in Ireland', *Economic Hist. Rev.* 7 (1954–5), 369–76.

18. D. McCourt, 'Rundale and its Social Concomitants' (M.A. thesis, Queen's University, Belfast, 1947), 38–54; 'The Rundale System in Ireland', 61–80.

19. *Devon Commission*, Dublin, 1845, I, 181; II, 420.

20. A. Young, *A Tour in Ireland 1776–78*, London, 1780, I, 113.

21. Seventeenth- and eighteenth- century estate maps of the Manor of Newtownlimavady: *Manor of Newtownlemavady Surveyed 1698; A Map of the Manor of Newtownlemavady, in County Londonderry, Surveyed in 1782 by Patt Roe* [Martin, King, French and Ingram, solicitors, Limavady; photostat copies in PRONI].

22. *Royal Commission on Congestion in Ireland* (1907), report IX, 129, sect. 28610.

Devon Commission, *loc. cit.*, I, 422.

23. D. McCourt, 'Surviving openfield in county Londonderry', *Ulster Folklife* 4 (1958), 27.

24. *Ibid.*, 23, 24, 27.

25. *Ibid.*

26. F. J. Byrne, 'Early Irish society, 1st–9th century', *The Course of Irish History*, Cork, 1967, 49.

M. Dillon and N. K. Chadwick, *The Celtic Realms*, London, 1967, 97.

P. W. Joyce, *A Social History of Ancient Ireland*, Dublin, 2nd ed., 1913, I, 167.

27. E. Jones, 'Settlement patterns in the Middle Teify Valley', *Geography* 30 (1945), 108.

28. R. H. Buchanan, 'The Barony of Lecale, Co. Down—A Study of Regional Personality' (Ph.D. thesis, Queen's University, Belfast, 1958), 109–20.

29. D. McCourt, 'The Rundale System in Ireland', 199–212.

30. H. Uhlig, *op. cit.*, 292.

31. *Devon Commission, loc. cit.*, II, 838.

32. D. McCourt, 'The Rundale System in Ireland', 310–23.

33. In the event of intestacy and lack of immediate heirs within such a group, property could pass to representatives of related but wider types of kin-group that existed for certain special functions: see E. O'Curry and W. K. O'Sullivan, *Manners and Customs of the Ancient Irish*, Dublin, 1873, 3 vols, I (Introduction by Sullivan), clxii; D. A. Binchy, 'Secular Institutions', *Early Irish Society*, Dublin, 1954, 58.

34. L. Ó Buachalla, 'Some researches on ancient Irish law', *J. of Cork Hist. and Archaeol. Soc.* 52 (1947), 43.

35. J. R. Fox, 'Kinship and land tenure on Tory Island', *Ulster Folklife* 12 (1966), 6–7.

36. *Estate Maps of the Manor of Limavady, loc. cit.*

37. T. W. Freeman, *Pre-Famine Ireland*, Manchester, 1957, 16.

38. *Minutes of Evidence of a Commission of Enquiry into the Working of the Landlord and Tenant (Ireland) Act of 1870*: 'Bessborough Commission', II (1880), 405.

39. W. S. Mason, *A Statistical and Parochial Survey of Ireland*, Dublin, 1814, 3 vols, I, 485.

40. *Devon Commission, loc. cit.*, I, 422.

41. T. J. Hughes, 'Society and settlement in nineteenth-century Ireland', *Irish Geography* 5, 2 (1965), 87–9.

42. T. J. Hughes, 'Landholding and settlement in the Cooley Peninsula of Louth', *loc. cit.*, 151–4.

43. T. W. Freeman, *op. cit.*, 56.

44. T. J. Hughes, 'Society and settlement in nineteenth-century Ireland', *loc. cit.*, 82–92.

T. W. Freeman, *op. cit.*, 67–73.

45. G. O'Brien, *Economic History of Ireland in the Seventeenth Century*, Dublin, 1919, 129–31.

46. K. H. Connell, *The Population of Ireland, 1750–1845*, Oxford, 1950, 90–3.

J. C. Beckett, *The Making of Modern Ireland 1603–1923*, London, 1966, 170–6.

F. H. A. Aalen, 'Enclosures in eastern Ireland', *Irish Geography* 5, 2 (1965), 32.

47. G. O'Brien, *op. cit.*, 37.

48. N. Taafe, *Observations on Affairs in Ireland*, Dublin, 1776, 12.

49. M. Wall, 'The age of the Penal Laws', *The Course of Irish History, loc. cit.*, 219–20.

50. G. O'Brien, *op. cit.*, 130.

51. A. J. Otway-Ruthven, 'The native Irish and English law in medieval Ireland', *Irish Hist. Studies* 7 (1950–1), 7.

52. A. J. Otway-Ruthven, 'Enclosures in the medieval period', *Irish Geography* 5, 2 (1965), 35.

53. A. J. Otway-Ruthven, 'The organisation of Anglo-Irish agriculture in the Middle Ages', *J. Roy. Soc. Antiq. Ireland* 81 (1951), 3, 12.

54. H. F. Hore, 'Colonel Thomas Smyth's settlement in the Ardes 1572', *Ulster J. Archaeol.* 9 (1861–2), 179.

55. For example in the following distributions: valuation of rural areas 1850, speakers of Irish 1851 [T. J. Hughes, *Irish Geography* 5 (1965), 82, 94]; farm size 1841, towns 1841 [T. W. Freeman, *op. cit.*, 26, 55]; jamb-wall, byre-dwelling, cap-flail [C. Ó Danachair, *Béaloideas* 25 (1957), 110, 119]; outshot-jamb-wall [D. McCourt, *Ulster Folklife* 2 (1956), 33; *Deutsches Jahrbuch für Volkskunde* 14 (1968), 247–60].

56. P. Flatrès, *op. cit.*, 78.

57. E. E. Evans, Historical Introduction to L. J. Symons (ed)., *Land Use in Northern Ireland*, London, 1963, 38–9.

58. A. Young, *op. cit.*, II, 244, 257.

59. *Ibid.*, 295; J. McParlan, *A Statistical Survey of the County of Leitrim*, Dublin, 1801, 43, 47, 62.

60. W. S. Mason, *op. cit.*, III, 314.

61. Ingeborg Leister, *Das Werden der Agrarlandschaft in der Grafschaft Tipperary*, Marburg, 1963, 88–117.

62. Sir H. Piers, 'A chorographical description of the county of West Meath. 1682', in C. Vallency, *Collectanea de rebus Hibericis*, Dublin, 1770, I, 116–17.

63. R. C. Simington, *Irish Manuscripts Commission: the Civil Survey, A.D. 1654–56*, Dublin, 1931–53, 9 vols.

64. For example: Tipperary, Vol. II, 101, 102, 138; Limerick, Vol. IV, 348.

65. For example: Tipperary, Vol. I, 106, 143, 271, 311.

66. R. E. Glasscock, 'Deserted villages in Ireland', *Studies in Deserted Villages*, M. W. Beresford and J. G. Hurst (eds) [forthcoming].

67. A. J. Otway-Ruthven, 'The organisation of Anglo-Irish agriculture in the Middle Ages', *loc. cit.*, 6.

68. R. E. Glasscock, *op. cit.*

69. A. Mahr, 'New aspects and problems in Irish prehistory', *Proc. Prehist. Soc.*, new ser., 3 (1937), pt. 2, 271.

70. R. E. Glasscock, *op. cit.*

71. E. Watson, 'Prehistoric sites in south Antrim', *Ulster J. Archaeol.* 3 (1940), pt. 2, 142–51.

72. V. B. Proudfoot, 'The economy of the Irish rath', *Med. Archaeol.* 5 (1961), 119.

73. E. Watson, *op. cit.*, 150.

74. D. M. Waterman, 'The Excavation of a House and Souterrain at Craig Hill, Co. Antrim', *Ulster J. Archaeol.* 19 (1956), 87–91.

75. E. E. Evans, 'Newly discovered souterrains in county Antrim', *Ulster J. Archaeol.* 9 (1946), 79.

76. V. B. Proudfoot, 'Clachans in Ireland', *Gwerin* 2, 3 (1959), 112.

77. L. M. Cullen, *Life in Ireland*, London, 1968, 26.

78. E. O'Curry and W. K. Sullivan, *op. cit.*, I, clvii–clix.

79. F. J. Byrne, *op. cit.*, 44.

80. E. O'Curry and W. K. Sullivan, *op. cit.*, I, xxiii, clii.

81. Northern Ireland Archaeological Survey, *An Archaeological Survey of County Down*, HMSO, 1966, 179.

82. S. P. Ó Ríordáin, *Proc. Roy. Irish. Acad.* 45C (1940), 83–181.

83. O. Davies, 'The Two Mile Stone, a prehistoric community in county Donegal', *J. Roy. Soc. Antiq. Ireland* 72 (1942), 98–105.

84. M. Duignan, 'Irish agriculture in early historic times', *J. Roy. Soc. Antiq. Ireland* 74 (1944), 128.

85. E. E. Evans, 'Some survivals of the Irish openfield system', *loc. cit.*, 28. D. McCourt, 'The Rundale System in Ireland', 296.

86. B. S. MacAodha, 'Clachan settlement in Iar-Connacht', *Irish Geography*, 5, 2 (1965), 27.

87. J. H. Johnson, 'The development of the rural settlement pattern of Ireland', *Geografiska Annaler*, 43, 1–2 (1961), 167.

88. B. S. MacAodha, *op. cit.*, 23.

89. S. MacAirt, 'Co. Armagh: toponymy and history', *Proc. Irish Catholic Hist. Committee* (1955), 2–3.

90. V. B. Proudfoot, 'Clachans in Ireland', *loc. cit.*, 112–15.

91. R. E. Glasscock, *op. cit.*

92. V. B. Proudfoot, 'Clachans in Ireland', *loc. cit.*, 112.

93. S. MacAirt, *op. cit.*, 3.

8
Hamlet and village

P. Flatrès

'Hamlet' and 'village' are old words which make one think of traditional settlements of ancient agricultural folk who, from Neolithic times onwards, have tilled the soil and provided the bread. These forms of settlement normally antedate towns and urban cultures. Their present network is the result of a complex evolution going back, directly or indirectly, to the primary pattern of settlement.

Though 'hamlet' and 'village' signify nucleated rural settlements as distinct from isolated farms, their differentiation has been thought necessary to distinguish different types of nucleation. An equivalent dual terminology exists in several European languages: *hameau* and *village* in French, *Weiler* and *Dorf* in German, *aldea* and *pueblo* in Spanish. However, these have not precisely the same meaning in all languages. In English the distinction is based on size, a hamlet being smaller than a village. In French some authors use *hameau* and *village* in much the same way as the English do 'hamlet' and 'village'. But generally, and officially, the difference between *village* and *hameau* is an administrative one. In the French system of local government the *commune* is the basic administrative division, and the seat of the *commune* authority is called the *chef-lieu* to distinguish it from the other places called *hameaux* or *écarts*. *École de hameau* means a school that is not sited at the *chef-lieu*. In some *communes* a *hameau* happens to be a bigger settlement than the *chef-lieu*. In German, generally, *Weiler* is supposed to be a smaller place than a *Dorf*, but the notion of *Weiler* also entails a kind of subordination, at least genetic, in relation to *Dörfer*. A *Dorf* may be very small but is never subordinate.

Moreover, this differentiation of rural nucleated settlements into hamlet and village types is not general in Europe. The Atlantic fringe from northern Portugal to Norway with the often comparable countries of the North Sea, from northern France to the Danish border, is a vast area where the hamlet–village dichotomy has little or no meaning. Here, indeed, the distinction between single farms and groups of farms is not felt to be fundamental. Most Celtic languages in fact use the same basic word for all kinds of agricultural settlement—isolated farms (provided they are fully independent holdings), groups of farms, and settlements which elsewhere would be called villages. In this way are used the Breton *ker*, Welsh *tre*, Irish *baile* and Manx *balla*. In Norway the word *gård* is used in exactly the same way. In the west of France the word *village* is used by the people to describe all kinds of agricultural settlements, most of which would never be called *villages* by other Frenchmen. In the same way 'village' may be used by the English-speaking peasantry of west Britain as an alternative for the more traditional word 'town', in its older sense of a small clustered group sometimes containing as few as two houses which would not even be a 'hamlet' in England.

These clusters of farms have long lacked a convenient terminology. German geographers have used the local word *Drubbel* to describe those of north-west Germany, and Professor Evans has most happily introduced the Ulster term 'clachan' for the clusters of the Atlantic fringe generally.

But the Atlantic fringe has other nucleated settlements which are bigger than, and fundamentally different in nature from, these clusters. Strangers indiscriminately call them 'villages', but for the natives they are something altogether different. Special local names are used for them, especially when they have developed around the parish church. In western France they are known by the word *bourg*, which was borrowed in early times by Bretons to become *borh* or *bourk*. In south-west England the corresponding term was 'churchtown' which is the equivalent of the Cornish *treveglos*, the Welsh *treflan* and the Scotch 'kirktown'. In Ireland non-agricultural settlements are often sited apart from the church and are sometimes known by the term *sráid-bhaile* or 'street-baile'.

In Norway geographers have coined the word *tettstet* for such settlements which are neither agricultural nor urban.

In all these Atlantic countries the indiscriminate use of 'village' and 'hamlet' to describe any kind of rather large rural nucleated settlement is entirely contrary to local usage and understanding, and leads to much confusion.

These difficulties of terminology show that the typology of rural settlements is far more complicated than the simple and familiar 'hamlet–village' dichotomy would suggest. To go further it is necessary to establish principles of classification as objectively as possible.

Size, the simplest criterion

The simplest, and in appearance clearest, criterion is the size of settlements. But here, also, difficulties arise; first of all in establishing the lower and upper size-limits of settlements designated 'hamlet' or 'village'—that is, in determining when a place is too small to qualify as even a little hamlet or when it is too big to be described as a large village.

The question of lower size-limit is essentially that of the differentiation between isolated and nucleated settlements. It has two aspects: distance and actual size. When may two neighbouring houses be said to be part of the same settlement group? If the houses are contiguous, or separated only by a lane or a street or even a small garden, no problem arises. But what is the position if the houses are separated by a large orchard or a field? There must be a distance beyond which it can be said that a house does not belong to the same settlement as its neighbour. This problem does not occur everywhere, which is why it has been rather neglected. In some regions, for example eastern France, south Germany and the Mediterranean islands, isolated farms are clearly separated, radically distinct from the nucleated villages. But in other districts every transition exists between village nuclei, with contiguous houses or houses separated by a few metres, and isolated farms scattered over the parish. At the fringe of the village the distance between the neighbouring houses gets greater and greater, and gradually, over a length of perhaps several kilometres, the village fades into the countryside in such a way that it is impossible to say where the village ends.

Such patterns are characteristic, for example, of the district of Pevèle in northern France, and of Tournaisis in Belgium. They also occur in northern Portugal, between Douro and Minho. Similar transitions between nucleated and dispersed settlements are peculiarly striking where associated with settlements of the *Haufendorf* type. Usually the distance between the farms is such that they may be considered isolated: for example in the regular French-Canadian *rang*, in the original linear defence settlements of Slavonia studied by A. Blanc, and in many marsh settlements of the North Sea countries, the older Dutch polders, the Maritime Plain and the Lys valley in northern France. But in certain places, for some reason, the original planned plots were divided longitudinally and subdivided, with the result that the front of each plot became narrower and narrower and the houses on them nearer and nearer. Eventually, as in parts of Slavonia, and in the dyke settlements of the Netherlands, in Côte de Beauport and Côte de Beaupré in Québec, the houses became almost contiguous and can on no account be described as isolated. How are we to classify such settlements? The most obvious way is to decide on the distance beyond which two houses may be said to be isolated from one another, and within which two houses may be considered as belonging to the same group.

The French statistical office, the INSEE, in its 1962 census, decided by what criteria an *agglomération chef-lieu de commune* might be defined. One of these is a maximal distance of 200 metres between neighbouring houses. This was certainly a step in the right direction but, unfortunately, the distance fixed proved to be too large for any practicable application, as Mlle Dufour in her studies on the *département* of Sarthe, a typical scattered settlement area, was able to show. Actually, in conducting the census most local authorities paid no heed to this criterion. The author of this paper, working on a rural settlement map of northern France, proposed 100 metres as the distance criterion. This estimate, for that area at least, appears to be satisfactory and has been adopted in principle by the Rural Commission of the French Geographical National Committee.

But is it, after all, necessary to use a numerical criterion? The feeling of belonging to a place, a community, might be considered as essential. A suggestion by M. de Planhol, to consider the hearing-limit of the human voice as the maximal distance between the houses constituting a settlement group, underlines the importance of the human links. But social, tribal and technical links can also unite spatially isolated settlements. The loose clusters of west Britain and Ireland, with their isolated houses set around the tillage areas, a pattern of tribal origin, are an example. In some mountainous parts of West Africa, officials and geographers have described as villages settlements what are in fact a scattering of farms over the well-defined area belonging to a tribal or patriarchal community. Such scattered settlements may indeed be considered as social units—community settlements or settlement cells (*cellules d'habitat*). But they must be distinguished from settlements as physical units (*unité d'habitat*) defined by locational criteria. In any case a complete description of a settlement must show the physical location of the houses and so must lead to their classification as isolated, grouped or nucleated.

Once we have decided which houses may be considered as part of the same settlement unit, we still have to decide which settlement units qualify as hamlets or villages. Here again the problem is more or less acute according to region. In eastern France and south Germany there is a wide gap between the villages (*villages; Dörfer*) with usually more than 100 and often several hundred inhabitants, and the isolated farms. But elsewhere, as in the Atlantic fringe, transitions occur, and we may find all kinds of settlement from the isolated farm to the *bourg, pentref* or *tettstet* of nearly 1,000 inhabitants, with groups of two, three, four farms or houses, and thence all the way to places with ten, twenty or fifty dwellings in between. Here again if we are to decide on a typology we must decide on the criteria.

The French INSEE definition of *agglomération chef-lieu de commune* is that it should have at least fifty inhabitants. The Statistical Office of the Republic of Ireland uses a slightly different, but comparable, criterion; it lists as towns all places with '20 houses or more'. These criteria—twenty houses or fifty inhabitants—are reasonably comparable and may be retained as the minimum size of a rural agglomeration.

Between isolated farms or houses and rural agglomerations there exists a third category—clusters of farms or houses—to which most 'clachans' belong and which is worthy of more consideration than it usually receives.

This category is rarely considered by itself. In some regions, such as Mediterranean Europe and Atlantic Europe, it would be regarded as part of the general dispersed pattern. But even small clusters may raise agrarian, sociological and technical problems of a kind that would on occasion justify their being considered villages in their own right. In Sweden the small clusters of farms that existed before the *storskifte* and *laga skifte* often had fewer than ten farms. Nevertheless they were regarded as villages (*by*), and M. St Helmfrid uses the German word *Dorf* to describe them, rightly, in our view, because they played the same role as ordinary villages. Because of the ambiguity arising from the classification of clusters, sometimes as nucleated, sometimes as dispersed settlement, it seems better and more valid to have a separate category for clusters of from two to about twenty farmhouses. Real hamlets and villages, rural agglomerations in general, would be places with more than twenty houses or fifty inhabitants.

The second limit, the upper one, distinguishing rural places from towns has been far more studied and indeed officially fixed in all countries compiling statistics of rural and urban population. The discrepancies in practice between the statistical offices of different countries have often been stressed by urban geographers working on the definition of a town, and there is no point in repeating their arguments here. It should suffice to notice that as far as numerical criteria are used there are two rather different levels at which the limit is usually set. One is at about 2,000 inhabitants—let us say 1,500–3,000. The other is much higher, at about 10,000, 15,000 or even 20,000, for, as E. Juillard has stressed, only places with at least 20,000 inhabitants may provide the essential urban services and functions. Here again, between the normal village and the real town, we have an intermediate type of settlement which in certain countries is classified as village, in others as small town. Most authors would agree that settlements of from 3,000 to 8,000 inhabitants predominantly engaged in agriculture, like certain African, Mediterranean or central European 'giant villages', have an indisputable rural character, whereas a settlement of 2,000 non-agricultural inhabitants is urban in nature. But to avoid ambiguities it is better, in a preliminary typological approach, to exclude settlements of from, say, 2,000 to 20,000 inhabitants.

In between the two intermediate categories of rural clusters and small towns the size of real villages and hamlets varies both in space and through time. The classical West European villages of central and southern Germany, Switzerland, France and England, with their few hundred inhabitants each, have long appeared to geographers as the most common type. But in some regions, as in the southern Jura, smaller villages with 50–150 inhabitants prevail. Recent researches reveal more and more regions with large villages of some thousands of inhabitants, as in western Africa and southern Asia. This category of 'large village' is perhaps the most numerous, but it is difficult to be definite as statistical data are lacking.

West European villages, moreover, fluctuate in size through time. After a long period of growth, interrupted sometimes by severe set-backs, they usually—on the Continent at least—reached their highest population towards the middle or end of the nineteenth century. Since then only the villages in industrial areas have continued to grow. The others declined, at first slowly, later often rather quickly, so that it is difficult, even for this acknowledged type of village, to specify a size bracket.

It is therefore difficult to establish a village typology based on size. Nevertheless considerations of size are important, and must be stressed first in all settlement studies. Differences of size may be of ethnic origin. For example, Cambodian villages are usually smaller than those of Vietnam, and the distinction between them may be sufficiently strong on the map to show the ethnic boundary. In other regions size is governed by economic factors. For example, in Belgium the agricultural villages of the Ardennes have many features in common with the agricultural villages of the loamy plains of middle Belgium, but they are definitely smaller. On the other hand, on some Atlantic shores the resources of the sea have allowed some old clusters to develop into real villages.

Man has sometimes deliberately influenced the size of villages. Many small Irish villages or clusters were replaced by isolated farms when the landlords 'striped' the land. More often governments with a fancy for bigger places try to concentrate population in huge settlements. This process is well known in times of strife, leading, as in Algeria and Vietnam, to the creation of so-called 'strategic hamlets'; the word 'hamlet' is a misnomer as these places are bigger and not smaller than normal villages. It is probable that the large size of south Italian villages is due to the conscious policy of medieval barons.

Size in itself is therefore an important and interesting factor. But there is another—the economic one.

The functions of villages and hamlets: the economic view

Villages from Neolithic times onward have been essentially, often exclusively, agricultural. Agriculture and village life appear, indeed, to be definitely linked, and many people tend to equate 'rural' and 'agricultural'—wrongly, as our review of regional terms has already shown. In fact the two notions are quite different in nature. There exists in some countries an urban agriculture conducted by farmers living in towns; traditional urban agriculture in certain south German towns, or the modern agriculture of town-dwelling farmers in the American Middle West, are examples. On the other hand, in some industrial countries the villages are inhabited mostly by workers, shopkeepers, etc., the agriculturists being in a minority; and indeed over entire regions rural agglomerations may be completely non-agricultural. There are fishing villages on most coasts and on the banks of lakes or large rivers. Less numerous are the villages of quarrymen like Ballyknockan, south of Dublin, or mining villages (at least during the earlier phases of mining). There is also an important type of rural agglomeration, particularly in regions of dispersed agricultural settlement, whose functions are tertiary, or in part secondary, but always non-agricultural.

Thus villages and rural agglomerations in general differ, not only in size but also in their functions, and villages of similar size but different functions are quite distinct geographical phenomena. Unfortunately this aspect of rural settlement has been often much neglected. It is true that it is difficult to collect accurate data in this field. Statistical data on the occupation of population are provided for large towns, but not for smaller places. Most large-scale maps use the same sign for a farm, a shop, an ordinary dwelling. The Scandinavian countries alone use special signs: for normal farms (*gård*), for small-holdings (*småbruk*), for non-agricultural houses and sometimes inns (*krug*). This helps the map analysis of rural settlement in those countries. Elsewhere it is necessary to do field work, and maps can be correctly interpreted only by those who have first-hand knowledge of the country.

Except in a few mining districts, agricultural settlements existed first, and the functional typology of rural settlements may therefore be studied as the gradual influx of tertiary and secondary activities into the countryside. Often this influx has affected the agricultural villages themselves, modifying them from the inside, metamorphosing them into multi-functional settlements without destroying the older structures. In other places the new functions have grown separately from, but side by side with, the ancient agricultural villages, creating settlements characterized by a locational segregation of economic functions. Elsewhere, again, the non-agricultural activities developed in new places, apart from the agricultural settlements, superimposing on the primitive agricultural settlement pattern a new pattern of non-agricultural settlements. These different processes may be studied separately.

The secondary and tertiary metamorphosis of villages

This phenomenon usually begins gradually, adding hardly any new constituents to the old patterns, though in certain circumstances it may develop rapidly in such a way that in some cases little will remain of the primitive functions and aspects of the village, through their having been largely engulfed by a mass influx of non-agricultural elements.

In some developing countries we witness the first stages of the tertiary metamorphosis of agricultural settlements. This phenomenon may be at first almost non-apparent. Trade is conducted in temporary markets, the primitive craftsmen are also cultivators of the soil as are their fellow villagers. But sooner or later permanent shops are set up; there is more and more specialization by craftsmen; government officials and ministers of religion appear. Usually the new developments are located at the centre of the village which may, in its small way, assume some of the functions, and even something of the outer look, of an urban centre. The metamorphosis thereby begun may spread outwards to the outskirts of the village. But the process may stop at different stages. In the big southern Mediterranean or central European villages, for example, only a few streets or squares at the centre have been urbanized, the rest of the village remaining a maze of peasant-inhabited streets and lanes. In the medium-sized villages of western Europe all stages of the evolution are documented both historically and in the present. The smaller villages usually set apart from farms have only a church, a school and an inn, and functionally do not differ much from their predecessors in the Dark Ages when the first rural parochial churches were established in the villages. Actually in many of the small villages recent rural depopulation has caused a reversal to earlier conditions: the one-class school has been closed; the priest no longer resides in the village; and one or two shop-keepers have ceased their activity.

In the larger villages, on the other hand, shops and workshops have multiplied; baker, butcher and grocer have been added to the inn; a hardware-shop, garages, service station have supplemented or replaced the traditional smith. A number of officials have been added to the priest and schoolmaster. The centre of the village then takes on a non-agricultural look, only a few farms remaining there, and only the farm-bordered side streets retain their traditional features. In some places the agricultural population is a minority and the farms form a rather secondary element of the village morphology. These are the rural centres around which the modern planners want to reorganize the whole countryside.

The last stages of metamorphosis are reached when local industrial employment causes a large increase of industrial workers in the village population, or when the proximity of a town enables commuters to settle in the village. This stage has been reached in parts of northern France, especially on the coalfield or near the Lille–Roubaix–Tourcoing conurbation, in Belgium and in some areas of Germany. There the original features of the village are hardly recognizable. Few farmers remain to till what industrial or urban developments have left of the arable land. Most former farm buildings have been transformed into shops or workers' dwellings. In the centre, only the plan and certain vernacular building features remind one of the traditional villages, while on the outskirts new streets have been laid and new estates built so that the non-agricultural elements are supreme. These settlements are quite characteristic of parts of industrial Europe, but unfortunately they lack a special name.

In some countries the old villages have been modified not only by the introduction of non-agricultural elements but also by the exodus of part of the agricultural population and the moving of farms outside the villages. The process has been spontaneous and gradual in some Mediterranean countries like central and northern Italy and Mediterranean France. There the old 'perched' villages have been losing part of their farming population since the latter part of the Middle Ages. New farms have been established, more or less scattered, in the agricultural plains and valleys below. In some places part of the countryside is still farmed from the village, part from the new scattered farms; *biens de village* and *biens de mas* are the respective terms for such holdings in southern France. Elsewhere all farmers have left the village, which is inhabited by farm labourers and craftsmen only, when it is not largely invaded by commuters from neighbouring industrial towns as happens in Lombardy.

In Denmark and England a similar process was accelerated by a conscious enclosure policy. The old Danish villages retain only one or two farms, the church, school, inn (*krug*) and a few houses. The English villages, even when they keep the vernacular styles of building that make their charm, have mostly lost what was once their paramount function—the farming activity. One or two farms at most are left. Most of the dwellings are agricultural labourers' cottages. The church, the vicarage, the squire's house are other traditional elements. When the village was well situated it may have attracted new tertiary functions and developed as a rural centre, but in the smaller places the new conditions have affected the traditional elements badly.

These 'metamorphosed' agricultural villages have therefore undergone varying processes of transformation which have left them at different stages, making for a wide variety of types.

Functional segregation in villages

The process of functional segregation occurs less frequently than metamorphosis and rarely develops in homogeneously populated areas. However, even when it does, professional specialization will entail some local separation of activities. In Europe functional segregation is mainly a feature of the past. During the rural phase of the textile industry, streets of spinners and weavers developed in the textile villages. On large rivers, boatmen's quarters extended along the banks side by side with the agricultural nucleus. The process also appears to be especially widespread in India, where it is dominated by the caste system, and some Indian villages are like conglomerations of cells, socially and functionally separated. A similar situation is found in the other developing countries. It started in the colonial period but still prevails in the post-colonial era. In some African villages there exist a church and school quarter originally set up by the Christian missions and now sometimes developed by the new governments. Trades and services are also often localized in new streets which make up a kind of new village juxtaposed with the old agricultural settlement. One may wonder what the future of these settlements will be. Will separatism vanish as a relict of a previous colonial and perhaps racial segregationist age, or will it be reinforced and reorganized as a rational element in village planning?

Superimposed non-agricultural settlements

Non-agricultural villages have a long history. Fishing settlements, going back to the Mesolithic, antedate agricultural villages, in Europe at least. And in Africa, the Mediterranean countries and some parts of the Atlantic coast, as in Norway, fishing villages are quite distinct from farming settlements; indeed sometimes, as in some Breton islands (Sein; Molène) or on the Norwegian *skiärgård*, they thrive where no agriculture is possible. Quarrying or mining villages also belong to an old tradition, and in such mineral-bearing districts as the hercynian massifs of central Europe, they may have constituted the first network of settlements. But all these examples belong to the primary sector of economic activities.

Far more widespread and interesting is the development of rural tertiary settlements. In many cases, as we have seen, farming villages have attracted new non-agricultural functions, but in other regions the reverse has occurred and farming settlements appear to have acted as a repellent to non-agricultural activities.

This has been marked in areas of nucleated settlement. Robequain and Gourou have described villages in North Vietnam of specialized craftsmen such as paper-makers, basket-makers, weavers, etc. In the same country, minute trading settlements developed around Chinese shops away from the surrounding and bigger Vietnamese agricultural or artisan villages. In areas of nucleated settlement in

Europe new tertiary settlements are quite exceptional. A few may have developed as road villages around a *relais de poste*, or at some crossroads near an inn. These new settlements are quite distinct from the agricultural villages in their location, having been attracted by the roads which nearly all agricultural villages ignore, in plan and in functions. Sometimes they are more or less an offshoot of older agricultural villages such as Vimy and Petit Vimy in Pas-de-Calais.

But it is mostly in regions of dispersed settlement that a new network of tertiary places has developed. In the extreme examples of farm scattering these non-agricultural settlements are the only form of nucleation, and there is a dual network of settlement: a scattered agricultural settlement and a more or less nucleated non-agricultural settlement. This dual pattern prevails in all lands of recent settlement with dispersed farmsteads: Canada, the U.S.A., Australia and New Zealand. The only forms of nucleation among the dispersed farmsteads are small service centres, at a crossroad or near a church, school or railway station. The Atlantic fringe of Europe from northern Portugal to Norway is the area *par excellence* of tertiary, rural, nucleated settlements. The continental North Sea countries from the Straits of Dover to the border of Denmark are of similar type.

In all these regions agricultural settlements are farms or clachans. Large rural nucleations were exceedingly rare until the last century. But with the progress of economic relations, the secondary and tertiary economic sectors quickly developed and gave rise to new nucleated settlements. Usually these tertiary settlements developed around the parish churches. In smaller parishes sometimes the only accretions to the parish church were an inn, perhaps a smithy and later on a school. But in the larger parishes, or in well situated or very active areas, substantial settlements appeared, made up of shops, schools, offices, retired people's dwellings and workshops. In Brittany some of these places, like Plougastel-Daoulas and Landivisiau, have attained a population of over 2,000 inhabitants, and are thus, according to French standards, automatically classified as towns. But by local people they are still referred to as *bourg* in French, or *bourk* in Breton, in the same way as their smaller counterparts. These parochial tertiary settlements are often called 'villages' by strangers, but the local people often resent that appellation.

A *bourg*, 'church-town', *treflan* or *pentref* is not a village. It is indeed urban in nature if not in size.

Parish churches have been the origin of most tertiary settlements in north-west Iberia, Brittany and the west of France generally, in Cornwall and Devon, in some parts of Wales (it is especially true of the larger *clas* parishes like Llanbadarn or Clynnog Fawr) and in Man. It is also the case in the Low Countries where such settlements occasionally get the same name as that for agricultural villages—*dorp*.

But tertiary settlements could grow around other nuclei such as the local ancient chapels in some of the larger Breton parishes (like St Jacques in Bannalec or Kergoat in Quéméneven). In Wales and sometimes in Cornwall Nonconformist chapels occasionally attracted such settlements. Some of these chapel-villages in Wales are recognizable from their Hebrew names (Bethel, Bethesda, Siloh), such names being usual for chapels among some of the Nonconformist denominations.

All along the Atlantic fringe, roadside settlements have developed. The name *sráid-bhaile*, which is used for them in the Gaeltacht of Ireland, is very appropriate. Place-names like Minffordd (Welsh: roadside) or Kroazhent (Breton: crossroads, usually mistranslated into French as Croissant) are also very good descriptions of such places.

The relationship of roadside settlements to the church-town is very interesting. In Brittany, where parish life has been very strong, the former developed late and were very often rather small. It is only in certain places and in recent years that some of them developed enough to compete successfully with the church-towns, though in some cases by the nineteenth century the attraction of the road was proving so strong that some *bourgs* were displaced, complete with parish church, cemetery, etc., to sites on a main road, examples being Quimerch, Finistère and, outside Brittany, Buais Manche. In Ireland the checkered religious history of the island was such that the traditional parish churches, once taken over by the Anglican church, lost all attraction and remained mostly isolated, while the new Catholic churches, built during the nineteenth and twentieth centuries, came too late to act as a nucleus. Indeed most tertiary rural settlements in Ireland are landlord foundations (embryo towns) or roadside settlements. Sometimes there is no nucleation at all, the churches, schools, post-offices and shops being as scattered as the farmhouses. In Norway also, for different reasons, many parish churches failed to attract such settlements. From the fourteenth century onwards only the most important churches (*herred*-churches) acted as real parish churches, the lesser ones (*sogn*-churches) being used as chapels. So it is not surprising that most tertiary settlements (*tettstet*) originated at a crossroad or near a railway station, or at a landing-place on a fjord.

This non-agricultural element in rural settlement thus seems to be more important than is usually suspected, especially in the most developed countries where it is more prominent in rural nucleations than the agricultural element. It really deserves more attention than has usually been devoted to it, particularly in view of the diverse ways in which it appears. It affects all aspects of village life and, notably, the one we have to deal with next—the internal organization of villages.

The internal organization of villages

We have just seen that the economic function of village settlement may affect its internal organization and that a centre or specialized area may appear as in a town. Many careful studies have been devoted to village plans, notably by German geographers, and elaborate typologies have been established which need not be repeated here. But it may be worthwhile to stress the importance of some factors in the spatial organization of villages.

One of these factors is orientation though it is not always significant. For example, it does not play any apparent role in the *Haufendörfer* of the European plains. But researchers at Nancy are exploring the preferential orientations that may have directed the planning of the street-villages of Lorraine. It is mostly in oceanic or in mountainous regions that the orientation factor is vital. In the Atlantic areas of Europe, and in the main European mountain regions, the orientation of the house-front towards the south—or in some Atlantic parts towards a point slightly east of south—is a basic factor. In the clachans of the Atlantic zone it is often the only element of order in what appears at first sight to be utter chaos. In some mountain valleys, orientation towards the south on a well-lit *adret* often combines with relief to create those sun-facing villages that the French compare to fruit trees against a wall (*villages-espaliers*).

A second factor that affects the layout of agricultural villages is the type of agriculture. Tillage usually has a subordinate influence. For example, the traditional Mediterranean corn-growers have set up more or less communal threshing-floors near their villages. These are mentioned in the Bible and may be seen today near Castile villages. But it is cattle rearing that has most affected the plan of agricultural villages. It has been noticed by ancient writers that the street-plan of the Lorraine village was well suited to the practice of communal herding. Other features are linked more directly to cattle rearing. Many types of villages in different parts of the world are characterized by the existence of an open space which is or was devoted to the herding or pasturing of cattle. The Zulu *kraal* is such an enclosure, and the word is often also used to describe the village around it. Many of the Atlantic clachans have on one side a small triangular grassy area linked by an old enclosed cattle way to the existing or former outer common pastures. This area is called *placître* in the west of France, *leurger* in Brittany; similar areas are called *dries* in Flemish. These green spaces are very ancient. They appear most clearly in the most archaic areas of the Atlantic fringe; and in Ostergötland in Sweden the remains of a second-century A.D. village show the same feature. It is probable that the classical English 'green', mostly rectangular and central, and related forms, which have been studied by Professor Thorpe, belong to the same pastoral tradition. Indeed in the 'green' villages of western Picardy one may still see an occasional tethered horse, or hens—a last remnant of former uses.

A third element dominates the structure of non-agricultural villages. It is the commercial element, spaces being marked off for markets and fairs. Thus the western French *bourgs* have no green but a square (French *place*; Breton *plasenn*) or even sometimes several squares. The square is not a grassy area; it is macadamized, or paved, or tarred, is bordered by shops, inns, etc., and sometimes a market hall has been built on it. Most squares are central, but fairgrounds, which have to be larger, are often on the outskirts of the village. Squares and fairgrounds are linked by shop-bordered streets and not by farm-skirted lanes.

A last factor in village structure is the presence or absence of a surrounding line of delimitation or, if we use the word in a very general way, of defence. In this connection E. Juillard distinguishes 'massed villages', bordered by a sharp boundary line, from 'loose villages' which gradually merge with the dispersed forms of the countryside.

Fortified villages, with defence lines of stakes, poles, etc., are still to be found in some south-east Asian areas. Villages surrounded by an earth rampart existed in medieval Europe, and some are still to be seen. But more common was, and is, the existence around the houses and their gardens or crofts (*courtils* in Lorraine; *meix* in Burgundy) of an encircling line sometimes followed by a lane or a fence separating the village and its enclosed gardens from the surrounding open fields. Where the main streets crossed this line, crosses were sometimes set up. In the past the line had legal significance, for it separated the village areas, owned and used in severalty, from the common fields. In the countries where these legal features have been retained the village plan tends to be more compact and sharply defined than elsewhere. In other areas the village has a looser structure and, as we have seen, gradually merges with the countryside. Some extreme examples, where the village structure is often hardly recognizable, occur in the Pevèle and the Pays-de-Caux.

The influence of the village: its agricultural territory

So far we have dealt with villages in themselves, seen from the inside. There remains the relation of villages with the surrounding areas, and the agricultural and non-agricultural aspects have to be examined separately.

Agricultural villages, large or small, use an agricultural territory which may be said, in a very general way, to belong to them. The old English notion of 'township' applied both to the village and its territory. The French used the word *finage* which applies only to the village lands and excludes the village itself. The distinction between *village* and *finage* was legally important in ancient France. The Germans have the well known word *Flur* which describes the cultivated territory only. This agricultural village territory has varied not only in extent but also in nature. In regions practising shifting cultivation the village territory is an extensive but in-

N

determinate area where the villagers have certain rights of cultivation, pasture, turbary, wood-cutting, etc. Lacking fixed boundaries, usually a kind of no-man's land intervenes between the ordinarily used area of one village and that of the next. This is particularly true in wooded areas. Where the several village territories impinge on such land it may be recognized as common to them, to a tribe or to a district.

This lack of definite boundaries is usually transitory however. When occupation becomes denser and the pressure on the land resources becomes greater—even in very extensive economies—neighbouring villages begin to compete with one another for the use of the former no-man's-land so that definition of boundaries becomes necessary. Often natural landmarks are agreed upon for this purpose in the beginning—a stream, a rock, an unusual tree—artificial elements like roads or boundary stones being introduced later. Then begins a second phase when the village territory is a single, well defined whole. Inside these boundaries the village has all agricultural, tillage, pasture, and forest rights. If regulations are enacted by the village authorities, they apply to the whole territory and to all the inhabitants thereof. This is a kind of classical stage in village history, when all rights of ownership, possession and agricultural regulation are vested in the same village community and apply to a single territory. This state of affairs is well documented in the east of France and Germany. The medieval word *banum* or *ban* expresses well in French this general power of some men over a defined territory.

But when occupation intensifies, when woodland wastes are replaced by tillage, and neighbouring cultivated territories meet, very soon a third stage develops. Villagers begin to own, or rent, or possess in some way parcels of land in another village territory. The boundaries of ownership and holdings are no longer coincident with the traditional limits of the *ban* of the village. The village is no longer a community but an assemblage of several holdings, each with its own parcels, and the lands cultivated by the village farms are just an assemblage of parcels possessed in severalty by the different tenants. This assemblage no longer deserves names such as *finage* or *Flur* which suggest a unit. It is better just to call it 'village agricultural territory'. This is the stage usually reached in the village regions of France. The study of these village agricultural territories is of some interest. First, some villages may have extended their territories at the expense of weaker neighbours. There are expanding villages and contracting villages, a feature which has been studied by Ph. Pinchemel in Picardy. Moreover, some village agricultural territories remain compact, massive areas; others have very irregular limits; some may comprise enclaves in neighbouring territories. In regions of loose villages and hamlets, the examination of village and hamlet territories is necessary to decide if such-and-such a place is an agricultural settlement in its own right or only an incidental offshoot of some other village.

The boundary lines or boundary zones of the agricultural village territories are not often accurately described and shown on maps. Usually they may be discovered only by the perusal of local deeds or by field work. But in some cases they have been delineated in field plans, as in Lorraine, or even in general maps. These maps usually oversimplify, rightly or wrongly portraying arrangements like those described by the author as the classical stage of village history. Thus the townlands of Ireland were in origin village territories, and so also were some of the *communautés rurales* shown in the recently published *Atlas historique de Normandie*.

But in general the boundaries that appear on large-scale maps, whether or not derived from agricultural boundaries, are in fact ecclesiastic or administrative boundaries. This brings us to the second aspect of the relationship between villages and surrounding areas.

Ecclesiastical and administrative villages

In Europe from the Dark Ages onwards ecclesiastical and, later, administrative boundaries were superimposed on the old *villages* and *finages*. In northern France and a large part of Germany it happened that at the time of the setting up of rural parishes the village and its territory were substantial enough to maintain a parish priest. The village therefore became a parish village, and the *finage*, on which the tithes were levied, became the parish territory. At the time of the 1789 Revolution, when administrative *communes* were established, there was, as a rule, a *commune* corresponding to each traditional parish. The *commune* boundaries in those areas, therefore, more or less represent the former limits of the *finage*.

A similar process took place in large parts of southern and central Germany. In other areas, on the other hand, the average village was either too small or too poor to maintain a priest, and therefore several villages were grouped to form one parish. Such was the case in the southern Jura of France, in some parts of the Auvergne, and often in England where many parishes each included several agricultural townships. In such instances an hierarchy of villages was initiated, the one where the parish church stood developing a kind of pre-eminence over the others. Here again the *commune* or civil parish was more or less modelled on the previous parish.

In dispersed settlement areas the parish church was sometimes sited near the home of the local chieftain, but often it appears to have had no obvious links with the agricultural settlement network. In some cases it remained isolated like many *sogn* churches in Norway, many churches in the smaller Welsh parishes and many Irish churches. But in other instances a nucleated settlement of tertiary functions grew up around the parish church, especially when that place became also the seat of a *commune*; we have already referred to these *bourgs* or 'church-towns'.

Western Europe is remarkable for its *commune* organization, Ireland being the sole exception. But we find comparable phenomena elsewhere. In the U.S.S.R. the village that is the seat of a multiple-village *kolkhoz* gets some kind of pre-eminence over the other villages. In Central and West Africa the villages that are the seat of traditional chieftainships also have a pre-eminence, notably over their recent offshoots of more or less dispersed farms (called *campements* in French Africa). This hierarchy tends to be strengthened as the traditional parishes and *communes* appear more and more to be too small as administrative units, and physical planners contemplate the creation of larger districts around larger villages—*villages-centres*, *centres-ruraux* or 'king-villages' where all modern developments should be concentrated.

Conclusion

The village and hamlet network, in spite of rural depopulation, is growing more complex, more hierarchical. In a parallel development the village economic functions become more and more diversified, less and less dominated by agricultural activity. The morphology of villages also gets more and more complicated with the concentration of shops and services at the centre of the most important places.

All these changes are aspects of the general process of the urbanization of the countryside which makes the villages, hamlets and isolated farms a less dense, looser variety of a general rural–urban settlement pattern.

9
The dispersed
habitat of Wales

E. G. Bowen

It is now exactly 30 years since Professor Estyn Evans discussed some survivals of the Irish open field system in Donegal in a classic paper in *Geography*.[1] It is not always appreciated that he was breaking new ground in the study of rural settlement patterns when he pointed out that there was 'abundant evidence that the type of settlement accompanying rundale cultivation before its decay was not the dispersed habitat which generally distinguishes the Irish landscape at the present day'. The scattered habitat, he maintained, was a 'secondary dispersion following the dissolution of this type of cultivation'. With these sentences we moved from a static to a dynamic conception of rural settlement patterns.

The monumental work of August Meitzen[2] at the close of the nineteenth century had popularized the view that dispersed and nucleated settlements could be traced back to different ethnic groups, and the association of *Einzelhöfe* with the Celtic lands was regarded as basic—a settlement pattern carried by Celtic peoples into the farthest ends of Europe. Geographers, lawyers and economic historians accepted Meitzen's general thesis. The geographers, in particular, adopted it without question and proceeded further to show how nucleated settlement, on the one hand, was restricted in prehistoric times to land that was fertile, but free of heavy forest, and that stock raising, on the other hand, with its need for enclosed fields, had been associated from the beginning with isolated farms established in forest clearings. It was equally easy to find a physical background for all this. The western climate with its cool summers and mild winters, its early spring and late autumn, was ideal for the long continued growth of grasses on which the basic pastoralism, associated with the scattered habitat, depended. After all, had not Demangeon[3] adopted exactly this approach in his contribution to the Report of the Commission on types of rural settlement presented to the International Geographical Union at its Paris meeting in 1931? Evans's pioneer work, however, substantiated the doubts of earlier workers,[4] and completely undermined this line of thought. 'It is now clear', he concluded, 'that throughout Western Britain and in many parts of Western and South-Western Europe, some kind of communal cultivation is of great antiquity—Meitzen's well-known map of *Dörfer* and *Einzelhöfe* needs drastic revision.'

The type of settlement described by Evans in Donegal is usually referred to as a 'clachan'. It consists of a cluster of farmhouses and associated out-buildings usually arranged without any formal plan. Geographers in Ireland developing Evans's ideas have shown that the clachan form of settlement, often accompanied by common arable fields, was widely distributed in other parts of the island down to recent times. Proudfoot[5] has suggested that this type of settlement was associated with serf cultivators who were the social inferiors of the free farmers, a minority of whom lived in raths, ring-forts and cashels in the Dark Ages. The upland mountain pastures were used for communal summer grazing. Similar evidence comes from Scotland. It is now clear that in historic times the typical rural settlement there was a cluster of farmsteads, similar to the Irish clachan, occupied by tenants who farmed the township lands jointly in in-field and out-field. As in Ireland, the extensive hill-pastures were utilized for summer grazing for cattle and sheep under a system of transhumance. The scattered farms and cottages of the present landscape are rarely older than the mid-eighteenth century.

In the years following the Second World War the late Professor T. Jones-Pierce[6] and G. R. J. Jones[7] revealed the outlines of a similar pattern of rural settlement in early Wales. Two distinct forms of settlement appear to have existed side by side. On the one hand there were small hamlets usually inhabited by communities of bondmen, while on the other there were clusters of semi-dispersed homesteads in which the freemen lived. The bondmen owed certain services and allegiances to the freemen.

Looked at in greater detail, the settlements of the bondmen took the form of a nucleation of usually nine adjacent houses surrounded by the open-field arable which they tilled in common. Within every territorial administrative unit there was a more important nucleated settlement—the *Maerdref* (the Mayor's settlement), which contained, in addition to the bondmen, the *llys* or court of the local lord or prince and his demesne lands. These lands were tilled for him by the local bondmen and also by serfs from other bond-vills around. The free tribesmen, the *élite*, formed originally a minority of the population, each clan occupying a *gwely* (resting place) which always contained a portion of arable land with extensive common pastures around. The dwellings of the free tribesmen were located on the margins of this arable patch, and because holdings were seldom large the grouping of homesteads resulted in a cluster rather more like a clachan than anything in the present day rural landscape. In addition, the upland areas in Wales, as in Scotland and Ireland, were available for summer grazing of sheep and cattle by all concerned, from prince to bondman. Thus, as Evans forecast, Meitzen's map of *Dörfer* and *Einzelhöfe* needs drastic revision. In place of his basic, long-established pattern of scattered farms associated with pastoralism, tribalism and semi-nomadism, we have created a picture of the rural habitat in Celtic lands in the Dark Ages consisting of a much more settled habitat, with a preponderance of nucleated settlements in which arable farming played a significant part. Neither is there any evidence for the semi-nomadic tribalism postulated by Seebohm[8] and other early workers.

The breakdown of the native system

With the evidence now at our disposal it is probably true to say that the transition from the landscape of the Dark Ages to that of modern times can best be studied in Wales. There is some evidence that this process of change began earlier here than in either Scotland or Ireland. Jones[9] has suggested that the evolution of the present scattered habitat was well advanced in Wales as early as the beginning of the sixteenth century. In any case, the *gwely* system contained the seeds of its own destruction. The free tribesmen practised equal division of their arable lands among all the male heirs. Thus, as the population grew in size, the arable area was split into smaller and smaller portions, and a stage reached when the continued subdivision of arable land led to the breakdown of the system. This situation was all the more acute where extensive stretches of good arable land were difficult to come by; and where it was difficult to find new areas of suitable soil for ploughing, the original patch or patches became increasingly fragmented. It was in response to this situation that portions of the common arable and pasture lands of the original *gwely* were enclosed to form some of the oldest isolated farmsteads we see today. As far as the bond-vills were concerned it would appear that they began to decay even earlier. Everyone seems to agree that they were more numerous before the year 1100 than afterwards and that there was, correspondingly, a marked decline in the bond population of Wales in the later Middle Ages. This was due, among other things, to the granting of bond-vills by the princes and overlords to younger free tribesmen or even to the Church. Once this occurred, further fragmentation took place, resulting ultimately in enclosure, as was the case with lands formerly associated with the free tribesmen. The cumulative result was to intensify still further the distribution of scattered farmsteads.

The Cistercians and the growth of pastoralism

One other matter associated with the developing situation in the late Middle Ages deserves mention because it helps indirectly to explain why the earlier students of rural settlements in the Celtic lands were so deeply impressed by the pastoral tradition they found associated with the scattered farms of the present day, and which, in turn, they mistook for an original attribute. Reference should be made to the fact that in the later Middle Ages the great religious Orders, particularly the Cistercians, had much to do with the intensification of the pastoral aspects of native farming in the Celtic west. The Normans in Wales, Scotland and Ireland occupied the lower, more fertile lands and introduced there a manorial system, with its open arable fields and nucleated settlements, leaving the higher ground to the Celtic peoples, who continued their traditional form of land tenure with only some slight modifications. The Cistercian monks, however, seem to have made it a part of their policy to penetrate into the native upland territories and to concentrate much of their economic activity on sheep farming and the wool trade.[10] There is abundant evidence of the way they integrated with the Celtic peoples in political and cultural matters, but integration with the native economy was equally evident.[11] They certainly helped in the improvement of sheep farming, and did much with their already available 'common market' to organize the export of British wool to European markets. In the organization of their estates they practised transhumance as the native farmers did, and it is worth noting that the great size of many of their granges anticipated in many ways the larger units necessary for remunerative sheep farming so strongly advocated today. Population decline after the great plagues of the fourteenth century was partly responsible for a rise in the number of sheep and a decline in arable land.[12] But in Ireland and western Britain the Cistercians played a major part in organizing and emphasizing the importance of sheep farming in their time. This helps us to appreciate that the pastoral tradition so long associated with our scattered farms in the West is not necessarily an original, deeply rooted factor of great antiquity, but largely the result of increasing specialization in later centuries.

Population growth and the spread of scattered farms

It would be absurd to think that the development and spread of scattered farms in Wales ceased when the open fields of the last *gwely* or bond-vill had been enclosed by the beginning of the sixteenth century, or, indeed, when the traditional custom of *gavelkind*, which had resulted in the pronounced fragmentation of the arable fields of the free tribesmen and thereby accelerated the process of consolidation, was abolished by the Act of Union of 1536. As the population grew in numbers in the seventeenth and eighteenth centuries the pressure on the land became considerable. Many of the farms were too small to maintain a large family at subsistence level, while in the background was the pronounced hostility of the landowners. Under these conditions it became extremely difficult for farmers' sons to find a new farm on marriage—a situation that was particularly acute before the industrial revolution provided the possibility of new sources of employment both inside and outside Wales. Many newly-established families failed completely to find new homes and were forced to emigrate overseas, more particularly to seek 'pastures new' in the vast expanses of the Great Republic across the water. Others solved the problem by 'squatting' on the commons and waste lands, particularly on the margins of the uplands, a process which involved the creation of a new farm from what was virtually virgin land. Every time it occurred the scattered nature of the farmsteads became more and more pronounced. Squatting amounted to illegal enclosure and it was completed surreptitiously at night time. It was claimed that if a newly married couple could raise a rough dwelling of clods and timber on the margins of the common or open land on their wedding night, and arrange to have smoke emitting from the chimney by daylight, then the freehold of the site became theirs for ever. Accordingly, the wedding party, including the bride and bridegroom, together with their parents and well-wishers, worked through the night to satisfy these basic conditions and, finally, the bridegroom stood near the newly erected cabin and threw his wood axe in all directions. Where it fell marked the perimeter of the land the new settlers were allowed to enclose. Such were the squatter cottages, or the *tai un nos* ('houses of one night') as they were called. These crude dwellings became in time more permanent homesteads with little to distinguish them from the traditional *tyddynnod* or single farms. In many parts of Wales this custom went on until the middle of the nineteenth century, especially in areas where common land remained unenclosed or where estate bailiffs lacked vigilance. The establishment of *tai un nos* was very prevalent in central Cardiganshire, particularly in the early part of the nineteenth century. Figure 8, based on the first edition of the Ordnance Survey, shows a marked cluster of these squatter settlements in the neighbourhood of Penuwch, high up on the flanks of Mynydd Bach. The map indicates clearly the process of upland expansion whereby the newcomers ate into the very margins of the high ground, especially in the vicinity of the 900 foot contour, leaving great embayments in the original extensive rough grazing. The patches of upland pasture that still remain are indicated on the map.

There is one further point of interest regarding this late expansion of the single farm in Wales. Such newly-settled neighbourhoods naturally had no centres or focus of any kind, with the possible exception of the Nonconformist chapels, the majority of which were set up during the late eighteenth and early nineteenth centuries. It is, therefore, not unusual to find a particular neighbourhood bearing the name of the chapel concerned—the local farmer maintaining that he hails from Jerusalem or Nazareth, or it may be from Nebo or Joppa.[13] Much of the western area shown on Figure 8 is known officially as Bethania, from the name of the chapel established there among the profusion of scattered farms. The present-day Ordnance Survey map shows a small nucleation with a sub-post office and a few houses near the junction of the secondary roads nearby, but the neighbourhood still carries the name Bethania.

The decay of the scattered farm in the uplands

The proliferation of squatter settlements marked the final phase in the expansion of the single farm. At the same time this upward movement again carried with it the seeds of its own destruction. In brief, the squatters had moved up too high and had entered what may be described as marginal land in the physical sense. Many of the present social and agricultural problems in upland Wales stem from this upward movement of subsistence farmers who find it increasingly difficult in such circumstances to produce the beef, wool and mutton needed in the home market. The upland farm is, therefore, marginal both in the physical and in the economic sense; it is no longer a viable unit. This position has been accentuated by the mechanization of agriculture in modern times. Mechanization is, undoubtedly, the greatest innovation that has taken place in British farming since the Iron Age, yet its effects are not felt to the same extent in all areas. The dairy farms on the lower lands in Wales have been able to respond easily, backed as they are by an efficient national marketing organization—the Milk Marketing Board. On the contrary, the smaller sheep and store cattle farms of the uplands, and especially those whose life began as squatter settlements, have not been able to respond to anything like the same extent. There are several reasons for this, the majority of which are closely related to the physical environment.[14] The results are to be seen in the serious depopulation of the uplands and in the rapid amalgamation of farm holdings, both involving the abandonment of many of the *tyddynnod*. All this stands out in sharp contrast to the relative prosperity of the lowland farms. The overall situation

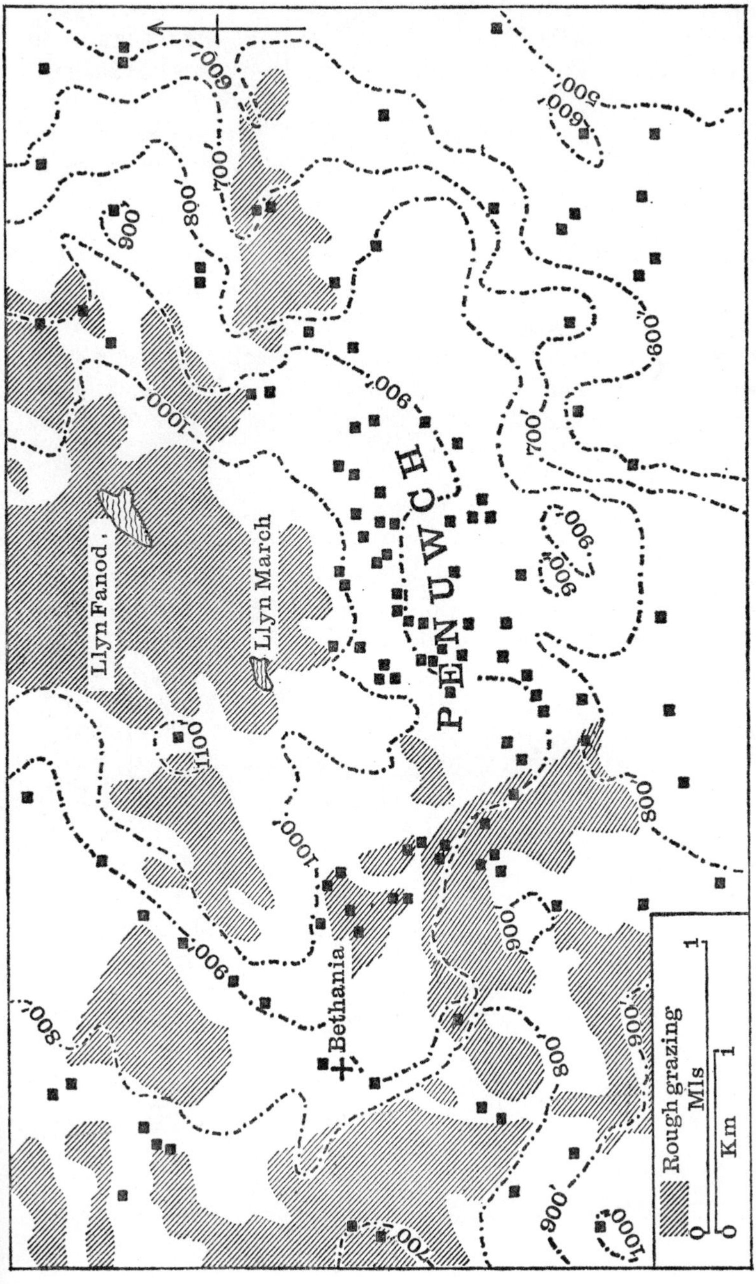

Figure 8 Squatters in the Penuwch area of central Cardiganshire, 1834 (based on the 1st edition O.S. 1834)

is that the single farms in the lowlands have been able to adapt their traditional pastoralism—and with it much of their culture—to modern conditions, while the hill farms remain virtually uneconomic, but, nevertheless, retain a great deal of their traditional culture. The plight of the upland farms is a cause of great anxiety not only to the agricultural specialist,[15] but also to all those interested in the life and culture of modern Wales.

The regeneration of the uplands

It is clear that the human use of the uplands must be looked at anew and every effort made to adjust the natural endowments of these areas to the needs of the present. Several suggestions have been put forward and they are examined here with reference to the extent to which they are likely to modify the existing settlement pattern. The five most important are :

1. That the best agricultural land could most appropriately be used for large-scale sheep and cattle farming in units of over 1,000 acres, coupled with the corresponding elimination of many of the smaller farms by a process of amalgamation. Changes of this nature are already taking place naturally, without inducements or Government interference of any kind. Such a development would, of course, lead to fewer and fewer scattered farmsteads. It would not necessarily lead to further depopulation because there is a growing tendency for farm workers to live away from the farms on which they work in new well-appointed houses built around minor service centres among the hills. Many of these workers are now lorry drivers and motor mechanics in charge of tractors and other mechanized equipment. They all have their own motorized transport and travel to work each morning on the sheep and cattle grazing grounds very much as the medieval villager went out to work daily to the open fields and common pastures. The overall effect on the settlement pattern would be the diminution of scattered farms and the intensification of minor nucleations.

2. More land of poorer quality with steeper slopes and higher elevation could be developed by the Forestry Commission. Considerable areas in the Welsh uplands have already been developed in this way over the last 40 years, and areas that are suitable for further afforestation have already been mapped. The Commission

has given special attention to the establishment of new houses as homes for forestry workers. These often take the form of some two or three isolated semi-detached houses, or sometimes larger groupings which form completely new villages. At the same time the Commission is keen to integrate forestry with agriculture, and many of the single farms in and around the forested areas have been reconditioned, while the occupier becomes a part-time forester and a part-time farmer.[16] On the whole, it can be said that the vast extent of forested countryside has reduced considerably the number of single farms, while the Commission has helped to intensify nucleation in the form of new villages and dwelling clusters.

3. A combination of physical factors such as the excessive steepness of many of the slopes, the high aggregate of rainfall and the poor quality of the soil make much of the upland area ideal for water conservation. Wales has great water resources which could be utilized for the production of electrical power as well as for storage purposes. It is from such sources that the large ranches envisaged, after further amalgamation of the smaller holdings, could be supplied with electricity and with piped water for both agricultural and domestic purposes. Any surplus water or power would find a very ready market in industrial areas both within and outside Wales. In the context of the present analysis it should, however, be remembered that the installation of such schemes, even on a fairly large scale, will not necessarily affect the existing settlement pattern, as the number of technical and engineering staff employed is not great. In these days of mechanized transport there will be no need of another Elan Village as set up at the beginning of the century by the Birmingham Corporation near the Elan Valley dams in Radnorshire.

4. Modern reservoir schemes envisage a close link with the tourist industry. The maxim concerning the 'alternative use of land' must be applied equally to the alternative use of water surfaces. Many of the reservoirs could be used for fishing and boating, sailing and skin-diving, speed boats and water polo. In other words they could be turned into recreation areas and thus attract the tourist industry into the heart of the countryside. It should be noted, however, that such schemes—some of which are already far advanced—will have little, if any, effect on the permanent settlement pattern. Such developments tend to attract only a seasonal

population and in most cases the day-visitor who travels by car. They can, however, help to provide a secondary source of income for some of the small farmers in the vicinity who could offer temporary accommodation or bed and breakfast. Other aspects of the tourist industry, particularly pony-trekking, cannot be overlooked in this context, but again the effect on the settlement pattern is negligible.

5. Mention must be made of other solutions designed to arrest the flow of population from the uplands, or more exactly, to retain as many people as possible in Wales. These involve either the building of completely new towns at suitable sites, or doubling the size of some of the already existing towns, as is envisaged for places like Rhayader in Radnorshire or Newtown in Montgomeryshire. Such solutions will most certainly affect the overall settlement pattern, but they cannot appropriately be discussed in this essay, which is concerned exclusively with rural settlements.

Afforestation and new settlements

Afforestation illustrates some of the ways in which such suggestions have modified the landscape of upland Wales. The changes produced by the Forestry Commission, in both land use and settlement pattern, are certainly more spectacular than anything yet associated with the other suggestions considered above.

On the borders of Carmarthenshire and Breconshire some 9 miles north-west of Llandovery (Llanymddyfri) the Commission acquired 9,429 acres of land, of which 8,900 acres have been planted to form the Crychan Forest. In developing the forest they have modified the previous settlement pattern of scattered farms and established, in addition, an entirely new settlement known as Llandulas (Tir Abad) intended primarily for forest workers. The extent of the change can be gauged if one examines the first edition of the Ordnance Survey in 1834 when the Llandulas district consisted of the church and a large farm, Glan Dulas, situated near the confluence of the Dulas and one of its easterly-flowing tributaries. In addition there was a large number of scattered farms (Figure 9). Slightly to the north-west of the church was a farmhouse bearing the historic name of Ty'r Abad (the Abbot's house), a reminder that the area (significantly in the present context) once formed part of one of the granges of the Cistercian Abbey of Strata Florida in Cardiganshire. After 1834, within an area of approximately 10 square miles, additions were made to the settlement at different times; these included an inn and a Nonconformist chapel, some distance away from Glan Dulas farm along a secondary road leading to Llanymddyfri, while nearer the farm and the church

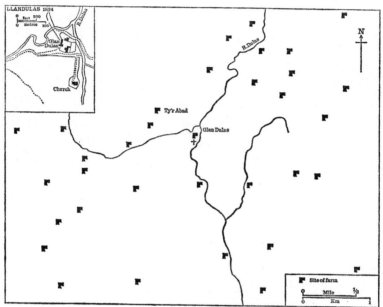

Figure 9   Llandulas, 1834 (based on the 1st edition O.S. 1834)

a small primary school (now disused) and a sub-post office were erected. In this way the seeds of nucleation were present before the Forestry Commission took over. In the 1930s the Commission acquired several of the scattered farms, and the War Department acquired a number of others for an artillery range. In 1938-9 the Forestry Commission built their first block of three houses, but it was after the Second World War, in 1953, that a further twenty new houses were erected around this nucleus to form the present village. Two years later a village hall was built by the Commission and let to the community at a nominal rent. It was used in the daytime as a primary school. At the same time, a lock-up shop was erected and this is now the combined village stores and post office.* The Breconshire County Council added a clinic in 1963 and 2 years later built a new primary school just north of the stream confluence (Fig. 10). In the same year the Forestry Commission built a new

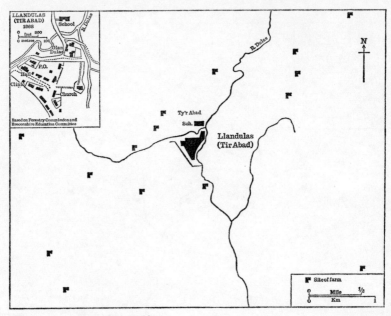

Figure 10   Llandulas, 1968

timber house for the chief forester. It is interesting to note that when the twenty houses became available for occupation in 1953 no local inhabitants were anxious to live in the new village, and the first tenants were brought from far outside the area, many of them displaced miners from South Wales. Here, then, was a new village located in a forest area but by no means a village for forestry

* Information kindly supplied by H. C. Cooke Esq., Land Agent, South Wales Conservancy Forestry Commission, Cardiff.

I wish to thank Michael Hicks Esq., Administrative Officer, Breconshire Education Committee, for much help and assistance regarding the Committee's work at Llandulas.

workers alone. At the present time the village has developed a community life of its own, and is in every way very conscious of its identity. We can complete the picture by drawing attention to the fact that in the same 10 square miles the number of inhabited single farms declined from thirty-four in 1834 to sixteen in 1968, including Glan Dulas itself, a reduction of just over 50 per cent. While some of the farms that were inhabited in 1834 have in recent times been taken over by the Forestry Commission and by the War Office, we must not overlook the fact that other farm houses, now abandoned, have been taken over by farmers living on the better lowlands. They allow the upland farm houses to fall into decay and farm their lands by remote control. This process is just another version of the amalgamation of holdings mentioned above. In this way the changing settlement pattern in the Llandulas area serves to cover several aspects of the suggestions for change which were made above.

The life-cycle of settlement evolution

It is often claimed by modern geographers studying the settlement pattern in highland Britain that what we see today represents the end-product of a long and complicated process of development with some residual features here and there. This, of course, is basically true. The present study has shown, however, that there may be more in what we see than the term 'end-product' implies. We are almost certainly witnessing the final stages in the usefulness of the small single farm as an operational unit in upland Wales. The farms are rapidly contracting in numbers and are being replaced by new clusters of homesteads of various types. The picture is more that of a life-cycle, beginning with an original cluster, then passing through a stage of maximum dispersal, and finally returning once more to a cluster pattern.

Finally, the changing pattern of settlement shown on Figures 9 and 10 may be examined statistically by using the Clarke and Evans nearest neighbour formula. After processing the material for the computer, we find that the Clarke and Evans R value in 1834 was 1·1722, showing a well-nigh fully random pattern for the scattered settlements. A fully random sample would give R as Unity. The

1968 pattern, however, yielded a value for R of 0·8474, showing the extent of the change towards greater nucleation.*

In spite of clear warnings of the dangers involved in drawing superficial analogies between one field of study and another, it is tempting to speculate that in the Celtic lands of Britain we are witnessing a life-cycle in settlement pattern comparable with that pattern which modern astronomers would have us believe operates in the stellar universe. Our attention is directed to the great nebulae, or star clusters, whose individual stars appear to be moving away from one another at great speeds into outer space. Now it is reported that somewhere in these outermost areas new and fascinating objects called 'quasars' have been discovered by radio astronomy, with the suggestion that they might be new 'nebulae', representing newer and more concentrated clusters than the rapidly expanding nebulae we have been accustomed to hear about in conventional astronomy.

Notes

1. E. E. Evans, 'Some survivals of the Irish open field system', *Geography* 24 (1939).

2. A. Meitzen, *Siedelung und Agrarwesen* 1–3 (1895).

3. A. Demangeon, 'La géographie de l'habitat rurale', *Union Géographique Internationale* 4 (1931).

4. S. Harris, 'Settlement and field studies in Guernsey', *Studies in Regional Consciousness and Environment*, 1930.

5. V. B. Proudfoot, 'Ireland' in 'Rural Settlement in Ireland and Western Britain', *Brit. Assoc. Adv. Sci.* 15 (1959).

6. T. Jones-Pierce, 'Medieval settlement in Anglesey', *Anglesey Antiq. Soc. Trans.* (1951).

7. G. R. J. Jones, 'Some medieval rural settlements in North Wales', *Trans. Inst. Brit. Geog.* 19 (1953).

8. F. Seebohm, *The Tribal System in Wales*, 1895.

9. G. R. J. Jones, 'The tribal system in Wales: a reassessment in the light of settlement studies', *Welsh Historical Review* 1 (1961).

10. R. A. Donkin, 'Cistercian sheep farming and wool sales in the thirteenth century', *Agri. Hist. Rev.* 6 (1958).

11. E. G. Bowen, 'The monastic economy of the Cistercians at Strata Florida', *Ceredigion* 1 (1950–1).

* I wish to thank Mr J. W. Aitchison, Lecturer in Geography at the University College of Wales, Aberystwyth, for much help in the processing of the data.

12. W. Rees, *South Wales and the March, 1284–1415*, 1924.

13. J. G. Thomas, 'Settlement patterns; rural' in E. G. Bowen (ed.), *Wales, a Physical, Historical and Regional Geography*, 1957.

14. E. G. Bowen, 'Le pays de Galles', *Trans. Inst. Brit. Geog.* 26 (1959).

15. HMSO, *Mid-Wales Investigation Report*, 1955.

16. M. L. Davies, 'The rural community in Central Wales', *Geography at Aberystwyth*, 1968.

10
Mountain glory and mountain gloom in New England

J. K. Wright

Estyn Evans loves mountains. His charming volume, *Mourne Country*,[1] reveals remarkable sensitivity and understanding of a small range of hills in Northern Ireland. Hence it would seem fitting that a chapter in this present book should be concerned with the lure and lore of certain mountains which resemble and yet are sufficiently unlike those of the British Isles to make a comparison geographically interesting.

Most of this chapter, accordingly, is derived from personal records that I have kept of mountaineering experiences in New England, and stress will be laid upon impressions that differed from those I would have gained if the locale of my mountaineering had been in Britain or Ireland. This general topic was first suggested by a visit to Skye and an ascent of Ben Nevis in 1920. The memory of that trip prompted me to contrast mountain climbing in Scotland and in the north-eastern United States.[2] The contrasts in question arise partly from difference in the mountains and partly from dissimilar social and economic conditions.

Although not so high, the Scottish Highlands have many more Alpine features than do our White Mountains or Adirondacks. Slice off the uppermost 3,251 feet of an Alpine massif, set it down at sea level, melt away the glaciers and snow fields, and you will have a range resembling the rugged Cuillin hills of Skye. In the northern and western Highlands there are not a few mountains— like the striking Suilven—that rise precipitously on all sides. The summits of the Cairngorms and of Ben Nevis form the highest parts of wide plateau-like surfaces, but on these surfaces corries, or glacial cirques, have been etched on a far grander scale than is to be found in their counterparts of the Presidential Range in the White Mountains of New Hampshire, and Katahdin in Maine. In the corries and on the exposed ridges the snow in winter and spring forms névés and cornices closely akin to those of the Alps, and snow avalanches are not uncommon. These features have given rise to types of mountain climbing almost unknown in the eastern United States, rock climbing and snow climbing, with the elaborate techniques that have been brought to perfection in the Alps and the Canadian Rockies. As in these loftier ranges, many of the crags and pinnacles of Scotland have long resisted attempts to scale them, and the guidebooks make much of the records of first ascents, and of climbs by particularly difficult routes. For this kind of mountaineering the mountains of New England offer practically no scope whatever. On the other hand, an almost complete absence of forests has meant that the techniques of woodcraft and trail cutting have played no part in Scottish mountaineering. The American climber regards the forests as one of the main elements that give charm to the mountains. A British mountaineer finds charm in heather and rocks and writes of the Cuillins that 'their sides are not disfigured with monotonous pine forests of a uniform light green colour'.

In parts of the Highlands mountaineering formerly seemed to be predominantly the sport of the 'gentleman and scholar'. Early guidebooks themselves bear silent witness to this, with their discussions of geology, meteorology, botany, and place names, their historical allusions and their bibliographies, their quotations from poems, and their literary flavour of good sportsmanship. 'Gentlemen and scholars' also visited the White Mountains and Adirondacks,[3] but in addition and in ever-increasing numbers came climbers of all kinds and ages. The American mountains are somewhat nearer the main centres of population. Whereas Mount Washington is only 280 miles from New York, Ben Nevis is 410 miles from London. The almost universal use of the automobile and the extensive development of that peculiarly American institution, the summer camp, bring trampers to our mountains from all over the country. Our mountains, moreover, are open to visitors at all times of the year. Most of the tracts not included in the

National Forests belong to lumber companies, which have no
objection to trespassers. In Scotland, during the most favourable
climbing season—late summer and autumn—the public is excluded
from extensive mountain and moorland areas set aside as deer and
grouse preserves.[4]

In the last few decades changes have occurred in both mountain
regions: the British mountains have become far more accessible to
the general public, and in the north-eastern United States there
have been interesting developments in the arts of rock climbing
(on such rock as there is), and of snow and ice climbing in winter;
and, of course, the advent of skiing has altered the aspect of many
of our mountain slopes and valleys. The essential differences,
however—those that spring from the contrast between forest and
moorland—remain unchanged.

Let us now turn to five aspects of this topic: The first I want to
deal with are 'mountain glory' and 'mountain gloom', titles taken
from two chapters in Ruskin's *Modern Painters*.[5] The meanings
in which I use them do not conform exactly to those of Ruskin.
By these terms I have in mind emotions aroused by the passing
sights, sounds or smells of mountain environments, or by thoughts
about those environments, rather than long-enduring traditional
attitudes that have crystallized in the consciousness of artists or
of poets. This paper, in other words, is concerned with the subjec-
tive element in geographical field studies and not with literary or
artistic history. Because of its well-known association I take
Monadnock as the locale for illustrating some experiences of
'mountain glory', and to illustrate 'mountain gloom' I draw upon
certain emotions aroused by forest fires.

I shall then say something of the allure of remoteness, for which
John Ruskin and Thomas Starr King were responsible to a small
degree in my early education; and lastly of the kind of response
for which Ruskin professed disdain.

Mountain glory on Monadnock

Neither the loftiest nor the most rugged of the New England
summits, Monadnock has nevertheless a magical appeal to
Emersonians and a terminological appeal to geographers.

One afternoon before the turn of the century and before I could read Emerson (or anything else), I was taken high up on a pasture in south-western New Hampshire. Under a sinking sun, Monadnock loomed blue and mysterious a dozen miles or so away, and it then and there acquired for me an aura of mountain glory. In later years this aura sometimes took on a poetic and sometimes a scientific colouring, Ralph Waldo Emerson being an indirect cause of the former and William Morris Davis a direct cause of the latter.

Once when I had fallen ill at the age of 12, Professor Davis, who was a neighbour, gave me a copy of his *Elementary Physical Geography* to console and educate me, and in it I liked to look at a halftone of a photograph of 'The Upland of New England, with Mt. Monadnock in the Distance and a Valley in the foreground'. I dare say that all but the most recent generation of geographers know that Davis adapted the Indian word 'monadnock' as a generic term meaning, as he put it non-Emersonianly: 'a residual elevation rising somewhat above the general upland and evidently to be regarded as the unconsumed remnant of the denudation of a former cycle'.[6]

In 1866 Emerson spent a night on this remnant, where he found that 'every glance below appraises you how you are projected into stellar space, as a sailor on a ship's bowsprit out at sea'.[7] According to Starr King, 'the genius of Mr. Emerson has made Monadnock the noblest mountain in literature'.

I have climbed Monadnock (3,165 ft) several times—and I am well aware that it is not *comme il faut* to say 'climbed' in this context. The summit of Monadnock can be reached in normal conditions without any 'climbing' as the word is generally used today, without any mountain knowledge, and without qualifications beyond what the older guidebooks called 'soundness of wind and limb'. I remember, on one of my earlier journeys, that the road to the hotel —which then stood midway on the flank of Monadnock—wound up through the open pastures on the lower southern slopes of the mountains. Used to the scale of Mount Washington (6,288 ft), I was agreeably surprised when we reached the hotel after passing through a short stretch of woods above the pastureland. We found the hotel highly respectable, clean, and well kept—an absolutely typical New England summer boarding house, inhabited by typical New England boarders. The hotel, alas, is no more. It is shown as 'Halfway House (ruins)' on a map dated 1953. It was a characteristically American specimen. The life expectancy of those magnificent, monstrous white-painted wooden structures—with their mighty piazzas and rows of rocking chairs—has never been long: Fabyans', Profile House, old Summit House (Mt Washington), Ravine House, Glen House, the maplewoody-like Moby Dick, all are gone; unlike Moby Dick, generally by fire. But to get back to Monadnock.

We made the ascent to the top of the mountain after dinner. It was already growing dark when we climbed over the great ledges that surround the peak. The air was hazy and laden with heavy blue-grey clouds; in the east a shower drew its fine curtains across the valley, but the wind was brisk and brought from the north-west a promise of better weather. Huge mountains of dark cloud hung over Vermont, their edges burning with sunlight as if from a tremendous forest fire.

The next day I climbed to the top of Monadnock again, and spent practically the entire morning sitting in the lee of a rock, absorbing the view. The air was a little hazy. Everything was blue and immense. Southward the country stretched out level to a straight horizon broken only by the rounded summit of Wachusett, which seems to be the leader of a great procession of hills marching south out of New Hampshire into Massachusetts. Everywhere in the south and east lakes gleamed and blazed in the bright sunshine. While we sat looking at the view a fire warden arrived. He carried a lunch box, a copy of The Human Body, an enormous map wrapped up in oilcloth, and a gigantic field glass which he let us look through frequently. One might think that there is not much variety and change in the view from a mountain, but in this case a great deal was going on: a man flashed from East Jaffrey, another from Rindge, another from far off in Massachusetts, to all of whom the warden religiously flashed back; the sun struck some polished surface on a roof 6 or more miles away and shone like a small arc light for about three-quarters of an hour. We saw smoke rising, examined it and fixed its locality on the map, but since it grew no worse we decided that it was not a serious fire. We also saw smoke over near the railroad, and more smoke in Massachusetts; we watched an automobile on the road at the foot of the mountain; and so it went. The life of a fire warden was far from dull. When he saw a pretty bad fire he reported it from a telephone in a stone shanty near the summit.

Mountain gloom when smoke is in the air

'June 24, 1904. Forest fire on Mt. Success. Causes great excitement throughout the whole place. Great cloud of smoke across the sky . . .'

These observations are in a letter to my brother written from Philbrook Farm, in Shelburne, New Hampshire, a summer resort among the White Mountains. Four years later my journal, written also in Shelburne, reads:

There was a feeling of horror all that day and the next
[July 12th, 1908], for there were great forest fires on Mt. Hayes.
Whenever the smoke would blow across the sun, everything
would turn either a thin yellow or a deep red, and the sun
itself could be looked at, a red disk among ruddy clouds.[8]

Although now aesthetically agreeable to remember, at the time these fires made us gloomy and uneasy, if they did not exactly terrify us. There were continuous forests between us and Mt. Success in 1904, and between us and Mt. Hayes in 1908, and had the wind shifted or strengthened or persisted, things might have been bad. What a blessed relief when cold rains came not long after!

I spent the summer of 1914 at Shelburne, trying to study for a doctoral examination, and recorded other fires:

Aug. 6. Smoke from forest fires in the air, rendering the
mountains almost invisible in a dull greenish-yellow haze.
Aug. 9. The mountains were swimming in a thick combination
of haze and smoke. Towards the outlines of Mt. Moriah
were faintly discernible, a cap of pale white cloud clinging
clammily to its crests. The atmosphere was hot, damp, almost
choky. There has been a slight suggestion of the sinister
in the weather ever since the great war began; others besides
myself have remarked on this.

One midsummer night in 1916, while in Cambridge, Massachusetts, I wrote:

It has been a hot dull heavy, lifeless day with humidity 93

(says the paper), but now, late in the evening, a cool breeze is blowing in from the north, laden with the smell of burning woods. They must be far away, for the summer has been unusually damp here. The smell of forest fires, however, is unmistakable and very different from the pungent wood-smoke scent of neighbouring chimneys or of camp-fires. Kipling has vividly described the enchantment that the whiff of the campfire exercises over men; equally strong is that of a breeze bearing the suggestion of distant burning forests. It brings back my vague childish fear when a huge pall of smoke loomed behind Moriah all day and in the evening we could see trees burst into flame against the sky. Forest fires are a characteristically American institution: the true flavour of this continent, of its immense extents of wild land, its ruthless waste, with the suggestion of open lakes, burned black stumps against a ruddy sunset, or a lumber town, with its mills and roughness and flames on the mountainsides above—all this comes in the breath of the forest fires. . . .

Recently I read the above to an American professor of geography, a Southerner. He expressed surprise that I should have thus responded to forest fires. To him and his forebears—farmers—they were benevolent, the means of clearing the land.[9] The lumber-man or the dweller on the edge of unbroken and unprotected woodlands views the matter differently. Perhaps, however, a distinction should be drawn between a 'forest fire', which, raging like a wild beast out of control, strikes terror in the hearts of those who behold or smell it, and a domesticated woodland fire set to accomplish a useful purpose.

Ruskin, Starr King, and 'The White Hills'

Ruskin wrote: 'To myself mountains are the beginning and the end of all natural scenery; in them, and in the forms of inferior landscape that lead up to them, my affections are wholly bound up.'[10] Though Ruskin was no mountaineer—preferring to look up at the mountains from below rather than risk life, limb, or comfort while climbing them—his writings gave a powerful impetus to the mid-nineteenth-century vogue of mountaineering on both sides of the Atlantic.

Since beauty, like goodness, is incomprehensible without reference to its opposite, ugliness, Ruskin had something to say of the latter in mountains. In Chapter X of *Mountain Beauty* he describes certain slaty declivities in the Alps, which

> form those landscapes of which the purpose appears to be to impress us with a sense of horror and pain, as a foil to the neighbouring scenes of extreme beauty. Foul ravines branch down immeasurable slopes of barrenness . . . and the snow lies in wasted and sorrowful fields, covered with sooty dust. . . . I know of no other scenes so appalling as these in storm or so woeful in sunshine.

Among our New England mountains the counterparts are those bare spurs, where fire or ruthless logging or gales of wind have left abominations of desolation, and at the time when I did most of my mountaineering (*c.* 1908–14) these were probably at their greatest extent and maximum hideousness.[11] Since then, improved fire protection, more enlightened methods of forestry, and the inclusion of large tracts in the National Forests have healed many of the old scars.

Ruskin distinguished between the 'beauty' and the 'grandeur' of mountains, both being deemed components of their 'glory'. Though conceding the possibility that his opinion might be warped by idiosyncrasy, Ruskin 'knew' that it

> is not idiosyncrasy, in so far as there may be proved to be indeed an increase of the absolute beauty of all scenery in exact proportion to its mountainous character, providing that character be healthily mountainous. . . . The best image which the world can give of Paradise is in the slope of meadows, orchards, corn-fields on the sides of a great Alp, with its purple rocks and eternal snows above; this excellence not being in any wise a matter referable to feeling, or individual preferences, but demonstrable by calm enumeration of the number of lovely colours on the rocks, the vivid grouping of the trees, and the quantity of noble incidents in stream, crag, or cloud, presented to the eye at any given moment. . . . All of these superiorities are matters plainly measurable and

calculable, not in any wise to be referred to estimate of sensation.[12]

Thus Ruskin seems to have considered the beauty of mountains as a quality of which the intensity might theoretically be ascertained by holding up an instrument like a cloud filter to register it. Ruskin refrained, however, from treating mountain grandeur in a similar fashion:

> How far the hills are great or strong or terrible I do not for a moment consider, because vastness and strength and terror are not to all minds subjects of desired contemplation.[13]

The Rev. Thomas Starr King (1824–64) was a Unitarian minister who had a church in Boston and later in San Francisco. He was an American counterpart of those stalwart nineteenth-century clergymen-mountaineers who distinguished themselves in the Alps. Between 1849 and 1859 Starr King spent his summer vacations among the White Mountains of New Hampshire, walking, reading poetry and Ruskin, and rhapsodizing about the views, which afforded him immense spiritual uplift, verging on the ecstatic. His book, *The White Hills: Their Legends, Landscape, and Poetry*,[14] enabled the summer boarders and transient visitors of the later decades of the nineteenth century to look at the mountains through Ruskinian, Wordsworthian, and Whittierian spectacles that screened out the gloom and enhanced the glory.

On the whole *The White Hills* is both geographically and historically interesting; and is full of perceptive descriptions as, for example, the following:

> Frequently it has been our fortune to see a shower . . . sweep down the Androscoggin Valley, and, as it thinned out, trail the softest veils over the Moriah range. And how much more gentle and soothing its outline appeared when the warm rain-drops were woven into broad webs of gossamer to mark the ridges more distinctly, line behind line, and show their figure in more refined pencilling against the damp sky. . . . Nothing can be more graceful and seductive than the flow of these lines of Mount Moriah seen through such a veil.[15]

Starr King felt that 'childlike animation, perpetual surprise and enthusiasm are signs of healthy and tutored taste',[16] and his enthusiasm for the White Mountains is infectious. His book was one of the factors that helped bring about the burst of mountain tourism and 'exploration' among the highlands of New England on the part of professors, clergymen, and other persons of 'tutored taste' (i.e. 'gentlemen and scholars') during the last three decades of the nineteenth century and the first of the twentieth. *The White Hills* was the 'bible' for the region among the summer boarders in Shelburne during my boyhood.

'Terrae incognitae' in the New England highlands

As we drew near the mountains I was very much impressed by
their purple greyness and by the vastness of their forests. How
much wilder and how much more savage are our mountains
than the lower mountains of Europe. There hangs
a mystery . . . the mystery of wilderness, lost and uninhabited.
That mystery lures me to the region north of Mt. Success;
there the forest reaches 40 miles with no house or road.

I wrote this early in 1908 of the approach to Shelburne by rail from Portland. A few days later, from the summit of trackless Green Mountain, overlooking the sources of the Ingalls River,

The great view fully repaid the exertion of the climb through
dense scrub spruce. Beyond the great gulf of a deep valley
rose the wilderness peaks of Success, Goose Eye, and further
mountains. To the north stretched the wilds, broken only here
and there by clearings. As far as the eye could see there were
mountains, grading from the dark blue of the nearer ones to the
almost silvery colour of those on the horizon.

During the next few years I 'explored' the nearer portion of the *terra incognita* that had spread before us so enticingly as we lay in the sun on the summit of Green Mountain.[17]

'Unknown-ness' and 'unexploredness' as attributes of geographic areas are relative, not absolute; they depend upon our definitions, our standards of judgement, and our scale of reference. As a mountaineering youth I was prone to regard the parts of the New England highlands that had not yet been mapped topographically by the United States Geological Survey on the scale of 1:62,500 or larger as *terrae incognitae*. Green Mountain then lay in the 'unknown' and all to the northward and eastward of it within 50 miles. At that time the difference on the maps of the location of various ponds, mountains, etc., and the general absence of exact knowledge concerning camps, logging roads, and clearings, made you feel that even in New England there remains hope for those who wish to have a flavour of exploring.

The challenge of mountains

Having rarely attempted any rock climbing I know little of that intricate art, but I gather that it affords a sensation of athletic-plus-aesthetic euphoria exceeding in intensity anything else imaginable. Part of this springs from the supreme delight of exercising one's entire body and thereby, with the aid of highly technical knowledge, of overcoming danger, difficulty, and discomfort and reaching points to which no person has ever climbed before, or has ever reached by the same route, or has ever reached in such a short time and so on. Besides the satisfaction of doing things that one feels sure are far beyond the ability of the common run of humanity, to many mountaineers rock climbing would seem to provide a spiritual, even mystical, feeling of exaltation.

In my youthful days there were two lowly equivalents in New England of the rock climbing that flourished then and still flourishes in the British Isles. These also involved discomfort, danger, difficulty, and the exercise of bodily skill. The discomforts and the difficulties, though of different kinds, were probably no less great than those that beset rock climbers in the British Isles. The dangers were not so great; they included the risk of becoming lost in the woods or caught in bear traps, spraining one's ankle or breaking one's leg, or putting out one's eyes on briars and brambles. The skills required were also of a lesser order, skills comparable to those of the slugger as contrasted with the fencer, or of the bricklayer as contrasted with the matador. The two equivalents were: first, climbing mountains by routes followed by no paths or trails and hence of finding one's way through the trackless forest and second, marking and clearing trails and sometimes building paths and bridges along them. I did a good deal of the first on the north-eastern outliers of the White Mountains, but never any trail-making, a more sociable and socially useful form of mountaineering enterprise.

The following excerpts from a journal kept in the summer of 1910 may illustrate what it was like in those days to climb trail-less mountains in New Hampshire. Our base of operations was Philbrook Farm, and our objective Mount Goose Eye (3,850 ft), a peak that neither I nor my companion had ever climbed though we had often seen it beckoning us from afar.

We started at 5.30 a.m. The pinkish mists were just drifting down the valley, leaving a prodigious dampness in the meadow grass, so that by the time we reached Ingalls River we felt as if we had waded to our waists through fifteen rivers. . . . Between eight and nine we walked along a well-marked logging road running by the brook for many miles. But this road became less well-marked the further we progressed, till soon we were forcing our way through bushes twelve feet high. We passed here, on a track choked with bushes and blocked with windfalls, a collapsed logging camp. Beyond this the road led up into a most disagreeable country and finally petered out in a labyrinth of branches and blind leads, no one of which could be followed more than twenty yards. Such are all logging roads; like so many other things, they start out with admirable directness and straight forwardness, as if they know where they are going and mean to go there without any shilly-shally; but before long they begin to vacillate and wobble, and finally end up in a hopeless collapse of purpose and aim. . . . Finding now that it was impossible to keep to the road any longer we consulted our compass . . . and set our course toward mountain ledges visible through the tree tops. Then after fighting our way for two hours through the most unpleasant scrub I have ever met save perhaps on Moriah, we came out on the open summit—only to find that it was not that of the mountain we thought we were climbing, whose two peaks we could now see towering up magnificently some three miles away to the north-east. The hot haze took all the vigor out of the hills, leaving them vast, languid and faint; Mount Washington filled the sky to the south-west; the Moriah ridges with their smooth gentle lines and utter monotony of

P

form were depressing in the extreme.

Later in the same summer I described the scrub on Moriah thus:

... it fills and chokes great pockets between perpendicular
walls of rock. Some of these troughs are ten or more feet
deep. You have to force your way down into them at the risk
of scratching your skin off. Then it is necessary to worm in
and out on hands and knees between the robust and pitchy
stems of the trees, and after that the precipitous opposite
wall of the trough must be climbed with the thousand hands of
the scrub all trying to pull you back into the trough again.
The worst part is the deception. The rocks are covered with
a moss much the color of the scrub, and since the scrub in
the troughs rises to about the level of the tops of the blocks of
rock, at a short distance this horrible tangle looks as if it
were a smooth and easy slope over which to pass.

Today there are good trails on Goose Eye, Success, and Shelburne
Moriah, but to climb any one of them in 1910 surely must have
required as much energy, if not as much *finesse*, as it would have
taken to climb the Matterhorn or the original Monte Rosa. In later
years I no longer relished this kind of climbing and had become
reconciled to being transported to the summit of Mount Washington
(6,288 ft) in an auto-stage. These are my impressions of this journey
of more than 30 years ago.

The arrival of the train furnished a sensation. No train in
the world—unless it be the one on Pike's Peak—makes such
a fuss for its size. Clouds of black smoke pour from the
bulbous chimney, jets of steam shoot out from the cylinders,
the air is filled with hissing and rattling and clanking sounds.
Everybody gathers to watch the little engine come pushing
its toy car up the slope at a pace not much faster than a man
can walk. When the train finally stops, the curious gather
round the engine, bombard the engineer and fireman with
questions, and peer into the machinery.
    After watching the train for a while, we stood at the
south side of the hotel. As we were standing there a very old
man and a youngish man came up over the rocks. The old

man looked somewhat done up, but nevertheless shouted in a
hale and hearty voice for the benefit of all who could hear,
'Well, here we are!' There was something rather grand and
imperial in his air. He is, it appears, the Rev. Dr. Harry P.
Nichols, who has a church in New York, is 83 years old; and
this was his eightieth ascent of Mt. Washington. When he
was 79 he climbed the mountain 13 times. All this struck
a fat and prosperous-looking New York business man—with
whom I spoke later—as very remarkable indeed. The business
man had been conveyed up in the train and was waiting to
be conveyed down.

This interesting encounter on the top of Mount Washington
confirmed me in the belief that 'gentlemen and scholars' frequented
the New England mountains as well as those of Britain and Ireland
—and, if there are any left, they still do, for all I know.

Conclusion

We have been concerned with certain types of mountain lures as
human beings feel them, and with their opposites or *antilures*. We
have seen that the aesthetic and recreational lures of mountains may
generate a sense of mountain glory (as we have defined that term),
and, conversely, that their antilures may produce mountain gloom.
Mountain environments, however, exert lures and antilures of
many other kinds: social, sociable, cultural, cultured, gastronomic,
etc., and the same, of course, is true of geographic environments
of other kinds. The urge to ascertain how people of different kinds
respond to these environmental lures and antilures, and to classify,
organize, interpret and apply such knowledge, has given rise to
a school of thought, in which much is made of the philosophy,
psychology, and geography of human perception.[18] If this embry-
onic science ever is born as a genuine science and grows to maturity,
perhaps its central consideration may be the balance of lures and
antilures, somewhat as the balance of supply and demand formed
the central consideration in classical economics.

At any rate human mobility, both intellectual and physical, is
a function of this balance, or, strictly, of the varying degrees to
which there is imbalance, and this is seldom a simple matter. The

aesthetic lure of beautiful mountain scenery at a particular place may finally cease to counteract the gastronomic antilure of tasteless meals at the resort where the scenery is found when combined with the counterlure of a neighbouring resort having less aesthetic but greater gastronomic lure; and under these combined circumstances there might be a migration of tourists from the former to the latter resort. When such a delicate balance is upset mountain glory may suddenly yield to mountain gloom.

The antilure of one place may enhance the lure of a different place as, when 'city gloom' makes us yearn for the mountains, or when, revelling in mountain glory, we recoil with aversion from the prospect of having to return to the city. Frank Bolles wrote feelingly of 'city gloom' in a chapter entitled 'My Heart's in the Highlands', the 'highlands' being the vicinity of Chocorua Peak.[19] With another graduate student, I, too, was impelled by city gloom to seek the very same 'highlands' in the winter of 1915:

Jan. 15. These are slushy days in Cambridge, Massachusetts, when the streets are hideous; everything is foggy and watery. I detest winter. . . . Jan. 26. Keith Vosburg and I go to Chocorua next Saturday to get out of the mill. . . .
Feb. 17. We had a delightful leave at Chocorua last week; one has only to leave Cambridge for a while to understand what an abominable place it is to live in in the winter. Why the deuce did John Harvard found his college in such a hole? One physically mildews here all winter. Keith and I skied and tobogganed, took snow baths, and attempted without success to climb Chocorua Peak on a blue-gray day. Everything looked far away, the lines of the mountains gentle and languid, with that peculiarly mournful, *aged* look that characterizes New England scenery when the sunlight is shut off.

Why 'mournful'? why 'aged'? No computer, whether animate or inanimate and however sophisticated, could answer that question satisfactorily—so how could I? In any case, were there neither the lures nor the antilures nor the counterlures of places there would be no human mobility, nor any geography, nor would you be reading this.

Notes

1. E. E. Evans, *Mourne Country: Landscape and Life in South Down*, Dundalk, Dundalgan Press, 1951.

2. *Geographical Review* 24 (1934), 148-9.

3. E.g. M. F. Sweetser (ed.), *The White Mountains: A Handbook for Travellers* . . ., Boston, James R. Osgood, 1st ed., 1876; known as either 'Sweetser's' or 'Osgood's White Mountains'.

4. R. W. Clark and E. C. Pyatt, *Mountaineering in Britain: A History from the Earliest Times to the Present Day*, London, Phoenix House, 1957.

5. John Ruskin, *Modern Painters*, London, 5 vols, 1843-60, vol. 5, containing Part v, 'Mountain Beauty'.

6. W. M. Davis in *Geographical Journal* 5 (1895), as quoted in L. D. Stamp (ed.), *A Glossary of Geographical Terms*, London, Longmans, 1961, 322.

7. Bliss Perry (ed.), *The Heart of Emerson's Journals*, Boston, Houghton Mifflin, 1909, 316.

8. A 'dark day' over an immense area in north-eastern North America caused by forest-fire smoke occurred on 19 May 1780, and is described in Jeremy Belknap's *History of New-Hampshire*, 3, first ed., Boston, 1792, Ch. II; see also 'Belknap Papers', *Collections, Massachusetts Historical Society*, 5th Ser., 42, Boston, 1877, 52-5, 58, 425.

9. See, for example, John Leighly (ed.), *Land and Life: A Selection from the Writings of Carl O. Sauer* (Berkeley and Los Angeles, Univ. of California Press, 1963), and C. J. Glacken, *Traces on the Rhodian Shore*, University of California Press, 1967, index s.u. 'fire' in both books.

10. Ruskin, *op. cit.* Part v, Ch. xx, p. 1.

11. See the fascinating account of forest fires and their effects in the New Hampshire mountains in R. E. Pike, *Tall Trees, Tall Men*, New York, Norton, 1967, Ch. 18.

12. Ruskin, *op. cit.* Part v, Ch. xx, pp. 3, 9.

13. *Ibid.*, p. 9.

14. Thomas Starr King, *The White Hills: Their Legends, Landscape, and Poetry*, Boston, Andrews, 1859, 327.

15. *Ibid.*, p. 259.

16. *Ibid.*, p. 58.

17. On these 'explorations', see J. K. Wright, 'The Northern Mahoosucs, 1910-1911: Terra Incognita', *Appalachia* 141 (15 December 1965), 626-54.

18. David Lowenthal (ed.), *Environmental Perception and Behavior*, Univ. of Chicago, Department of Geography Research Paper No. 109, 1967; also David Lowenthal, 'Geography, Experiences and Imagination', *Annals Assoc. of Amer. Geographers* 51 (1961), 241-60.

19. F. Bolles, *North of Bearcamp Water*, Boston, Hougton Mifflin, 1893, 157-67.

11
The Canadian habitat

Andrew Clark

In 1949 the accession of Newfoundland completed the rather haphazard assemblage of the lands now under Canadian sovereignty. Straddling roughly 90° of longitude and 45° of latitude it comprises not far short of 4 million square miles, somewhat more territory than that conventionally called European and second in size among the world's national territories only to that of the U.S.S.R. Yet, although relatively closer settlement loops northward in the western plains to latitudes greater than 65°, the vast majority of Canada's 20-odd million people live—and for most of the past three centuries have lived—south of the fiftieth parallel. Ninety per cent of them live within 300 miles of the southern border with the U.S.A. and more than three-quarters of them within 100 miles of it. There, too, are most of the cities and, as in most countries of the western world, Canada's people are mostly urban and even the three in ten classified as rural also are closely concentrated in the south. Thus, when one speaks today of the Canadian habitat, one could limit one's attention to a very limited part of the vast national territory. Nevertheless, people have lived, however sparsely distributed, in all parts of it, for many thousands of years and a consideration of the geographically variable habitat qualities of all of it may help to explain the varying intensity of use and occupation of different areas through different periods of time.

One of the most interesting aspects of the habitat of any people or peoples is the degree to which its natural characteristics have changed through centuries and millennia. Even if these aspects of nature had remained unchanged their significance might have altered substantially because of location relative to natural or cultural changes elsewhere or because of changing human evaluation through cultural evolution or diffusion and technological advance. In other parts of the world occupying cultures appear to have wrought great changes in the endowments of nature. But our first concern here is with spectacular changes in the Canadian lands over the past 20,000 years to which human culture has contributed very little.

From what was, very largely, an ice-covered non-ecumene, not unlike present Antarctica for the most part, it slowly changed over the following 12,000 or 15,000 years to become, perhaps by 5,000 B.P., remarkably like what it is now. From the human viewpoint, there have been minor ameliorations of climate (and perhaps one major one) since the last remnant blocks of lowland ice were dissipated, but the main characteristics and circumstances of climate and biota have changed very little in those last five millennia. During climatic amelioration the tree line advanced poleward (nearly 200 miles from its present position), and crept up the sides of mountains, reflections of lengthened growing seasons and higher summer temperatures. Fire, we think, was endemic in the northern forests and perhaps in the grasslands as well. Yet, in that sweep of time, there would appear to have been little change in the species composition of plants. Animals or insects were perhaps more variable; even large mammals appear to have altered their range substantially. Deer and moose, for example, may be rather late entrants of the Labrador–Ungava peninsula. The grassland–woodland border very likely fluctuated a good deal, moving out from the grassland core in warmer, drier phases, when the dry heart of the grassland may have shown desertic aspects, and retreating with more available ground moisture.

The enduring characteristics of the post-glacial geography of the habitat are revealed in the fact that the *gross pattern* of population distribution today has much in common with that of 500, 1,000 or perhaps even several thousand years ago. Now Canada's population is heavily concentrated in the St Lawrence and Interlake–Ontario Lowland and in southern coastal British Columbia (which areas contain the country's two metropolises, Montreal and Toronto, and their nearest challenger, Vancouver). People are somewhat less densely scattered on the grasslands and their parkland borders and in the southern maritime areas of the east. It is believed that at the time of Cabot's landfall, of the Icelandic visits, or possibly for long ages before, these same areas contained about the same proportions of all the peoples living in the Canadian lands. The populations of Canada's vast northlands (divided by the tree line into Arctic and Subarctic) and its western Cordillera have always been thin and spotty in the extreme. This pattern has persisted, or repeated itself, despite the great technological changes of the periods involved and the immigration to the area of millions of exotic peoples from other continents.

There are many divisions of the Canadian habitat that could be made for convenience of description. Here we will employ one which is based upon the more conspicuous elements of terrain quality, climate and biota: the Arctic, Subarctic, Western Cordillera, Western Littoral, Western Grasslands, the St Lawrence–Interlake–Ontario Lowlands and the Maritimes. No mystique, or any special validity other than the above, is attached to this regionalization. The first three subdivisions contain the vast preponderance of territory, but are very lightly peopled. Even in the final four there are substantial differences in population density. Before considering the latter, the habitats that man has consistently found most favourable, we will turn to those, equally consistently, neglected lands of the north and the mountains. Perhaps perversely, perhaps naturally, these lands have done far more to create the image of 'Canada' in the eyes of the world than have those which for so many millennia have been the principal habitat of most inhabitants of the Canadian lands.

The Arctic

Canada's Arctic, well over 1 million square miles of land enclosing vast additional extents of water in its bays and archipelagic straits, to repeat, is now, always has been, and seems likely for long to continue to be largely non-ecumene. It is a country dominated by winter cold relieved only from 1 to 3 months each year by a meagre approximation to a mid-latitude summer. In landforms there is a great variety. Although more than half of the area has the Precambrian base rock of the Laurentian (Canadian) Shield, it is joined by Paleozoic rocks of the bordering area including the Shield, with a generally low relief in the south-west coast of Baffin Island, in the Mackenzie delta, and in the western archipelago, nevertheless, exhibits distinctly alpine character in Devon and Ellesmere Islands, the spectacularly fiorded, towering eastern coasts of which face north-eastern Greenland.

The nature of the bedrock, perhaps important for future mineral exploitation, has not hitherto been of much significance to man. Of much more importance is the morainic debris and interrupted drainage which, over so much of the area, is a legacy from Pleistocene glaciation. In the north-eastern mountains large bodies of surface ice remain, and in those north-western islands which may have been ice-free throughout the Pleistocene the surfaces often are of unconsolidated later Tertiary and Pleistocene sands and gravels yielding a regolith not dissimilar to that derived from the morainic aprons.

The Arctic climate, a winter one for most of the year, shows the expected low temperatures, snow and wind, that the name 'Arctic' conjures up in our minds. Chief regional differences are associated with the greater winter storminess and precipitation throughout the year of the Atlantic areas as contrasted to the ominous droughty quiet of the vast tundras west of Hudson Bay. To this may be added the further contrast of low cloud, fog and depressed temperatures of more maritime locations at the warmest time of year to the long periods of sunlight and occasional high temperatures on interior locations where (granted the usual heavy clothing-need to contend with the clouds of insects and the cool to cold nights) heat stroke has been experienced in July. The very light snow of the western Arctic, together with high winds from time to time, may leave large stretches of rock, sand and gravel uncovered in the winter, to the detriment of sledding, but elsewhere the snow may lie for 9–10 months and never entirely disappear from thousands of shady draws.

Perhaps the most important feature of the terrain is not among the visible ones, such as the lack of trees, but in its subterranean permafrost. Virtually everywhere below a variable shallow layer (which may thaw for a few feet in summer) the soil and subsoil is frozen to depths which may reach 1,500 feet or more. The resulting inhibition of ground-water percolation accentuates the effect of glacial disorganization of surface drainage and is reflected in vegetation and soil characteristics. The problems of construction above permafrost, or of excavation within it, had little relevance to human technology before this last century; but today they are among the most severe faced by those who would conduct open-pit mining, erect large buildings, build highways or rail lines, or provide water and sewerage at any distance from major lakes and rivers.

The lack of trees has not only meant shortages of wood for fuel and shelter but has also severely limited the kinds of game available to hunters. The caribou spent much of each year in or near the forest fringes to the south and the graze and browse from the tundra never supported a great density of muskoxen. The short warm period with its long daylight hours attracted a rich population of migratory waterfowl and the rabbits, lemmings and foxes could be locally numerous. But the season for land hunting or fowling, or for freshwater fishing, was exceedingly short and one of its major features, the teeming insect life, did much to negate its other attractions.

None of these problems was insuperable for the circumpolar cultures of the post-Pleistocene period or, indeed, for the first Europeans who attempted to exploit its local resources of animal life. But the harsh climate, the low productivity of land fauna, and the 'summer' insect plague forced most of the attention to the sea; the exploitation of sea fauna, on, or through the ice for most of the year could not, and did not, support a population of more than small scattered groups. That it ever reached a density of one person per 50 square miles is extremely doubtful. It is true that the deeply ice-covered surfaces of the western Arctic waters allow good travelling conditions in winter, turning an archipelago into a subcontinental expanse, if the severe climate can be adapted to, but it is equally true that the major resources of marine life (fish, mammals and birds) are found in the east, where the rough and treacherous conditions of sea ice have made their exploitation hazardous for pre-European and European alike.

The history of the search for a north-west passage, begun within a century of voyages of Columbus and Cabot (if not, indeed, *with* them!) and not realized until two generations ago (1903–6), is one of bitter testimony to the extreme difficulties of coping with the icy marine environment. The people of the initial Arctic Small Tool culture, and its successor, the Dorset, may have made little use of whales, but the people of the next Arctic cultural stage, the

Thule, did so, increasing their resources considerably for a relatively short time early in the present millennium. Then, for whatever reason, climatic or simply over-exploitation, whales disappeared from most of the central Arctic by, or shortly within, the first period of European contact. The flurry of European attacks on the whales of the eastern Arctic—which lasted for most of the first half-century of Canadian nationhood—involved the equipment and technology born of the European industrial revolution and used the native peoples as casual labour. These contacts, rather than failing resources or the exigencies of the habitat, were calamitous and almost fatal for the Eskimo; the population was decimated by most of the same vicious effects of European contact the debilitating impact of which, from the time of Columbus's first voyage, has been rarely relieved in the New World.

A few scattered bands have attempted to exploit the resources away from the coasts more than by the distinctly auxiliary activities of the largely coastal native peoples, who have always made some use of the caribou, muskoxen, bird life, foxes, berries and the like of the inland barrens. These few hundred (at most) of inland peoples lived largely by following the seasonally migrating herds of caribou. But the formidable problems of life in that habitat held the population in close check. Despite a slaughter, by Europeans or under their inducement, paralleling that of the plains buffalo, there still may be 200,000 or 300,000 caribou in the Canadian Arctic. Moreover, the domesticated European reindeer has been introduced and would thrive, by what evidence we have. But the Eskimo and northern Indian people have shown little interest in becoming herders. A market for hides of the muskoxen (in part to fill the void left by the virtual extinction of the source of buffalo robes) led to that animal's near disappearance in the mainland Arctic, although a few hundred muskoxen do survive there under conservation policies, and a few thousand remain in the archipelago north of Lancaster Sound—chiefly in Ellesmere Island and well north of areas where the Eskimo have found it profitable to try to live.

Perhaps tragically, but perhaps inevitably, the habitat of most of the present inhabitants of the Arctic, whether European or native in origin, is concentrated near a variety of chiefly governmental posts established for military, communication, weather observation, trans-Arctic transport, fur-trading, or other like purposes. Today the Arctic generally is emptier of people than it has been through several millennia, although actual numbers of Eskimo, which reached a nadir of some 10,000 or fewer a generation ago, may have climbed again to roughly 15,000. There are settlements, which include large numbers of Eskimo, of from 1,500 to 2,000 on the edge of the region (as at Inuvik in the Mackenzie delta and Churchill on Hudson Bay) but most of the truly Arctic posts are much smaller. The largest of them, Frobisher Bay on Baffin Island, probably has fewer than 1,500. More and more the Eskimo are divorcing themselves from the resources of the Arctic habitat and are accommodating themselves to the exotic food, housing, and ways of life introduced by the Europeans, to whom the Arctic is simply space on the earth's surface which must be observed and flown over but otherwise not really utilized. No doubt there will be some mineral exploitation in the future (and optimistic prospecting is in train at present) and perhaps artificial habitats will allow substantial nuclei of exotic populations to be established (if the price is right) but, to an increasing degree, the Arctic, as a habitat, is becoming virtually a non-ecumene as it was for so long before the arrival of the Arctic Small Tool folk scarcely 5,000 years ago.

The Subarctic

The Subarctic, as here defined, includes not only the boreal forests but, on its southern margins, near the Great Lakes and the Ontario interlake peninsula, part of what is often termed the 'Great Lakes Forest' area with its white and red pines, maples and other trees demanding higher temperatures and a longer growing period in summer. Everywhere, indeed, the southern border of the Subarctic is not a well-defined line but a transition zone to other regional habitat types. The boreal forest which clothes so much of it is well enough known in terms of species composition from its Eurasian counterparts. The local dominance of one or more of birch, aspen, spruce, fir or tamarack (larch) varies a good deal with local conditions. Generally the Canadian Subarctic experiences a much more severe winter than does the Scandinavian forest area, or even that of Russia west of the Urals, although it shares a ground moraine—bare rock—muskeg legacy from Pleistocene glaciation with its comparable European region. Contrasts to the Siberian taiga lie more in species composition; larch, although very wide-spread, has rather less importance in the Canadian lands. The forest extends over half the District of Mackenzie east of the Cordillera, more than half of the 'prairie' provinces north of its parkland transition border with the grasslands, virtually all of Ontario north of the Great Lakes and the southern settled peninsula, most of Quebec and Labrador north of the St Lawrence lowlands and south of the tundra, and the island of Newfoundland.

For the past five or more millennia, since the final wastage of the ice, at least, most of the Subarctic has been the habitat of hunting, fishing and gathering peoples rather thinly spread from the Mac-kenzie delta to the Avalon peninsula. Material culture was sur-prisingly uniform throughout, despite the fact that west of Churchill on Hudson Bay the language family shifted abruptly from Algonkian to Athapaskan. As with the Eskimo, individual clusters of people were usually small and widely scattered. The ubiquitous water surfaces offered by the glacially disarranged drainage were the focus of their life, for along them lay the principal means of transport—by birchbark canoe in summer and, over their treeless frozen surfaces, by snowshoe and toboggan in winter. The land did provide very important resources of game in the moose, deer and a wide variety of fur-bearers. But the fish and most valuable avifauna were taken on or near the waters and perhaps most of the animals were killed or trapped near the water's edge. Permanent camps away from the water-side were virtually unknown and it is likely that large areas of the Subarctic literally never were 'trod by the foot of man'. The very few larger concentrations of people appeared near the larger lakes and rivers from Great Bear and the Mackenzie (where they were rare) to Superior, Huron and the St Lawrence.

Much of the flora was little used, including the ubiquitous aspen and balsam fir and the magnificent pines on the southern borders. But the paper birch, spruce roots for 'thread' and spruce gum for adhesive (boiled with animal fat) were as widely used as they were generally available. Many kinds of berries, led by the magnificent blueberry, provided spice and vitamins in the diet, and scores of leaves, barks, roots and seed yielded dyes, herbal remedies and 'famine foods'; some, like the wild rice of the south-central border areas, became local staples. But the base of the economy, for food, clothing and shelter, was the animal life. There were regional specializations—caribou in the north-west in winter, excursions into the grasslands for bison in the summer, and the exploitation of marine resources on the east coast—but the widely distributed animals such as deer, moose, rabbit and beaver were of major importance nearly everywhere.

'Forest, rock and water—these are the strongest landscape impressions of the Subarctic.' Perhaps this generalization is a little less true—in terms of rock and water—in the non-Shield areas of the Mackenzie lowlands, northern Saskatchewan and Alberta, but this triad formed, with the brushy and herbaceous flora and the fauna, the climate (particularly its winter phase), the major features of the northern habitat for its long-time pre-European inhabitants. The thinness of their occupation reflected the poverty of the area in terms of the resources which could be used. When combined with the climatic hazards the soils are of little use for agriculture. It might be argued that the northern limits of plant husbandry reached on the borders of the Subarctic (or at least the Shield) in Huronia represented simply the temporal stage of the outer fringe of an expansion which had been going on for thousands of years from Middle America and that, with time, it might have pushed further poleward. Within the last century, it might be argued further, there have been several farming penetrations of the margins of the Subarctic near its southern borders and in the Ontario–Quebec clay belts. But even with all of twentieth-century technology and heavy governmental subsidies of various kinds, they have not been truly successful operations. We must conclude that the peoples of pre-Columbian times made the most effective possible use of the Subarctic that their technology allowed and that the 50,000 to 100,000 folk it sustained represented an effective adaptation to the available resources.

This is not to imply that the peoples, in tribes or smaller groups, were static in location or that cultural diffusion and territorial aggression had ceased in the fifteenth century. Conflicts in pursuit of hunting-lands or mobile resources (as for caribou and seals off the Labrador coasts with the Eskimo) are known to have taken place. The point is that, at any time within the past 5,000 years, invaders or visitors from Europe would have found the boreal forest, from end to end, occupied by about the same numbers of people, living in about the same kind of economic way, even though individual tribes, and various aspects of non-material culture, such as language, may have shifted markedly the regions of their hegemony.

In the twentieth century the boreal forest has undergone much of the same process of territorial depopulation and nodal concentration of the descendants of its pre-Columbian occupants as has the Arctic. For most of the Canadian Indians within its borders it is far less of a habitat than at any time since their ancestors followed the retreating ice-edge into the area. Today most of them are clustered in straggling quasi-villages within reserves or in semi-urban slums on the fringes of larger centres like Kenora, the lakehead city of Thunder Bay, or Sudbury. They retain some knowledge of bush-craft and many of the men make additional money as guides, cutting pulpwood and the like. Women and children may be heavily engaged in berrying and wild-rice harvesting in season and in fishing at all times. Skills with axe and knife, the ability to track game, the almost uncanny knowledge or mystical insight as to where the fish will be biting at any day or hour are not dead. But the art of, and interest in, most of the traditional technology is gone. For example, the use of canoes has virtually disappeared among them; for the few families that still possess them paddling is considered only women's work. In many years of roaming about the environs of the Lake of the Woods, with one of the heaviest Indian populations in the Subarctic, I have rarely seen a man paddling a canoe. I hasten to add that, over the years, I have known and travelled with many excellent canoemen in many parts of the Subarctic who were essentially Indian in genetic and cultural inheritance. But, today, most guiding and general transportation is by boat and outboard motor or by jalopy on the bush roads; even the cedar and canvas canoe which succeeded the birchbark vessel has been replaced in turn by one of aluminium or fibreglass; the muscle power of the voyageur has given way to that of the internal combustion engine. Paddling is now being relegated to expensive summer camps for young people or the romantic, nostalgic expeditions of middle-aged city folk into the wilderness.

The Indian culture that seemed so well adapted to the habitat for so long has become almost completely Europeanized in its external and material aspects and it is entirely possible that, as a group very largely supported by governmental largesse, they are so divorced from their habitat and traditions of using it that they could be resettled entirely outside the area with little disturbance to their way of life and little effect on the general character of the Subarctic. Although these judgments are less applicable to the far north-west than to most of the centre and east, present trends suggest that, inexorably, its inhabitants similarly will soon face the same, almost complete, separation from their traditional ecology. Briefly, natural habitat characteristics are becoming increasingly irrelevant to Indian culture and economy.

Coincident with this progressive Indian withdrawal from the occupation and exploitation of the resources of the Subarctic, European invasion and use of them has gone on apace. For most of two centuries it was based on the use of the Indians themselves as hunters, trappers and transporters of furs; it was in that process that the chief material alterations in Indian culture, with the introduction of metal (for tools, firearms, pots, traps and the like), of cloth, alcohol, and exotic diseases, occurred. Then, within the past two centuries, the assault on today's three primary resources of the Subarctic, again 'forest, rock and water', began. The largely unsuccessful attempts to use its few patches of third-rate soils for agriculture (now largely in retreat) have been commented upon. But the central triumvirate have been exploited successfully and to a degree that has provided Canada with a major portion of its export staples (to replace fur—and far outdistance wheat) and with an abundance of power not only for extensive local processing to greatly increase the value of such staples, but also to supply much of the energy needed by the highly industrialized economies on its southern borders where most Canadians live and work. It should be added that 'forest, rock and water' also provide magnificent recreational opportunities for the burgeoning North American population to the south, and recreation is yielding perhaps a fuller territorial use of the habitat than any of the other activities of man. Finally, it should be noted, to exploit these resources it has been necessary to cope with the problems of providing adequate transport and of creating amenities of life, in cities and towns and outlying camps, which would attract and maintain the necessary managerial, technical, labouring and service manpower.

The first forestry exploitation of the white pine on the southern margins of the area was spectacular, but limited in time by the rapid exhaustion of the resource—usually a matter of one human generation, at most, in any given area. Today, lumbering as such is of very limited importance in the Subarctic and largely limited to spruce. (Recently, I bought some boards in Kenora for my island cottage on the Winnipeg river flowage and was startled to find that they were from northern Saskatchewan—coals, from such a traditionally unlikely source, to Newcastle!) About a century ago the pulping of wood, and the use of chemical aids in the process, was introduced. Today there are well over 100 sizeable pulp mills (128 in 1960) in Canada, many of them outside of the Subarctic area on its southern fringe, but depending chiefly on its resources. Gradually nearly all the common species of trees have been brought into use. Slow growth of trees, heavy fixed investments in plant and problems of transportation—together with government regulation —have forced the adoption of sustained-yield 'tree-farming' policies. Today, the making of pulp and paper, which is almost entirely from the Subarctic forests, has become Canada's leading industry in value of production, value of exports, total wages paid and total capital invested. Within the area many, perhaps most, of the ostensible farming operations are supported chiefly from pulpwood sales (in addition to various forms of government aid and the sale of casual labour). Perhaps, needless to say, this exploitation has been heaviest in the Subarctic east of the 'prairie' provinces and will spread west (into a poorer pulpwood resource consonant with a less attractive climate) only as the returns justify greater transport costs.

Mineral exploitation of the Subarctic is very important in the total economy of Canada but the actual mining, chiefly in the Precambrian rocks of the Shield, is necessarily extremely spotty, for most of the Shield consists of granites and other plutonic rocks in which mineralization of economic importance is rare. What are exploitable (and to a large degree already explored and in use) are found in 'islands' of volcanic and sedimentary rocks scattered irregularly and thinly through the wilderness. Gold and silver were early important and remain so, but the present strength of mining is for the industrial metals: iron (Canada is now the fourth leading producer and largest exporter among the world's nations), copper, lead, nickel, zinc and many others. Uranium resources are great but

Q

the market is fickle and their large-scale exploitation appears to lie in the future. Similarly the enormous quantities of petroleum in the oil sands of northern Alberta (perhaps half of the world's total known reserves) are a resource for the future and, situated on the south-western margin of the region, will likely have little effect on it. Although mineral exploitation has created railways and roads (permanent and winter) through the area and a remarkable number of air services (pontoon or ski aircraft exploiting the extensive and ubiquitous water surfaces) which, briefly, gave Canada world leadership in ton-mile air freight traffic in the 1930s, transport of bulky minerals remains a problem inhibiting the development of scores of small, isolated deposits.

The power resources of the Subarctic, even ignoring the mineral fuels (uranium and petroleum) in the Mackenzie river drainage, are very large. Roughly two-thirds of the installed hydro-electric power in Canada is in the Subarctic and only about one-third of the latter's potential has yet been developed. It not only supports—indeed may be said to have made possible—the pulp and paper industry, and contributes heavily to mining, smelting and refining, but, because concentrations of population are unlikely to develop in the Subarctic except for the needs of such industries and their transport requirements, most of the future power developed will be exported from the region. Indeed it is possible that much of the water-power potential never will be developed. The local abundance of nuclear fuels may make it uneconomic to do so within another generation.

The abundance of water depends more on interrupted drainage and low evaporation and transpiration than upon heavy precipitation, although the fact that so much of it falls as snow (the Subarctic has 5–7 months a year with snow cover of 1 inch or more) contributes greatly to the amount available and stored in its myriad lakes and swamps. Indeed most of Canada's stream flow derives from snowmelt waters with sources preponderantly in this region. Unquestionably these water resources will be tapped ever more extensively for the rapidly expanding southern Canadian (and American) peoples but, within the region, their use, apart from the supply of hydro-electric power and a minor role in transport (especially for planes and winter tractor roads on ice), is now, and increasingly will be, for recreation. Of course one must be careful not to underplay the importance of that use. The habitat is magnificently suited for it, and, if fire and water pollution can be controlled and wild life conserved, a summer population, perhaps largely American (for the United States is rapidly running out of, or destroying, its own wilderness areas), equal to half of the present population of Canada, may be found scattered over the Subarctic in the not-too-distant future summers.

Thus, if the affluent North American society continues on its upward economic course, providing increasingly more time and money for recreation for increasing numbers of people to enjoy it, the Subarctic may once again be a habitat for a significant proportion of the continent's people each year, if only on a seasonal basis from June to September. Since most of the accessible Subarctic lacks good skiing potential, winter recreational use is likely, as at present, to be confined to the Laurentians on its south-eastern flank. The winter, which restricts the Subarctic's warm-season recreational use to a scant 3-4 months over most of the area, continues to play its role as perhaps the most striking, and dominant, habitat characteristic.

The Western Cordillera

The Canadian lands contain a massive block of the western North American Cordilleran complex. Generally it is considered to have three sections: a Cordilleran continental façade, a Pacific mountain system, and, between them, an intermontane belt of plateaux, basins and valleys with isolated small ranges and peaks. Much of what has been said of the Subarctic region applies to most of it, but it has many distinct habitat characteristics. Except on its coastal fringes it does not appear ever to have been a favoured living area for pre-European man. Unquestionably he used it occasionally as a refuge region and for seasonal hunting but, like much of its southward extension in the United States, it represented a negative ecumene, a barrier to movement rather than a desirable place to live. Frequently a summer hunting ground for the bordering lowland forest peoples, as the grasslands may have been in part, the severity of the winter at higher altitudes, the roughness of terrain, and the threat of dangerous predators generally prevented the exploitation of the floral and faunal variety offered by the great ecological contrasts within short distances. The opportunity for refuge from human enemies afforded by the scores of secluded valleys (some unknown even to the far-ranging fur-traders and alluvial-gold seekers, and finally revealed only by aerial reconnaissance) appears largely to have been ignored. When it was taken, the difficulties of life and isolation from cultural diffusion appear to have led to a retrogression of material culture. Yet folk from both the eastern piedmont and the western littoral did make forays into the Cordilleran lands for hunting and trade (as for the hair and wool of mountain sheep) and pathways through it appear to have been known, if often obstinately concealed from the first European explorers.

In habitat terms, it may be that, at the height of the Wisconsin glaciation, when the putative piedmont corridor to the east may have been closed by the meeting of continental and Cordilleran ice fronts, ice-free valleys in the mountains offered 'islands' of plant and animal life, as nunatak peaks above the ice probably could not have done, for the support of human movement from the unglaciated Yukon River basin to the lands beyond the southern margin of the ice. Or, granted the existence of the piedmont corridor, such unglaciated areas may have made access to it possible from the open lowlands of the continental vestibule to the north-west.

Yet the Cordillera, as habitat, had little custom in pre-European times. Moreover, until the late eighteenth century its isolated relative location led to its neglect by invading Europeans. Then followed the three-quarter-century rape of its beaver and other valuable fur-bearers and the mid-nineteenth-century push up the Fraser valley to the Cariboo placers. In the early 1860s, as in the Sierras a decade earlier, large temporary populations established themselves there and in the coastal entrôpot (Victoria, on Vancouver Island); indeed, these formed the largest concentrations of people in the Canadian lands of the time west of present Ontario. This kind of rush, to be paralleled in the northern valleys of the Cordillera (the present Yukon) half a century later, was quite different from anything that had taken place (or ever would do so) on the Shield. With the dissipation of the Cariboo rush the interior valleys were used only very lightly for cattle ranching or small-scale farming with a large subsistence component, and, in the 1880s, for the locus of the first transcontinental railway in the Canadian lands. 'Whereas this environment could be admired for its scenic beauty by later generations, to the European [and Asiatic] people of the 1880s, the mountains were a barrier and a hindrance, the trees were a nuisance and there was little level land to attract agricultural settlers.' Not until the present century was well launched did the Cordilleran lands contribute much to the coastal nodes of population except as the locus of their one land connection with the rest of the country. Mining had developed in the 1890s in the Kootenays, in the extreme south-east, but these were largely tributary to the U.S.A. It is only a little more than 50 years since the first all-Canadian rail route was opened through southern British Columbia. By that time sawmills were exploiting the spotty, but locally very productive, forests although, like those of its fellow rubber industry, the resulting establishments were impermanent. Gradually irrigated agriculture on the dry valley-bottom terraces along the many linear trenches permitted commercial fruit growing and the raising of supplementary fodder to allow ranching to expand. Finally, one large industrial plant was established at Trail on the Columbia river, barely north of the U.S.A. border, for refining and smelting metals and, in very recent years, lumbering has again picked up. But prospects for substantial increases in population anywhere are meagre and the Cordillera seems likely to continue to contain a very small proportion of British Columbia's people.

As in the Subarctic the recreational potential of the area is great but, as in the broad expanses of the western Subarctic, much of it will remain for later generations to exploit. The coastal population concentrations have such extensive and varied opportunities of their own that, as yet, they have made slim use of the Cordillera for the purpose, although more and more distantly located North Americans now drive through it to enjoy it and relax in its magnificent scenery. The region's hydro-electric power resources, apart from those directly on the coast, have been little developed (although the near-coastal installations have made the province of British Columbia second only to Ontario and Quebec in available power, and the provincial potential is second to that of Quebec). The lower Columbia valley serves only to store water for U.S.A. power development (although there is a reciprocal return of developed power). However, one major north-eastern project (near Portage Mountain on the upper Peace River) is in current progress.

The Western Littoral

Abruptly on the seaward slopes of the western Pacific flank of the Cordillera the habitat possibilities and characteristics change spectacularly. Man has taken advantage of the attractive opportunities there for at least 5,000 years, although the broken nature of the fiorded, archipelagic shoreline, and barriers to land communication, appear to have contributed to a considerable variety in the inheritance of non-material culture. Material culture was remarkably uniform, however, and the economy it reflected supported what was, for the pre-Columbian Canadian lands, a substantial density of people.

Here and there the usually sharp boundary between sea and mountain was interrupted by small pockets of land of low relief. There the villages, impressive in their buildings wrought of wedge-cut planks from the huge trees of the Pacific rain forest, sheltered populations which were better fed and housed, and at least as well clothed for their climate, as the majority of Europeans of the time. That climate was benign and the sea that lapped at the roots of the truly magnificent trees literally teemed with fish and aquatic mammals. In a sense the habitat was as much sea as land and, in its resources, even more so. Whale, seal, halibut, salmon and sea otter, amongst the vast variety, existed in a profusion almost beyond the dream of hope.

Relative location which, except in the sense of refuge, was unfavourable to the pre-Columbian inhabitants in terms of contacts for trade and cultural diffusion, became of great importance with international competition of Europeans and eastern North Americans in the eighteenth century. Russian, Spanish, British and, in the early nineteenth century, American, interests met and, clashed in the area. Its resources of beaver on land and seal or sea otter in the coastal waters formed the first economic magnet but, with increasing Pacific trade in the nineteenth century, a base on that ocean, tied to eastern British North America by land, became of vital interest both to imperial strategists in London and to those British North Americans in the colonies along the lower Great Lakes and St Lawrence who dreamed of a continental empire of their own. Thus a very short stretch of the coastline (from the Strait of Georgia to 54° 40′ North Latitude) was secured between the insistent

Spanish, American and Russian claims and, as habitat, its greatest value lay, perhaps, in its role as a gateway to the Pacific.

In these narrow coastal lands, the only segments of Canadian territory apart from a few Cordilleran valleys to the east to escape the bitter frosts of the Canadian winter, a substantial population grew up, the only major concentration—as indeed in pre-Columbian times—west of the immediate hinterlands of the St Lawrence–Great Lakes drainage. The substantial inherent attractions of the habitat—the scenic splendour, wealth of potential lumber, moderate marine climate (which made it the 'California' of Canada), plentiful water power, and the prolific salmon in the coastal waters—all added attractive force to the central magnet of location relative to the great ocean. Many cities, led by the Greater Vancouver complex between Burrard Inlet and the Fraser delta on the mainland and Victoria and Nanaimo on Vancouver Island, grew up and the Vancouver conurbation is now well on its way toward becoming Canada's third million population node. Near to the cities the urban demands and the climatic attraction have created a relatively intense agricultural land use of the small patches of sufficiently level land.

The Western Grasslands

In a large, roughly semi-circular area, east of the Cordillera, south-west of the Subarctic boreal forest and north of the American border, lies the poleward extension of the great North American interior grassland. In present Manitoba there was a little of the tallgrass bluestem prairie, but more of the southern grassland area of that province was so intermixed with aspen and oak groves that it is usually called an 'aspen-grove complex'; indeed toward its northern margin the prairie is restricted to ever smaller enclaves and spruce and larch begin to appear as the transition to the boreal forest is made. In present Saskatchewan and Alberta the northern parkland area, often 100 or more miles in width, is one of almost pure aspen in its tree clumps. To the south of the parkland lies the great expanse of open grassland with only occasional riverine strips and odd patches of broken land (as in the breaks of the plains and on the Cypress Hills) with a restricted growth of, chiefly, poplar. At its heart, in the driest climate in Canada outside of Cordilleran valley pockets, are the short, grama-grass dominated swards of the northern Great Plains. On all of its borders this merges into the mixed grass (needle, wheat) formation which blends, in turn, into the outer parkland borders.

In this droughty expanse of grassland the primary resource of interest to pre-European man was the vast bison herd. For how many centuries or millennia a culture had existed based primarily on the plains, and primarily on the exploitation of this resource, is uncertain. There is artifactual evidence which goes back 2,000 years or more which suggests it, but it is possible that, in the half-millennium from 1500 to 1000 B.P., it was exploited largely as a summer hunting ground by folk coming from the forest and parkland perimeter who had an essentially Subarctic forest culture.

The habitat is a difficult one in which to live at any time of year. Water is hard to come by over much of the area, and in many a summer, as tributary creeks and sloughs ponded in the ground moraine go dry, there is very little available except from the major water-courses, tributaries of the Saskatchewan and Assiniboine rivers. It is true that on the floors of the former pro-glacial lakes (as Regina, Souris and Agassiz) there is a good deal of very flat land on which water lay in most spring seasons, as on the wet Illinois prairies, but this did little to relieve the situation. In winter the riverine forest strips provided meagre shelter at best from the howling blizzards, and deeply sub-zero temperatures can persist there for weeks. Nor, except in the great sweeps of sky and the atmospheric glory of spectacular sunsets and thunderstorms, can it be called an aesthetically pleasing land.

These 'prairie' areas (the term is inaccurate, but inescapable) were first appraised as a notably barren region by the fur traders, their waterways simply paths to the more distant beaver and other furs of the north-western and Cordilleran forests. Soon, however, the logistics of food supply turned attention to the bison resource and systematic hunts were organized to provide solid meat, the dried and pounded pieces of leather-like sun-dried flesh that in a matrix of fat or tallow often flavoured with sun-dried berries like the ubiquitous Saskatoon (*Amelanchier* spp.) formed the basis of the rawhide sacks of pemmican which sustained the voyageurs of the canoe brigades. Because the Indians were notoriously averse to the discipline of long-sustained buffalo hunts, this function became associated with a rising group of *métis*, offspring initially (and by repeated adoption) of the English, Scottish and, predominantly, French members of the fur-trading community and the accommodating daughters of the various Indian tribes but, gradually, forming a self-conscious group, or *nation*, based on the lower Red River Valley.

The effective agricultural occupation of these grasslands by Europeans was late and subsequent to their incorporation in the new Canadian nation and the provision of rail transport to east and west coasts. The climate and soils were exploited effectively for wheat and small grains for which, granted the often extreme year-to-year fluctuations in rainfall, in which crop failures alternated with bonanza productivity, the habitat was magnificently suited. The building of rail lines, again granted the need to import wood for ties and the long haul for the rails, was as uncomplicated as anywhere on the continent. Aspen supplied cordwood to heat the homes; western pine from the Cordillera, and spruce (and a little white and red pine) from the Subarctic forest to the east, the wood to build them. In terms of living it was scarcely a more attractive habitat for the *métis* or the European farming population than it had been for the Indians. Most of the encomia about the magnificent, stimulating environment have been written nostalgically by ex-prairie folk safely ensconced in more benign climates. But small-grain farming of the excellent grassland soils, however marginal it often was, offered the gambler's chance of an occasional year or two of big returns if the yields were high and the price was right.

The frequent downward trends of yields and prices (or even both at once, as in the 1930s) have often caused widespread distress and, on a national, or even continental, comparison, the prairie habitat has proved increasingly difficult agriculturally although agriculture has been sustained by diversification and various politically inspired subsidies. Fortunately for the economy (although sustaining mainly urban populations who must still cope with the climate) the exploitation of very extensive reserves of petroleum, natural gas and potash has provided new staples and diversified the economic base. But the habitat remains the least attractive in what we may call 'settled' Canada, and the three prairie provinces as a unit (Alberta has been a recent, and perhaps temporary, exception) have had a strong outflow of population to the west coast, central Canada and the United States.

St Lawrence and Interlake Ontario Lowlands

For perhaps much longer than 7,000 years the interlake peninsulas of Ontario and the St Lawrence lowland have had human occupants. Even when the ice fronts were as far south as Ohio we have evidence of living-sites which were covered by their late readvances and it seems likely that, from Paleo-Indian times, the Great Lakes–St Lawrence drainage area had a population supported by hunting, fishing and gathering. In the subsequent 10,000 years or so the environment changed a good deal as the margins of the pro-glacial lakes advanced and receded with changes of outlets for meltwater controlled by ice dams and the effect of isostatic recoil. For long successions of centuries much of the upper St Lawrence valley was flooded by salt water, a deep inward extension of the Gulf of St Lawrence. The advance of vegetation into the regolith of morainic and outwash debris and the exposed floors of receding lakes and estuaries must have been rapid. Bare rock was clothed with lichens, mosses and, surprisingly rapidly, with woody and herbaceous cover. The shallow lakes filled in with marsh vegetation and a new, if at first irregular, post-glacial drainage system became established. The base rocks, except for the one extension of the Precambrian Shield through eastern Ontario to the Adirondacks, were Paleozoic sedimentaries. There was much limestone and the regolith had, along with its extensive patches of sand, some areas which allowed the development of quite rich soil.

Warmer and longer summers, better soils, and proximity to a richer floral assemblage to the south gave this region a relatively luxuriant forest cover. Maple, beech, basswood, white elm, white and red oaks were dominants. In southernmost Ontario, a millennium ago, there were hickories, pawpaws, tulip trees and other trees characteristic of a more southern flora. Indeed it is believed that these spread well north of that range in the period of major climatic amelioration, as the Great Lakes forest, in turn, may have pushed north into the Subarctic lands. In general, the sandier areas tended to be dominated by white and red pine and, with increasing latitude, the key elements of the boreal forest—fir, spruce, paper birch, poplar and jackpine—became more common. In general it is seen as a transition area between the deciduous forests of the north-east–central United States and the true boreal forest. Within its shelter,

land game—moose, deer, rabbit and a wide variety of fur-bearers—
were plentiful, nuts and berries were profuse in season and the
lakes and streams were most productive of fish. These were the
opportunities that were exploited, perhaps without many marked
changes in material culture, for several millennia.

Then, perhaps 900 to 1,000 years ago, the edge of the diffusion
of New World agriculture reached the area and its resources of soil
and climate proved adequate for the growing of early maturing
maize. How large a place Indian corn played in the sustenance of
the regional population is still a matter of dispute; its great
advantages as a portable, storable food for the long journeys of the
fur trade and for the sharp increase in long-distance warlike forays,
both of which are clearly subsequent to, and consequences of,
European contact, may have greatly expanded the role of maize
agriculture in the early seventeenth century when we begin to get
our first written descriptions (apart from those of Cartier). Certainly this was the only part of the Canadian lands in which
agriculture played a significant economic role. That of the Malecites
of the St John River was, essentially, incidental to their economy.

It has often been supposed that agriculture arrived with, and was
established in the region by, an invasion of Iroquoian-speaking
peoples and that the coincidence of the borders of, first, this region
with the boreal forest, and, second, of Iroquoian and Algonkian's
speech, represented a conscious recognition of habitat quality by
an expanding agricultural folk. At present, however, there is a
strongly supported hypothesis that much of the Iroquoian culture
was indigenous and that agriculture diffused to, and not with,
the Iroquois.

The Iroquoian (and agricultural) area was contracting in the late
sixteenth and early seventeenth centuries, but not, we think,
because of any changes in the habitat. A very likely explanation of
its retreat westward from the St Lawrence lowland, where Cartier
had described its north-eastward extension in the 1530s, to the
lower Great Lakes region to the west, is that the Algonkian hunting
tribes first acquired metal, for pots and weapons, from the desultory
fur trade of the St Lawrence gulf and estuary in the later sixteenth
century and that this gave them an edge in the competition for
territorial control. But this may be too neat and easy an explanation.
It is highly likely that, even before the rippling disturbances of

European contact had spread inland, there had been a long and continuous state of flux in tribal and linguistic boundaries—as witness the great migration of Athabaskan people from the present Canadian north-west to the present American south-west. It is even possible that, since the St Lawrence lowland is marginal at best for maize growing, a few successive bad years, in terms of expectable small climatic fluctuations, could have led to the Iroquoian withdrawal.

By the mid-nineteenth century the habitat advantages for European occupation (pine lumber and potash to pay the costs of clearing and a soil and climate warmly encouraging to the extensive grain–livestock agriculture to maintain it) had given the area the densest and most prosperous population in British North America —in the interlake Ontario peninsula at least—a position which habitat qualities, including location relative to the American mid-west and water transport by lake, canal, and river, were of much importance. Today, in this small part of the national territory more than two-thirds of the Canadian people live; a fifth of the nation, indeed, is found in the two major conurbations of Montreal and Toronto. It is a four-season land with a lasting snow cover of only 3–4 months, a long, warm summer, and short but pleasant springs and autumns. The adjacency of lakes, rivers and the vast forested Subarctic to the north provide its folk with superb recreational facilities. This is, as it long has proved to be, one of the most favourable habitats in North America for man, whether primitive hunter or a member of one of the world's most prosperous and technologically advanced societies of the late twentieth century.

The Maritimes

The least attractive part of the St Lawrence–Great Lakes Lowland is in its south-eastern borderlands where it merges rapidly into the roughest section of the north-eastward extension of the Appalachian roughlands. These areas are not, and in the record of human occupation of North America have never been, closely settled. To the east of them is the last of the Canadian habitat regions, 'the Maritimes'. Although still considered part of the same Appalachian roughlands, they contain many patches of land of low relief (Prince Edward Island, Canada's smallest province, has no land over

500 feet in elevation) and, east of New Brunswick's central highland, only the massif of north-western Cape Breton could be considered geomorphologically forbidding. Since 1949, with the accession of Newfoundland, there has been a somewhat artificial attempt to include that island with the three traditional 'Maritime' provinces as a new regional entity, 'Atlantic Canada'. However, in habitat terms, apart from the coastal climate and situation (particularly in relation to Maritime resources), Newfoundland belongs to the Sub-arctic region and, were its people French-speaking (in fact it has fewer people of French origin than any other Canadian province), doubt-less would be included with Quebec in any regional grouping. The island itself, as well as the province's mainland territory of Labrador, have very much in common with La Belle Province north of the St Lawrence lowland.

The most distinctive habitat characteristics of the Maritimes are associated with their name. Most of the European population of the past four centuries, as today, lives close to tidewater. This was not so obviously true of the Algonkian-speaking tribes who lived there—the Malecites of the St John River basin and the Micmac of the rest of the area (Gaspe, Nova Scotia and Prince Edward Island)—as it was for their European successors. Even so, large numbers of them migrated seasonally to the seashore even if their preferred winter quarters usually were deep in the woods. The migratory life and lack of agriculture, together with the ease of movement by inland waterways and along the coasts, militated against even the degree of permanence of occupance found among the northern forest people whose economies and material culture had so much in common with their own. The combination of habit and habitat gave them less locational identity than probably any other major pre-European group in the Canadian lands. To the geographically unsophisticated eye, most of the interior of Nova Scotia and New Brunswick is almost indistinguishable from the glaciated boreal forest region of the Shield and, in the extensive granite country of western Nova Scotia, the similarity of the lake-and-rock-strewn landscape of forest, swamp and muskeg is very close indeed. However, in the seventeenth century the vegetation differed signifi-cantly, with a much larger broadleaf component and the latter's greater variety: two maples, an oak, yellow birch, beech and other trees common to more southerly latitudes, as well as white pine and larch. But these were mixed with the fir, spruces, white birches and poplars of the Canadian taiga. The animal life—deer, moose, rabbit, many of the other small fur-bearers, fresh-water fish and an abundant bird life—were remarkably similar to those of the Sub-arctic. But to these were added the great resources of the littoral seas and the offshore banks: seals, walrus and occasional stranded whales; lobsters, oysters and clams; the anadromous salmon and shad; the pelagic mackerel and herring; and the demersal cod, hake, haddock and halibut.

But resources of food, fur, skin, and oil do not tell the full story of the Maritime habitat. Winter was slightly warmer than further inland on the continent and summer distinctly cooler. The cold offshore waters induce frequent and long-lasting coastal fogs. Precipitation both as summer rain and winter snow is heavier. The pronounced lag in the seasons, a most distinctive Maritime character-istic, may give the area its special climatic individuality. Spring is cold, wet and late; summer comes on with dilatory reluctance. In contrast autumn, also late, is long and glorious and a permanent snow cover over much of the area may be delayed until the new year. March through May has always been the 'dying time' in the Maritimes when the promise of warmth from higher suns and longer days is denied, fortnight after frustrating fortnight, by the chilling winds from the sea.

The intricate serration of the Atlantic coastline, so like that of adjacent Maine, offered excellent harbours and coves for shelter from one of the world's stormier seas; a matter of some importance if those same seas were to be exploited effectively for what was long their most valuable resource—the cod of the littoral waters and offshore banks. Even tiny coves could provide havens and facilities for curing fish for the small vessels from Europe of the sixteenth and seventeenth centuries and the fishing shallops and schooners in which the fishery of later years was conducted.

And cod it was that brought European ships to the area from the early sixteenth century (if not well before) and, first in dozens, and then in scores and hundreds, they came from Spain, Portugal, France and the British Isles. Increasingly the shores were utilized to cure the fish on the ubiquitous bare rock or coarse gravel beaches or on roughly constructed tables (stages). The sea breezes, humidity and frequent cloud cover kept the fish from drying too rapidly (burning) and a fine quality, lightly salted cod that brought a premium price in the European markets was produced. Even when the banks were more fully exploited for larger fish, the shore stations retained, and even expanded, their functions.

Thus, by the beginning of the seventeenth century, when the attraction of fur led to the development of more elaborate and long-lived establishments to further that trade, the coastal habitat had been long, if only peripherally, exploited and known and, through the Indians, peddling their bundles of furs with increasing persistence in order to obtain metal goods, cloth and alcohol, more of the characteristics of the interior became known. The discovery of the utility of another major habitat characteristic, generally a negative one to navigators, was made by one of the early fur-trading entrepreneurs, established in Port Royal (Annapolis) Basin. The extraordinarily high tidal range of the Bay of Fundy leaves substantial areas of flats uncovered at low tide. At Port Royal, Charles Menou d'Aulnay had brought out several scores of settlers to attempt to make his establishment as self-sustaining as possible; some of them came from his own and his mother's estates in Poitou. These were well inland (north of Poitiers) but some of them may have made the trip down the Loire to the Biscayan coasts where, under similar conditions, Dutch engineers had been imported to dyke-in the tidal flats to make rich farmland; indeed some of the settlers may have come from such areas. At any rate, before the middle of the seventeenth century, the practice was well established in 'Acadia', as the region came to be known, and it spread with the expansion of the Acadian population to all the dykable lands of the Fundy shores within the next century. The rich reclaimed soil proved adequate for most of the needs of the Acadians (there were 10,000–15,000 of them by the mid-eighteenth century) and the other lands of the region were virtually untouched. The most important habitat feature for the Acadians thus was, in its final form, an artificial one, but they did some hunting in, cut their large, essential supplies of wood from, and pastured their animals through, the adjacent forested *terra firma*. Eventually, they made use of many of the lake–portage–stream route ways of the Indians, with whom they established an almost symbiotic coexistence. But, for their century or more of undisputed occupance of the area (before their forcible dispersal in the 1750s), the major feature of their habitat was the patchwork of remarkable fertile fields of silt behind the dykes and sluices.

The warmest summers of this Maritime region are found in the Fundy area which was a distinct advantage for the favourite Acadian crops of wheat and peas. Even those who ventured on to 'upland' soils, of substantially less fertility, in Isle St Jean (present Prince Edward Island) found the warmer summer suitable for them. But in Cape Breton, along the Atlantic coasts, and through much of the interior, cooler summers and poor soils were to present serious barriers to most forms of agriculture when the Acadians were uprooted and largely replaced by New Englanders (and others of colonial American origin) around the Fundy shores and by Highland Scots in eastern mainland Nova Scotia and on the two islands of Cape Breton and St John. The technology of dyked land farming was unfamiliar to the Yankees and they concentrated on trying to farm the uncharitable soils of the lowland patches back from the sea and in fishing and trading from the inviting south-western harbours; they did some lumbering and shipbuilding too, making rather a substantial accomplishment in the latter enterprise. In the circumstances of the habitat and the opportunities of local and world trade of the century following the American Revolution, together with the predilections and goals of the occupiers, the western areas of the Maritimes managed, by combining farming, fishery, trade and the harvesting and processing of forest products, to work out a satisfactory, if far from luxurious, mode of life. But the Highland crofters to the east who concentrated their attention on a meagre kind of mixed farming, or the Irish peasants who laboured in the pineries of New Brunswick, never really achieved what, as early as the late eighteenth century, had come to be regarded as a North American standard of living. Immigrants to North America from Europe who had more sophisticated agricultural, commercial or industrial traditions would appear to have recognized the limitations of the habitat and they generally had the means to avoid settling in it. Then, in the late nineteenth and early twentieth centuries, as information about the comparative regional limitations diffused through the area, it experienced a virtual haemorrhage of its youth.

Some 500 years ago, location relative to the main streams of cultural diffusion from the Far East, the Middle East and Middle

America in the previous 10,000 years had made this Maritime area one of the most distant and ignored corners of the world, comparable in many ways to Australia and the southern tip of South Africa. The last push north-westwards from across the Atlantic had petered out *c*. A.D. 1000 when the Icelanders and Greenlanders inspected, and rejected, the habitat opportunities. The farthest ripple of diffusion of the great dietary trio of maize, beans and squash had only lapped the edges of the area.

As a theatre of conflict between English and French empires and a marginal sector of the North American base of North Atlantic trading triangles, the Maritimes rose to some prominence in the eyes of the world for the first time in the seventeenth and eighteenth centuries. But the direction of the main streams of world economic activity and cultural diffusion shifted course in the nineteenth century and within the past 100 years the area has again suffered from a relative location that has made it the site of little but marginal eddies of those streams. It is now the most disadvantaged region of the Canadian ecumene; indeed it may be seen as the northernmost extension of the continental Appalachian problem that extends from Alabama to Newfoundland. Habitat limitations, both of nature and of location relative to concentrations of economic and cultural activity, have relegated it to a low place in the economic regional hierarchy of Anglo-French North America.

Yet there is, in the Maritimes, a beauty of landscape and a glory of climate in the summer and autumn that holds the hearts of its expatriate children to the third and fourth generations and that is making it a primary focus of recreational activity for those of the tens of millions in Ontario, Quebec and the American north-east, who prefer something less rugged than the Subarctic offers, or who simply enjoy the sea and the bountiful sea-food menus it makes possible. It will certainly become another major North American summer playground, and for its permanent residents the rewards may justify coping with the problems of living through its January–May climate.

Conclusion

No aspects of the Canadian habitat are of a piece over its vast area and variety. The winter, so widely advertised by Voltaire ('quelques

R

arpents de neige') and by Kipling ('Our Lady of the Snows') is, indeed, most pervasive, but its negative aspects stop short of the heavily peopled Pacific littoral. The Precambrian Shield, so prominent a topographic feature over so much of the heart of the Arctic and Subarctic, has been rather fondly adopted as 'Canadian' by the Canadian people and does contribute heavily to the nation's major exports of forest and mineral products and to its supply of hydro-electric power. But it still is not *habitat* for most of them except for brief summer excursions. 'Forest' is a rubric that, although comprehensive enough, never embraced the great sweep of Arctic lands, or the country's twentieth-century breadbasket, the Western Grasslands. The qualities of the habitat, together with the habits of the people and the course of world events, have made Canada, like Australia, New Zealand and Argentina, one of the world's greatest exporters of primary staples, raw and processed, but most of the highly urbanized population lives out its life with only indirect reference to the machinery of production, processing, or transport which place them on the world market. The country is too wide, the habitat too various, to allow any single, neat epithet.

If it is legitimate to think of size of national territory as a habitat characteristic—and it may deserve such nomination only less than does relative national location—Canada shares this fully with others of the world's territorial giants: the U.S.S.R., the U.S.A., China, Australia and Brazil. And as for all of them (although perhaps least the U.S.A.) the problems of connecting scattered pockets of favourable local habitats across and around great expanses of unattractive lands have placed substantial burdens on the rate and dimension of economic growth. It may be that the size and distribution of what we may call Canada's negative areas—large regions with some, or all, of poor soil, harsh climate, rugged terrain and unattractive vegetation—may constitute the major national habitat characteristic in relation to other nations. But of great, and perhaps prime importance, surely, is Canada's relative world position, lying as it does latitudinally between the two greatest oceans, facing China and Japan or western Europe, and, longitudinally, lying between the late twentieth century's two economic and military colossi, Russia and America. Studies of habitat have tended to neglect relative location but, in today's world, it may be the most important single aspect of Canada's habitat for its occupying people.

12
The future habitat

Emrys Jones

Professor H. J. Fleure, whose particular kind of scholarship so inspired Estyn Evans, once wrote: 'Geography, history and anthropology are a trilogy, to be broken only with severe loss of truth.' The truth lay in the historical explanation of the present, and time was a familiar dimension essential to all understanding. For Fleure the 'corridors of time' went back to the earliest phases of man's story, and with no perceptible break they also lie before us in the future. It signified no new departure when Estyn Evans saw the past in the present and had to turn to the spade to make sense of the human geography of Ulster. In so doing he made the most notable contribution to the archaeology of the province. The link between this archaeological research and the present lies in his extremely sensitive studies of folk life. In these studies elements from a distant past are seen to be subtly intertwined with those of a recent past, and the whole is a pattern which modern society is merely expanding. To Estyn Evans continuity pervades land and life. It may be that in the Celtic fringes of these islands one is more aware of continuity, less aware of the magnitude of changes today. Here, unquestionably, the present embodies the past. Much of that past is alive, much is redundant; some of it enriches, some encumbers. And to an extent this is true of the whole of Britain. Not even the most sophisticated society can ignore the past. Culture is learned behaviour, and neither the present nor the future can be understood without reference to the past. We are constantly posed with the dilemma of the extent we must turn to the past in solving the problems of the present, for we also face another fundamental characteristic of society—it is always changing.

The need to accommodate change

The major problem is how to accommodate change without destroying the structure of society. Change is constant, however gradual, however much resisted, in the simplest and in the most complex society. Change is particularly characteristic of urban society, though it would be very mistaken to assume that rural societies are in any way static. Williams, in his study of a Devon parish, stresses the ecological ties that constitute a stable element in an otherwise constantly changing rural situation, and describes the result as a 'dynamic equilibrium'.[1] Militating against change is a universal feeling of reluctance to upset an existing way of life. To accommodate change some part of the existing pattern must go, and yet the entire structure must not be damaged. The familiarity of the pattern of everyday existence which spells out the relationships between society and the environment on the one hand and between various members of the society on the other is a strong shelter from the unknown. Against this comforting stability, society faces innovations from within and without which at once threaten and promise, and it is not surprising that many of those who look at the stars and dream of utopias are regarded with suspicion. To many people 'planning' is a bad word, not only because it suggests a measure of control and loss of personal freedom, but because it also threatens an established and accepted pattern of life. Yet in one sense planning means dealing with change, making more orderly a natural sequence of events, shaping them, perhaps hastening them, but not destroying the past in the process. Indeed, planning should ease the process of accommodating change.

If, in planning the future, the break with the past is too sudden and too severe, then there may be severe dislocation in society. This is also the case if physical planning places a constraint on social customs which are held in high esteem. A simple case in point might be the disappearance of the parlour in planning modern houses. More than one study in rural Wales has stressed the particular role of the parlour.[2] This room often becomes a shrine—small, rather overcrowded with the best furniture, rarely used except on special occasions, and recording in photographs and snapshots and bric-a-brac all the important stages in the life of the family—the rites of passage—such as christenings and weddings. There is a strong parallel in the 'west room' described in Arensberg's *Irish Countryman*, often the room where the old folk retire, but also having many of the characteristics of a shrine.[3] It serves its final function when there is death in the house, for here the body is laid out. It is hardly surprising that open planning is looked upon with suspicion by country folk (whatever arguments can be put forward for the better use of space), for in their case the open plan places a constraint on a well established pattern.

Change does not affect the whole of society in the same way or at the same time. Generally speaking changes are more common in an urban than in a rural context, for two reasons. The first is that rural society must set itself in equilibrium with a physical, natural environment which if it changes at all does so very slowly indeed. The whole rhythm of life of a peasant community is tied to summer and winter, to day and night, to planting and harvesting. Urban society has divorced itself from this pattern. In towns and cities we are regimented by clocks and time zones. Our lives may be dominated by television series which have a Newtonian regularity, but this is a pattern of our own devising, a change brought about by society, and conceivably it could be changed again. Secondly, the city may be regarded as the centre of innovation—begging the question of the link between the urban process and innovation being a causal one. From earliest times the city has been the symbol of increasing organizational and social complexity. Commerce, class structure, industrialization, increasing communications, are all inextricably part and parcel of the life of a western city. To some extent the control of some of these processes involves planning. In the western world change is overwhelmingly urban change, and planners are products of the city.

In looking into the future the planner must forecast in some way or another what kind of changes might arise within the society in order to create the kind of structure—whether of a city or of a society—which will be acceptable in the future. There are two kinds of forecasting and planning. 'Trend planning' consists of extrapolating from the existing situation, assuming that nothing will seriously upset the trend. This does not involve any value judgments on the changes taking place. For example, if one of the changes is a continuing increase in population, then it is a simple job to project that increase into the next 20 or 30 years, assuming that fertility and mortality rates are not going to change radically. One can refine the projection. If there is a known decline in the rate at which fertility increases, this can be used to modify the projection. But there is no value judgment. The other kind of planning is 'normative'. One assumes that a certain goal is desirable and then plans a programme to achieve the goal: a value judgment is essential. Both approaches may be combined. For example, in looking at the future of the south-east in 1944 it was assumed that population was going to continue growing. But as the established goal was that London itself should not grow, it was necessary to plan the expansion of cities outside the metropolitan area to take an overspill population.[4]

Trend forecasting and planning is much more easily accommodated by society than normative planning. It is nothing more than a tidying process. The changes that are occurring are taken at their face value, and if they can be brought about with less rather than more disruption all the better. In this way the values that are already enshrined in the society are retained, disturbance is minimal, and most of the elements in the old pattern are carried into the new. But the acknowledged planners of the world are the normative planners, who try to free themselves from their existing environmental framework in order to create something quite new. The utopias of this world bear little relation to life as it is. So many have wanted 'to change the sorry scheme of things entire', and this calls for drastic action:

> Would we not shatter it to bits, and then
> Remould it nearer to our heart's desire?

The break must be complete, the old must be shattered, the start must be from scratch. But most utopian plans retain their ideal only because they never descend to ground level:

> The city is built
> To music, therefore never built at all,
> And therefore built forever.

Perfect, unchanging—never having come to life! Even normative planners have to come to terms with reality. They dare not look too far ahead. Indeed the majority have been more tied to the past than ever they realized, for even the visionary can operate only within his own cultural framework. To take a simple example: the geometric city of early Renaissance times, such as Palma Nuovo in north Italy, is a clear reflection of Vitruvius's ideal design of 1,000 years before. Again, when L'Enfant designed a new city for the emerging United States of America, however fresh the start or new the site or clear the ideals, the instructions from Jefferson were to build a city on the Greek model. At that time classical designs were dominating city growth in Europe, and in the correspondence preserved between L'Enfant and Jefferson the former asks Jefferson to bring home the designs of the new cities of Germany and Italy and the latter gives a long list of the plans he is sending L'Enfant. It is true that new elements also were introduced, such as the symbolizing of executive, legislative and judiciary in three main avenues. L'Enfant was looking very far into the future, too, when he planned for a city the size of Paris, then about 800,000. Nevertheless the plan was deeply rooted in the enlightened culture of the late eighteenth century.

How far are we tied to the past and to what extent can we or should we free ourselves from it? The questions are more difficult to answer because, in a physical sense, most of us are living in the past. The countryman wrestles with a field system which is largely the outcome of the seventeenth century, or possibly much older. In south-east England the eighteenth century is firmly printed on the rural landscape, in regular fields, hedgerows and avenues of trees, in parks and country roads with wide grass verges. In upland Wales the pattern may be much older, or, on the moorland fringes, may reflect the haphazard enclosures of the early and mid-nineteenth century. One way or another the farmer is severely constrained by the past—I had nearly said hedged in by it.

Living in the past is even more familiar to dwellers in towns and cities. They have inherited structures from past centuries which in no way ideally serve our purposes today. Only a minority live in relatively modern houses, i.e. of the last 30 years or so. Millions are living in houses built in Victorian times, and many in older houses. Our cities echo the past, mainly because most people seem to want to build for eternity, permanent and stable and unchanging. This is why our traffic crawls uncomfortably down medieval lanes, or comes to a complete halt in market squares meant for pedestrians. Between cities our major road system until recently was only a slightly modified version of the Roman network, and our rail system reflects the industrial revolution at its height. Too much is invested in the existing environment to expect rapid alteration, but there is a danger that we will be utterly strait-jacketed by the past. We are expert, too, in investing the past with certain social values which militate against change. The Victorian row house may be a slum but the Regency terrace is highly desirable. Indeed the further back we go in time the richer one has to be to meet the values set upon seventeenth-century or even medieval houses—suitably fitted with twentieth-century heating and air conditioning of course!

But this use of past housing stock is natural. If there is no alternative then there is some justification for trying to adapt ourselves to an outworn environment. On the other hand there may be little or no justification for continuing to create a similar environment without planning for future change. The difficulty is in breaking out of past constraints.

The traditional model of the city

An example of this is the physical form of the western city during its long history. One can trace back many elements in the western European city to the very early civilizations of the Middle East. Lopez reminds us that the earliest known symbol for a city is an Egyptian hieroglyph, and that it is simply a circle with a cross inside it.[5] This very simple symbol is a model of our own cities. The circle represents the separation of the urban from the non-urban. In a physical sense it could well be the wall which from time immemorial has been a cardinal feature of towns and cities, from Jericho down to late-nineteenth-century Paris. The division between urban and rural in Europe, and, until recently, in this country, is sudden and complete. In a social sense the circle symbolizes the closed society, and the feeling of belonging within a city. To be 'without the walls' was formerly a sign of rejection—as for example in medieval Caernarfon, where the walled town was a symbol of

English domination, and the Welsh were relegated to *Y Maes*—i.e., outside. The cross in the circle is a symbol of communication within the walls, physically the roads leading to the centre which was and is literally the focal point of city life. In medieval towns this would be the market—often the *raison d'être* of a city; in classical times it was the *agora* or the *forum*, and in Renaissance Europe the *place* or *plaza*. These were the economic, social, political or religious foci.

Our cities are still based very much on this model. The wall has often disappeared, but it has been replaced by a green belt. Although more pleasant to look at, the green belt is almost as effective as a wall. Its purpose is much the same, because it symbolizes the containment of the city, the effort to preserve the distinction between urban and rural, and it is meant to ensure that development beyond the green belt will be very different from that inside the belt. Its dangers lie in its rigidity and inviolability. The latest equivalent to the wall is the boundary of a designated area, and this is even more inviolable. When a planning team is asked to design a new city it is restricted absolutely to a set designated area. This is like building a wall before building a city—a doubtful step at all times, but deplorable in a planning sense because it assumes that the old model is the right one. Strangely enough the people in the vicinity of such a designated area may feel safer outside this boundary than inside, so that in one sense it certainly differs from the medieval wall. Again, as in the old model, the centre of our cities is a focal point, where all roads meet. The market, or its equivalent, the stock exchange, is still in the centre. Here is accumulated the capital of a region, and the attraction of the central area has gone on increasing as the value of the land has increased, leading to the cumulation there of activities and to the congestion from which we are suffering today.

How far this traditional model has become part and parcel of our thinking can be judged by looking at the post-war new towns around London. In part their very existence stems from the policy of containment—in this case the desirability of containing London—and this was done by designating a green belt. Beyond the green belt the new towns are suspiciously like the model referred to above. There are radial roads leading from the outside to the centre, which is a traditional centre with its market, shops, town hall and principal buildings. Each town is contained to a greater or less degree by its own green belt. The circle and the cross dominate. In parenthesis even the idea of the neighbourhood is of doubtful novelty. In the new towns the neighbourhood is nothing more than a focusing centre of areas lying between the radial roads. Looking again at the plan of the ideal city put forward by Vitruvius in the third century A.D., we find not only the radial roads leading to a central square, but subsidiary small squares between the radial roads looking suspiciously like neighbourhood centres.

The growth of the western city, in the last 50 or 60 years in particular, has spilt outwards far beyond any former confines in a low density sprawl that is particularly characteristic of our interwar suburbs. But this has not fundamentally changed the model. Economically the model is based on minimizing the cost of overcoming distance. Nearer the centre the rent increases as one approaches the most coveted sites. Further out the rent decreases as one faces an increase in cost of communication. Two things follow. One is the continuing need for compactness, the second is the recognition of the centre as the most desirable point in the city. Theoretically the centre of the city is the most accessible point to all the people in the city: this is why the *agora* and the *forum* were centrally placed, why the medieval market was central, why Woolworth is in the High Street. In the traditional city, centrality and accessibility were coincident. Even when the growth of cities led to expansive suburbs, those suburbs were still tied to the services at the centre. However much the inhabitants of suburbs were escaping from the city, no one wanted to run so far as to be beyond the convenient reach of what the city had to offer. Any centrifugal forces were always counteracted by the centripetal; these forces lie at the base of our simple model of the western city.

Until recently, planned cities have shared all the disadvantages of those which have grown naturally, precisely because planners have seen no further than the existing model. This tradition has been followed from Vitruvius and the ideal planners of the Renaissance period right down to those who planned our post-war new towns. A planned city of this traditional kind suffers most because the approach is monolithic—i.e. the city is planned as a complete entity: the end is seen before a beginning is made. The wall, or any form of containment, makes it a discrete, once and for all concept. Two criticisms arise from this: the first that it controls too rigidly the internal development of a city; the second that once the plan is fulfilled the city can grow no more. Deny change and growth to a city and you deny it life. The ideal city becomes static, unchanging. If it is preserved, as in Naarden in Holland or Palma Nuovo in Italy, strait-jacketed in massive wall and ditch defences, it is a museum piece. Ideal cities have little place in a changing world. To live at all a city must be able to accommodate change. We still tend to see our towns and cities in monolithic terms, looking for an ideal size, or using the green belt as a form of constraint. But the more perfect the plan and the more formalized, the more restrictive it becomes to functional change. This is why Mumford is so scathing on monolithic planners, from Hippodamus to Hausmann, for regimenting human functions and space.[6]

In many ways the traditional western city has failed, more particularly on a metropolitan scale. On a small scale the forces and tensions set up by the traditional model are tolerable; on a large scale they are liable to cause chaos. This is not necessarily in our own times only. Living conditions were by no means ideal in Rome at the height of its imperial power, when probably over a million people lived in a city of 5 square miles—at about the same density as cities like Calcutta today. Overcrowding was ten times worse than we experience in our cities. There were tenements of six to ten storeys, rickety houses which collapsed and caught fire easily. Augustus tried to limit the building height to 70 feet, i.e. about seven storeys, but many buildings were well over 100 feet high, though lanes were as narrow as 10 feet. Nero introduced what look suspiciously like our own planning bye-laws when he decreed that no building should exceed in height twice the measurement of the width of the street.[7] Conditions were intolerably crowded. This was the consequence of the need for accessibility, in a pedestrian city: its largest diameter was only 3 miles, so that everyone could get to the centre. Living outside the city deprived one of cheap bread, work and entertainment. But the price paid for the privilege of living in Rome was high.

The intolerable conditions of imperial Rome were repeated again and again in our own cities at various points in their history. There was extreme congestion in London prior to the Great Fire. In the nineteenth century we have Gustav Doré's magnificent drawings of an intolerably crowded city, backed by accounts ranging from Dickens to Mayhew. And our own complaint still centres on the heavy price one has to pay to maintain the traditional western city. The city is failing quite simply because centrality and accessibility no longer mean the same thing. No motorist would deny that the centre of London is no longer accessible. Indeed there is ample evidence to show that accessibility is now a function of the periphery. For many years much of the hotel service in the United States has been taken over by motels, which fringe the city because they cater for the car: they have successfully countered the congestion that the central situation implies. Even more significant, supermarts have become suburban features. In some cases—in this country as well as in America—they have been built outside the town altogether. It is paradoxical that the market— the very reason for the establishment of a town—can now only exist outside it, often where it is accessible to more than one town. If this reading of the western city model is correct it follows that we are facing the future with an utterly inadequate concept of what our urban environment should be like. The changes we are facing are likely to be more radical than any that have been faced before. To what extent are we justified in retaining the old, or alternatively in looking for something quite new? It could be argued that adaptations to change are already being made—for example the growth of peripheral markets, because these are firmly based on the same economic principles that formerly emphasized the dominance of the city centre. But it can also be argued that this uncontrolled departure from the existing pattern, determined by the economics of the situation only, may not be creating the best urban environment. In other words one element alone is determining the course of change.

The need for flexibility

Some planners are now specific in condemning the static approach, in stressing process only and ignoring any kind of completion: 'a new plan should not be a blue-print, but a draft for discussion'. More specifically still we find Lord Llewellyn Davies putting the view that in planning for change there should be no such thing as an ideal size, and that we should not plan for a specific centre in a new town.[8] His own plan for Washington, Co. Durham, goes some way towards this. Its grid system of roads will give equal accessibility to all points, and the traditional functions of the traditional centre will be dispersed throughout the town.

This leads to an extreme open-ended approach. It has been expressed most clearly by one of this country's most distinguished hospital designers, faced with a situation where a normal brief was almost impossible to obtain as no one can foretell the rapidly changing demands of the different branches of modern medicine. These can only be met by what he calls 'indeterminacy in architecture', and by designing to accommodate unforeseen changes.[9]

It may well be that a measure of indeterminacy is essential in urban planning, though this clearly will not apply in the same way to social goals. Possibly technical changes, suggesting new relations between social groups and their methods of building and presenting new urban environments, will occur much more rapidly than changes in the values which decide social goals. What, then, are the possible urban environments that might face our society in the future? These will clearly range from one extreme to another and the easiest measure of this range is compactness and density.

To increase density and emphasize compactness seems to be an architectural dream, only faintly hinted at in Manhattan or the Barbican. We are told that 20 million people could be comfortably accommodated within a cube with a side of 3 miles.[10] A recent article, visualizing Britain in 30 or 40 years' time,[11] suggested one possible future along these lines. The writer envisaged a series of towers, each 2 miles high and housing complete cities of 300,000 people. Each tower would have a central core, 600 feet in diameter, for factories, schools, hospitals and services, and on each of the 850 floors there would be an outer skin of housing, 100 families occupying each level. Movements would be fast and three-dimensional and no one would be further than a few minutes away from his work. Internally the environment would be controlled. There would be wonderful views—though we are not told what the cloud cover is at 2 miles high!—and an unspoilt countryside would be within easy reach by the 150,000 cars garaged in the basement floors. The interesting point is the technical feasibility of such a scheme. It will be technically possible before the end of the century.

However far-fetched this scheme may sound, it expresses,

albeit extremely, a commonly held notion that the city is a human ant-hill, and that men benefit from living in close proximity to one another. There is a tendency to equate urban-ness with density and this is held to be one of the attractions of high density schemes like Habitat in Expo '67.

The other extreme envisages a complete dispersion of the population in an attenuated suburban-like matrix. The technical basis of this possibility lies in our increasing freedom to communicate. The theory underlying it is that communication is the basis of the urban process, that it has been so in the past and will continue to be so.[12] We are now concerned with the urban process; that is, the social component rather than the physical, environmental component which we usually associate with the planning of cities. In the past communications have centred on the city, and the linking of the various functions within the city have depended upon face-to-face communication. It has previously been essential to have physical contact between the many activities—banks must be near the exchange, offices near banks, shops near offices, embassies near the seat of government and so on. For example, the disproportionately high number of engineering firms in and around Victoria Street in London stems from the mid-nineteenth century, when engineers, lobbying for acts permitting new railway lines, wished to be as near the Houses of Parliament as possible. The concentration of doctors in and around Harley Street reflects a desire to be near the large teaching hospitals of the country. To put it briefly, propinquity has been a necessary condition of city life. But with the development of communications over the last century, need this still be so? May we not be suffering from inertia? Is it still necessary for messengers to carry news from the Stock Exchange when a telephone would be more efficient? One can see how in Harley Street the reputation of its first practitioners has been transferred to the location, but in most urban situations propinquity is no longer essential. Radio and television are substitutes for face-to-face contact, and space is being diminished to an undreamt-of degree by road and air. Years ago the rare specialist stayed at home and the world came to him: this position is being reversed. The great scholar figure who once had students flocking to him is today replaced by the international scholar who dashes from a seminar in Tokyo to a class in New York, calling in for an informal lecture during a change of planes at London. In all spheres of human activity the *élite* are now an international *élite*. Some would argue that this ease of movement, as well as the use of communication media like television, will become available to more and more people, as education, real wealth and leisure increase, and as social barriers become lowered. Theoretically this means that the need for a city as a fixed location, in which specialized services are available, will diminish.[13]

The theoretical model based on these assumptions is one of complete dispersion, a scatter of houses served by a complex system of communications. The possibility becomes more real when we appreciate how many activities can now be spread without loss of efficiency. Industry is a case in point. The association of many of Britain's industrial areas with the coal fields is so automatic that we forget that this is a constraint of the industrial revolution which no longer operates rigidly. Our newest sources of power are near the sea (atomic energy stations) or under it (natural gas). Electricity and gas can be fed into a national grid, and both are easily sub-divisible and can serve any size of plant. Theoretically the pattern of industry determined by the industrial revolution could dissolve. In addition, with increasing automation, fewer and fewer people will be involved in manufacturing, more and more in service industries and in communication activities.

Neither the construction industry nor the locating of industrial activities have caught up with this fluid situation. The caravan is only a partial answer to freedom of house location. Architects have yet to design a free standing house which has, for example, its own waste disposal unit. Elimination of waste is important, for, in addition to all the other things that hold the traditional city together, drains must not be forgotten. Roads and power are more easily dealt with. But in the United States people are moving towards dispersal in spite of the difficulties—and in parts of America supplying water is the greatest difficulty. New towns are being built in Nevada at densities of two or three houses per acre. In Britain such dispersal would undoubtedly bring an outcry against destroying good agricultural land. There would certainly be no even scatter of houses all over Britain, however; the best agricultural land could be kept for an increasingly mechanized farming, other parts of the country could be protected for recreational purposes. There would still be enough land to allow the kind of density now enjoyed by a very small percentage of the upper and middle classes.

These, then, are two feasible futures. Not surprisingly both have in them much of the past. In a modified form—and one would hesitate to suggest that either extreme is going to sweep the country—they have very much of the past in them. The idea of a core city of great density, sharply demarcated from the countryside, is an extreme form of traditional urbanism, an expression of the propinquity which some claim is necessary for the cultivation of all that is best in urban civilizations.

The idea of dispersing houses more widely is only an extreme form of the trend in suburbanization in the last 50 or 60 years. The ideal that every house must have a garden was firmly established by Ebenezer Howard at the end of the last century. It has dominated the practice of building residential areas ever since. However much the architect stresses the possibilities of point blocks and the need for a feeling of urbanism, the planner has been happy in translating Howard's idea into bricks and mortar and lawns. The first post-war new towns were nothing more than garden cities at garden city densities, or, equally true, parcels of low-density suburbia focused on neighbourhood services. Although subsequent new towns, like Cumbernauld, have departed considerably from this pattern, the overwhelming trend is still towards lower densities. One very strong factor in this is the fact that middle-class housing already has such low densities. Three or four houses to the acre is becoming standard in the London region where houses cost over £12,000. If such a low density is seen as an index of a high standard of living then this may become a norm for the future. Looked at in that way, dispersion is no more than an existing trend which may well increase dramatically.

Between the two extremes is a variety of possibilities; of modified core cities, or of a combination of suburban-like dispersion and scattered nuclei of higher density. The choice should rest on the needs of society and its social values. However far dispersion may go, there will be a great reluctance to abandon high density cores altogether.

There is certainly a very strong feeling that the city in its traditional compact form has produced all that is best—as well as all that is worst—in civilization. The words city and civilization after all have the same root. It is debatable whether propinquity *alone* will produce advances in civilization, though this is often unwittingly assumed.

Although Ebenezer Howard thought the city to be physically—i.e. environmentally—bad, he considered urban society to be productive and good. To him the country was physically pleasant but socially dull, and that is why he tried to combine the best of both worlds. Dr Johnson, to whom London was life itself, said: 'Men thinly scattered make a shift, but a bad shift, without many things. . . . It is being concentrated which produces convenience.' He equated progress in the arts and sciences with cities. One of the most strongly argued pleas for the traditional compact city made recently is by Jane Jacobs.[14] She vigorously defends the tightly-knit community of the traditional high-density city, and sees nothing but evil in the suburban spread which is becoming characteristic of American cities. Los Angeles is sometimes taken as a prototype of the future dispersed city, and Miss Jacobs pulls no punches in condemning it. Her comparative statistics of crime rates in New York and Los Angeles are very striking, though the conclusion that dispersion positively encourages crime does not necessarily follow. She has done a service in reminding us that high density does not mean overcrowding, and that what we should retain in the old is not the evils of overcrowding but the positive good of propinquity. This rightly focuses attention again on the social rather than the environmental. If people wish to live in close contact we must devise the best environment to enable them to do this.

It was said above that innovations very often come in at one level of society and then tend to percolate downwards. This in itself is a great moderating force in the effect of change in the society as a whole, for two reasons. First, the majority of people are unable to afford innovations when they first appear. By the time the innovation has spread, another has appeared, again in the ranks of the rich or the *élite*. For example, 40 years ago comparatively few people had a radio. Twenty years ago the radio was ubiquitous, but few people had television. Today the television set is universal, but few people have colour television. By the time these are commonplace some people will have videophone—and so on. The percolation of innovations, governed by the ability to afford them, introduces a time lag which conserves. Secondly, there may be a tendency for the 'have-nots' of today to wish to emulate the 'haves'; and when they will be able to do so, tomorrow, they may reproduce a set upper-class fashion. This may be more so in planning because a house and its setting tends to be a symbol of class distinction. Some planners certainly act on these assumptions: that if the middle class today lives at four houses to the acre, then this will be the desirable standard for tomorrow's working class. This assumes too much about class rigidity, and different groups in society today are probably capable of producing new life styles without slavishly emulating those of richer groups. But if planners are presented with the prediction that in 30 years real income will have increased three times, then they are likely to act on the assumption that they must present today's middle-class environment to tomorrow's working class. This perpetuates existing forms: it does not encourage looking for new forms.

All things considered, we are unlikely to see a brand new Jerusalem in the near future. There is so much of the Old Babylon which we can't erase, so much inertia and conservatism. But where growth and expansion take place the future is theoretically open. There is a range of possibilities which leaves our planning open-ended. To predict an ultimate form is to commit the historic blunder of monolithic, idealistic end-planning. It leaves out of account society and its changing values. We have assumed too easily that form has an effect on society, that if we build a school catchment area, add a few shops, playing fields, a church and a pub, this will produce a neighbourhood. This is nonsense. A neighbourhood is the product of society. Our towns must be such that society can express itself within the least number of constraints. The most important element a planner has to deal with is the set of values society wishes to preserve; and accommodation must be made even for the changing of these values. Successful planning today is that which will enable the next generation to plan successfully. In so far as the past is enshrined in the present, much of this will be handed on to the future: not the trivial and banal, the bric-a-brac of society, but the fundamental and deep-rooted values that are basic to it. In this sense it behoves all planners to be students of the past.

Notes

1. W. M. Williams, *A West Country Village: Ashworthy*, 1963.
2. E. Jones, 'Tregaron, a Welsh Market Town', in A. Rees (ed.), *Welsh Rural Communities*, 1960, 95.
A. Rees, *Life in a Welsh Countryside*, 1950, 46.

3. C. M. Arensburg, *The Irish Countryman*, 1937, 29.
4. G. L. Abercrombie, *The Greater London Plan, 1944*, 1945.
5. R. S. Lopez, 'The Crossroads Within the Wall', in G. Haudlin and J. Burchard (eds), *The Historian and the City*, 1967.
6. L. Mumford, *The City in History*, 1961, 172.
7. W. Schneider, *Babylon is Everywhere*, 1963, 143.
8. R. L. Davies, 'Town Design', *Town Planning Review*, 37, iii (1966).
9. J. Weeks, 'Indeterminate Architecture', *Transactions Bartlett Society* 2, 1963-4.
10. K. Lynch, 'The Pattern of the Metropolis', in H. Rodwin (ed.), *The Future Metropolis*, 1962, 112.
11. W. Freichman, 'Cities in the Sky', *Drive* (Autumn 1968).
12. R. Mier, *A Communications Theory of Towns*, 1965.
13. M. W. Webber, 'Order in Diversity: Community Without Propinquity', in L. Wringo (ed.), *Cities and Space*, 1963.
14. J. Jacobs, *The Death and Life of Great American Cities*, 1967.

13
A Bibliography of the writings* of E. Estyn Evans

Compiled by M. L. Henry

(*excluding book reviews and articles in daily and weekly periodicals)

1927

'Bronze celt found near Carno, Mont.', *Archaeologia Cambrensis*
82, 390–1.
'Excavations on the Kerry Hills, Montgomeryshire' (with
John E. Daniel and Trevor Lewis), *Archaeologia Cambrensis*
82, 147–60.

1928

'An essay on the historical geography of the Shropshire-Mont-
gomeryshire borderland', *Collns Hist. Archaeological Mont.* 40,
1–30.

1929

'Denmark' [*in part*], in *Encyclopaedia Britannica*, 14th ed.

1930

'The Pyrenees: a geographical interpretation of their role in
human times', 45–68, in I. C. Peate, *Studies in Regional
Consciousness and Environment: Essays Presented to
H. J. Fleure*, Oxford, O.U.P.
'The sword-bearers', *Antiquity* 4, 157–72.

1931

'A Study of the Origins and Distributions of some Late Bronze Age Industries in Western Europe' (M.A. dissertation, Univ. of Wales).
'The late Bronze Age in Western Europe', *Man* 31, 207–13.

1932

'Ridgeways in north central Wales', *Bull. Brd. Celtic Studies* 6, 295–6.

1933

'The bronze spear-head in Great Britain and Ireland', *Archaeologia* 83, 188–202.
'Excavation of a horned cairn at Goward, Co. Down' (with O. Davies), *Man* 33, 114–17
'Goward Hill cairn, Co. Down' (with O. Davies), *Antiquity*, 7, 222.
'Ridgeways in north Wales', *Bull. Brd. Celtic Studies* 7, 86–8.

1934

'Excavation of a horned cairn at Ballyalton, Co. Down' (with O. Davies), *Man* 34, 88–9.
'Excavations at Clonlum small cairn, Co. Armagh' (with O. Davies), *County Louth Archaeological J.* 8, 165–8.
'Excavations at Goward, near Hilltown, Co. Down' (with O. Davies), *Proc. Rep. Belfast Nat. Hist. Phil. Soc.* (1932–3), 90–105.
'Prehistoric archaeology in Northern Ireland', *Antiquity*, 8, 329–30.

1935

'Archaeological investigations in Northern Ireland: a summary of recent work', *Antiquaries J.* 15, 165–73.
'Belfast Naturalists' Field Club Survey of Antiquities: megaliths and raths' (with M. Gaffikin), *Irish Naturalists' J.* 5, 242–52.
'A Bronze Age cist containing food vessel and cremation burial found at Ballynagross, near Downpatrick, Co. Down' (with M. Gaffikin), *J. R. Soc. Antiquaries Ir.* 65, 141–6.

S

'Excavation of a chambered horned cairn at Ballyalton,
Co. Down' (with O. Davies), *Proc. Rep. Belfast Nat. Hist.
Phil. Soc.* (1933–4), 79–103.
'Excavations at Aghnaskeagh, Co. Louth, Cairn A', *County Louth
Archaeological J.* 8, 235–55.
'Excavations at Clonlum, Co. Armagh' (with O. Davies),
County Louth Archaeological J. 8, 165–8.
'Notes on excavations in . . . Northern Ireland, 1934',
Proc. Prehistoric Soc. E. Anglia 7, 411–13.
'Ridgeways in north-west Wales', *Bull. Brd. Celtic Studies* 8,
84–7.

1936

'Doey's cairn, Dunloy', *Antiquaries J.* 16, 208–13.
'Excavation of a chambered horned cairn, Browndod, Co. Antrim'
(with O. Davies), *Proc. Rep. Belfast Nat. Hist. Phil. Soc.*
(1934–5), 70–87.
'Notes on excavations in . . . Northern Ireland, 1935',
Proc. Prehistoric Soc. 1, 140–2.
'Some recent finds of flint arrow heads', *Irish Naturalists' J.*
6, 9–11.

1937

France: A Geographical Introduction, London, Christophers,
183 pp. (New ed., 1959, 159 pp.; 3rd ed., London, 1966,
Chatto & Windus and New York, Praeger, 192 pp.)
'The Causeway Water, Co. Down, and its cairns', *Irish
Naturalists' J.* 6, 242–8.
'Excavations at Aghnaskeagh, Co. Louth, Cairn B', *County Louth
Archaeological J.* 9, 1–18.
'Human ecology: man and his environment', *New Era* 19, 273–6.
'Notes on excavations in . . . Northern Ireland, 1936',
Proc. Prehistoric Soc. 2, 221–3.
'The site of Belfast', *Geography* 22, 169–77.

1938

'A bronze spear-head from Caernarvonshire', *Archaeologia
Cambrensis* 93, 134–5.

'A chambered cairn in Ballyedmond Park, County Down', *Ulster J. Archaeology* 3rd s. 1, 49–58.

'Doey's cairn, Dunloy, County Antrim', *Ulster J. Archaeology* 3rd s. 1, 59–78.

'Giants' graves', *Ulster J. Archaeology* 3rd s. 1, 7–19.

'Megalithic civilisation in Northern Ireland', *Proc. Prehistoric Soc.* 3, 338–9.

'The multiple-cist cairn at Mount Stewart, Co. Down, Northern Ireland' (with B. R. S. Megaw), *Proc. Prehistoric Soc.* 3, 29–42.

'Notes on excavations in . . . Northern Ireland, 1937', *Proc. Prehistoric Soc.* 3, 453–4.

'Some results of recent excavations in Northern Ireland', *Q. Notes Belfast Munic. Mus. Art Gallery* 57, 7–10.

'An urn from Aghascrebagh, Co. Tyrone', *Ulster J. Archaeology* 3rd s. 1, 189–92.

1939

(Edited) *South Carpathian Studies: Roumania II* (with H. J. Fleure), London, The Le Play Society, 58 pp.

'Works submitted' (published papers presented for D.Sc., Univ. of Wales).

'A Bronze Age burial group from Kilskeery, County Antrim' (with T. G. F. Paterson), *Ulster J. Archaeology* 3rd s. 2, 65–71.

'The Celts in archaeology' (with O. Davies and C. Blake Whelan), *Ulster J. Archaeology* 3rd s. 2, 137–47.

'Donegal survivals', *Antiquity* 13, 207–22.

'Excavations at Carnanbane, County Londonderry: a double horned cairn', *Proc. R. Irish Acad.* 45C, 1–12.

'Killin Hill', *Ulster J. Archaeology* 3rd s. 2, 250–54.

'Notes on excavations in . . . Northern Ireland, 1938', *Proc. Prehistoric Soc.* 4, 322–3.

'The rowing-boat curraghs of Sheephaven', *Ulster J. Archaeology* 3rd s. 2, 28–31.

'Some survivals of the Irish openfield system', *Geography* 24, 24–36.

1940

(Sub-editor for Prehistoric Monuments) D. A. Chart,

A Preliminary Survey of the Ancient Monuments of Northern Ireland, Belfast, H.M.S.O., xxiv, 284 pp.

'Bibliography of the periodical literature relating to the archaeology of Ulster, 1939' (with B. R. S. Megaw), *Ulster J. Archaeology* 3rd s. 3, 170–1.

'Conditions of life in prehistoric Ireland'. Compiled by members of the Editorial Board (E. E. Evans, O. Davies and C. Blake Whelan), *Ulster J. Archaeology* 3rd s. 3, 5–16.

'An eskimo harpoon-head from Tara, Co. Down (?)' (with C. F. C. Hawkes), *Ulster J. Archaeology* 3rd s. 3, 127–33.

Introductory note to E. Watson, 'Prehistoric sites in South Antrim', *Ulster J. Archaeology* 3rd s. 3, 142.

'The Irish peasant house', *Ulster J. Archaeology* 3rd s. 3, 165–9.

'Lyles Hill: a prehistoric site in Co. Antrim', *Q. Notes Belfast Munic. Mus. Art Gallery* 64, 1–15.

'Notes on excavations in . . . Northern Ireland, 1939', *Proc. Prehistoric Soc.* 5, 255–6.

'Problems of Irish ethnology', *Irish Naturalists' J.* 7, 282–6.

'Sherds from a gravel-pit, Killaghy, Co. Armagh', *Ulster J. Archaeology* 3rd s. 3, 139–41.

✕ 'Seasonal nomadism in modern Europe and ancient Ireland', *Proc. Belfast Naturalists' Field Club* 2nd s. 10, 94–9.

✕ 'Transhumance in Europe', *Geography* 25, 172–80.

'Wooden trough from Tyrone', *Irish Naturalists' J.* 7, 246–7.

1941

'Bee transhumance', *Geography* 26, 76.

'Cist-burial at Loughry, Co. Tyrone', *Ulster J. Archaeology* 3rd s. 4, 145–8.

'Correspondence' [on Folk tales from Cadian, County Tyrone], *Ulster J. Archaeology* 3rd s. 4, 76–7.

'The flachter', *Ulster J. Archaeology* 3rd s. 4, 82–7.

'Grooved hammer-stones from Co. Antrim', *Ulster J. Archaeology* 3rd s. 4, 27–30.

'An interpretation of Irish culture'. Compiled by members of the Editorial Board (E. E. Evans, H. C. Lawlor and C. Blake Whelan), *Ulster J. Archaeology* 3rd s. 4, 12–18.

'Report on some sherds from Mount Druid', *Ulster J. Archaeology* 3rd s. 4, 55.

'Survey of Ancient Monuments. Additions' (contributions by E. E. Evans), *Ulster J. Archaeology* 3rd s. 4, 35–44.

'A sandhill site in Co. Donegal', *Ulster J. Archaeology* 3rd s. 4, 71–5.

1942

Irish Heritage: the Landscape, the People and their Work, Dundalk, W. Tempest, Dundalgan Press, xvi, 190 pp.

'Clermont cairn', *County Louth Archaeological J.* 10, 77–9.

'Coin hoards from Ulster: a hoard of coins from Rathlin Island', *Ulster J. Archaeology* 3rd s. 5, 66.

'A baking stone from Fermanagh' (with O. Davies), *Ulster J. Archaeology* 3rd s. 5, 76–7.

'A food-vessel from Ballynagarvy, Co. Antrim', *Ulster J. Archaeology* 3rd s. 5, 95–7.

'Pumice stone and neolithic sherds from Dundrum, Co. Down' (with A. McI. Cleland), *Ulster J. Archaeology* 3rd s. 5, 11–13.

'The stone houses, Tricloy, Co. Antrim' (with E. Watson), *Ulster J. Archaeology* 3rd s. 5, 62–5.

'The fireside', *County Louth Archaeological J.* 10, 196–9.

'Four bronze axes', *Ulster J. Archaeology* 3rd s. 6, 106–7.

'The horned cairns of Ulster' (with O. Davies), *Ulster J. Archaeology* 3rd s. 6, 7–23.

'Recent excavations', *Ulster J. Archaeology* 3rd s. 6, 23.

'Ten years' achievement: a summary of archaeological research in N. Ireland' (anon. editorial), *Ulster J. Archaeology* 3rd s. 6, 1–6.

1944

'Belfast: the site and the city', *Ulster J. Archaeology* 3rd s. 7, 5–29.

'A bronze axe from Co. Down', *Ulster J. Archaeology* 3rd s. 7, 98.

'A gold ornament and other Bronze Age finds from Rathlin', *Ulster J. Archaeology* 3rd s. 7, 61–4.

'The megaliths', *Geogr. Mag.* 17, 294–305.

'Souterrain at Ballyhornan, Co. Down', *Ulster J. Archaeology* 3rd s. 7, 102–4.

'Two food-vessels from Co. Tyrone', *Ulster J. Archaeology* 3rd s. 7, 105–8.

'Survey of Ancient Monuments', Third list of additions and corrections (contributions by E. E. Evans) *Ulster J. Archaeology* 3rd s. 7, 117–21.

'Unrecorded finds', *Ulster J. Archaeology* 3rd s. 7, 122.

1945

'A famine relic', *Ulster J. Archaeology* 3rd s. 8, 49.

'Field archaeology in the Ballycastle district', *Ulster J. Archaeology* 3rd s. 8, 14–32.

'Potatoes and man', *County Louth Archaeological J.* 11, 34–6.

'An urn from Culmore, Co. Antrim', *Ulster J. Archaeology* 3rd s. 8, 39–42.

1946

'Folk museums', *Ulster Countrywoman* June, 5–6.

'Newly discovered souterrains, County Antrim', *Ulster J. Archaeology* 3rd s. 9, 79–83.

'The origins of Irish agriculture', *Ulster J. Archaeology* 3rd s. 9, 87–90.

1947

The Ulster Countryside : report of the Planning Advisory Board on Amenities in Northern Ireland, Belfast, H.M.S.O. (Members of Committee on Amenities; E. E. Evans and others).

'Bog butter: another explanation', *Ulster J. Archaeology* 3rd s. 10, 59–62.

'Foreword', 5–6, in H. A. Boyd, *Rathlin Island, North of Ireland*, Ballycastle, Scarlett.

'Some newly reported bronze implements', *Ulster J. Archaeology* 3rd s. 10, 66–8.

1948

'General Introduction', pp. v–vi, in D. A. Hill; *The Land of Ulster : The Report of the Land Utilisation Survey of Northern Ireland. Part I : Belfast Region*, Belfast, H.M.S.O.

'Lands and peoples of the world: Western Europe', 97–121, in
Geography: The World and its Peoples, London, Odhams Press.
'A lost Mourne megalith—and a newly-discovered site'. *Ulster
J. Archaeology* 3rd s. 11, 43–7.
'Strange iron objects from Co. Fermanagh', *Ulster J. Archaeology*
3rd s. 11, 58–64.

1949

'Archaeological research in Ireland, 1939–1948', *Archaeology* 2,
69–72.
'Northern Ireland: the land and the people', *Geogr. Rev.* 39,
316–17.
'Old Ireland and New England', *Ulster J. Archaeology* 3rd s. 12,
104–12.

1950

'Antrim'; 'Belfast'; 'Donegal'; 'Down'; 'Fermanagh'; 'Ireland'
[*in part*]; 'Londonderry'; 'Louth'; 'Monaghan'; 'Northern
Ireland' [*in part*]; 'Tyrone' [and other articles] in *Chambers's
Encyclopaedia*, New ed. (Revised ed., 1967).
'Rath and souterrain at Shaneen Park, Belfast, townland of
Ballyaghagan, Co. Antrim', *Ulster J. Archaeology* 3rd s. 13,
6–27.
'Worked flints from boulder clay in Belfast', *Ulster J.
Archaeology* 3rd s. 13, 42–3.

1951

Mourne Country: Landscape and Life in South Down, Dundalk,
Dundalgan Press [12], 226 pp. (2nd ed., 1967, xvii, 244 pp.)
Northern Ireland: With a Portrait (About Britain 13), London,
Collins, 92 pp.
'Ancient fish weirs on the Co. Down coast', *Ulster J. Archaeology*
3rd s. 14, 48.
'R. A. S. Macalister and the archaeology of Ireland', *Ulster J.
Archaeology* 3rd s. 14, 2–6.
'Some archaic forms of agricultural transport in Ulster',
pp. 108–23, in W. F. Grimes *Aspects of Archaeology in*

Britain and beyond: Essays Presented to O. G. S. Crawford,
London, H. W. Edwards.

1952

'The physical background—the region and its parts', 15–28;
'The human background—prehistoric: Mesolithic, Neolithic
and Bronze Ages' (with E. M. Jope), 75–87; 'The human
background—protohistoric: the prehistoric Iron Age, early
Christian and Viking periods' (with E. M. Jope), 88–97 in
Belfast in Its Regional Setting: A Scientific Survey, Belfast,
British Association for the Advancement of Science. Local
Executive Committee.
'Two Belfast raths', *Ulster J. Archaeology* 3rd s. 15, 84–6.

1953

*Lyles Hill: a Late Neolithic site in County Antrim (Archaeological
Research Publications (Northern Ireland) no. 2),* Belfast,
H.M.S.O., viii, 71 pp.
'Archaeology in Northern Ireland, 1921–51', *Ulster J.
Archaeology* 3rd s. 16, 3–6.

1954

'Claude Blake Whelan', *Ulster J. Archaeology* 3rd s. 17, 6.
'Dairying in Ireland through the ages', *J. Soc. Dairy Technol.*
7, 179–87.
'Joseph Skillen', *Ulster J. Archaeology* 3rd s. 17, 2.
'The rural house', *The Landmark* 2, 5–6.
'Three bronze spearheads from Tattenamona, County Fermanagh'
(with G. F. Mitchell), *Ulster J. Archaeology* 3rd s. 17, 57–61.
'Ulster's place in British archaeology', *Trans. Lancashire &
Cheshire Antiquarian Soc.* 64, 19–23.

1955

'The black man and the white thorn', *Ulster J. Archaeology*
3rd s. 18, 109–12.
'The growth of Belfast' (with E. Jones), *Tn. Plann. Rev.* 26,
93–111.
'The Ulster farmhouse', *Ulster Folklife* 1, 27–31.

1956

'The ecology of peasant life in Western Europe', pp. 217–39, in
W. L. Thomas Jr. (ed.), *Man's Rôle in Changing the Face of the Earth: An International Symposium*, Chicago, Univ. of Chicago Press (revised ed., 1960).
'Fields, fences and gates', *Ulster Folklife* 2, 14–18.

1957

Irish Folk Ways, London, Routledge & Kegan Paul, xvi, 324 pp.
'A. H. Davison', *Ulster J. Archaeology* 3rd s. 20, 1–2.
'Changes in rural life and settlement', pp. 62–70, in
T. W. Moody and J. C. Beckett, *Ulster Since 1800, Second Series: A Social Survey*, London, British Broadcasting Corporation.
'Professor S. P. O'Riordain (with E. M. Jope), *Ulster J. Archaeology* 3rd s. 20, 2–3.
'The Ulster farmhouse: a comparative study', *Ulster Folklife* 3, 14–18.

1958

'The Atlantic ends of Europe', *Advancement of Science* 15, 54–64.
'The ecology of the rural house in Ireland', pp. 47–55, in
N. Anderson, *Recherches sur la famille, volume III: séminaires 1956 et 1957 du Séminaire International de Recherche sur la Famille et de l'Institut UNESCO des Sciences Sociales*, Cologne, Göttingen, Vandenhoeck & Ruprecht.
'Excavations at the Deer's Meadow' (with V. B. Proudfoot), *Ulster J. Archaeology* 3rd s. 21, 127–31.
'The Ulster landscape', *Ulster Folklife* 4, 9–14.

1959

'A fairy millstone', *Ulster Folklife* 5, 64.
'Miss Mary McMurry Gaffikin', *Ulster J. Archaeology* 3rd s. 22, 2–4.
'A Pennsylvanian folk festival', *Ulster Folklife* 5, 14–19.
'Rural settlement in Ireland and Western Britain' (with others), *Advancement of Science* 15, 333–45.

'A shell industry in County Londonderry', *Ulster Folklife* 5, 60.
'Social Sciences: Geography', 25–8, in *Pursuit of Knowledge: A Collection of Essays on Current Research*, Belfast, Queen's Univ.

1960

'Dicuil' in *Encyclopaedia Britannica*.
'The peasant and the past' (Presidential address to the Anthropology section of the British Association), *Advancement of Science* 17, 293–302.

1961

'The evolution of rural settlements in Scotland and beyond' (with R. A. Gailey), *Ulster Folklife* 7, 63–5.

1962

'Irish court cairns' (with O. Davies), *Ulster J. Archaeology* 3rd s. 24/25, 2–7.

1963

'Introduction' and 'Chapter 1 (Prehistoric and historic background)', pp. 19–44, in L. Symons, *Land Use in Northern Ireland: The General Report of the Survey*, London, Univ. of London Press.
'Ireland and Atlantic Europe', *Geogr. Z.* 52, 224–41.
'Northern Ireland'; 'Belfast' (and other articles) in (Grolier) *Encyclopedia International*.

1964

'Bann'; 'Erne'; 'Europe' [*in part*]; 'Mourne Mountains', in *Encyclopaedia Britannica*.
'County Londonderry: archaeology', pp. 49–62, in *County Londonderry Handbook*. [Coleraine, County Londonderry County Council.]
'Dame Dehra Parker', *Ulster J. Archaeology* 3rd s. 27, 2.
'Prehistoric geography', pp. 177–97, in J. Wreford Watson, *The British Isles: A Systematic Geography*, London, Nelson.

1965

'Cultural relics of the Ulster-Scots in the old west of North America', *Ulster Folklife* 11, 33–8.
'Folklife studies in Northern Ireland', *J. Folklore Inst.* 2, 355–63.
'Historic cities and boroughs: Belfast', *Munic. Rev.* 36, 24.
'Introduction', *Florin Guide to Northern Ireland.* Shell Petroleum Co.
'The Province', pp. 8–15, in R. Common, *Northern Ireland from the air.* [Dept. of Geography, Queen's University of Belfast.]
'The Scotch-Irish in the new world: an Atlantic heritage', *J. R. Soc. Antiquaries Ir.* 95, 39–49.

1966

Prehistoric and Early Christian Ireland: A Guide, London, Batsford, xiv. 241 pp. (New York, Barnes & Noble.)
'Culture and land-use in the old west of North America', *Heidelberg Geogr. Arb.* 15, 72–80 (*Festgabe fur Gottried Pfeiffer*).
'General introduction: geographical', pp. vii–xv, in Northern Ireland, Archaeological Survey. *An Archaeological Survey of County Down*, Belfast, H.M.S.O.
'George Barnett: an appreciation', *Ulster J. Archaeology* 3rd s. 29, 1–5.
'Some cruck roof-trusses in Ulster', *Ulster Folklife* 12, 35–40.

1967

'Flax-scutching', *Ulster Folklife* 13, 78–9.
'H. J. Fleure', in *International Encyclopaedia of the Social Sciences.*
'The geographical setting', pp. 1–13, in J. C. Beckett and R. E. Glasscock, *Belfast: the Origin and Growth of an Industrial City*, London, British Broadcasting Corporation.
'Lady Dorothy Lowry-Corry', *Ulster J. Archaeology* 3rd s. 30, 1.
'Preface', 17–18, in M. Rogers, *Prospect of Erne...*, [Enniskillin] Fermanagh Field Club.

1968

The Irishness of the Irish, Belfast, The Irish Association for Cultural, Economic and Social Relations, 8 pp.

'Archaeology in Ulster since 1920', *Ulster J. Archaeology* 3rd s. 31, 3–8.

'A cist burial at Carrickinab, Co. Down' (with A. E. P. Collins), *Ulster J. Archaeology* 3rd s. 31, 16–24.

'Ireland' [*in part*]; 'Northern Ireland' [*in part*]; 'Lough Neagh', in *Encyclopaedia Britannica*.

'Irish harvest', *Ulster Folklife* 14, 3–5.

'A late seventeenth-century farmhouse at Shantallow, near Londonderry' (with D. McCourt), *Ulster Folklife* 14, 14–23.

'The "Larne" material in Lord Antrim's collection at the Ashmolean Museum, Oxford', *Proc. R. Irish Acad.* 67C, 9–34.

1969

'A Cardiganshire mud-walled farmhouse', *Folk Life* 7, 92–100.

'The Scotch-Irish: their cultural adaptation and heritage in the American old west', pp. 69–86, in E. R. R. Green, *Essays in Scotch-Irish History*, London, Routledge & Kegan Paul.

'Sod and turf houses in Ireland', pp. 79–90, in G. Jenkins, *Studies in Folk Life: Essays in Honour of Iowerth C. Peate*, London, Routledge & Kegan Paul.

'Emeritus Professor Herbert John Fleure', *Geogr. J.* 135, 484–5.

'Foreword', 3–4, in Institute of Irish Studies, *Somerville and Ross: A Symposium*, Belfast, Queen's Univ.

1970

'Introduction', 1–9, in A. Gailey and A. Fenton, *The Spade in Northern and Atlantic Europe*, Belfast, Ulster Folk Museum and Institute of Irish Studies, Queen's Univ.

Notes on contributors

Harold John Fleure (1877–1969), M.A., D.Sc., LL.D., F.R.S., Professor of Geography, University of Manchester (1930–44); previously Professor of Geography and Anthropology, University of Wales. President Anthropology section, British Association (1926) and Geography section (1932). President Geographical Association (1948). Author of *Peoples of Europe* (1922); *Races of England and Wales* (1923); (with H. J. Peake), *Corridors of Time* (1924); *French life and its problems* (1942); *A natural history of man in Britain* (1951).

Bruce Proudfoot B.A., Ph.D., F.S.A., Professor of Geography, University of Alberta. Formerly lecturer in geography, University of Durham, and Visiting Fellow, University of Auckland, New Zealand. Lister Lecturer, British Association (1964). Author of *The Downpatrick gold find* (1958) and articles in geographical, archaeological and soil science journals.

Carl O. Sauer Ph.D., D.Phil., LL.D., Professor of Geography, University of California, Berkeley, since 1923. Formerly Professor of Geography, University of Michigan. Author of *The road to Cíbola* (1932); *Distribution of aboriginal tribes in New Mexico* (1934); *Man in Nature* (1939); *Agricultural origins and dispersals* (1952) and *Land and life* (1963).

Axel Steensberg D. Phil., Professor of Folk Culture, Copenhagen, 1959–70. Previously a keeper in the Danish Natural Museum. Has published books on rural dwellings, peasant furniture, field systems, and an *Atlas of the fields of Borup Village, 1000–1200 A.D.* Joint editor of *Tools and Tillage*.

John M. Mogey M.A., D.Sc., Professor of Sociology, Boston University. Formerly Professor of Sociology at Vanderbilt University, Nashville, lecturer in sociology at Oxford and lecturer in geography at Reading. Author of *Rural life in Northern Ireland* (1947); *A study of geography* (1950); (with R. N. Morris), *The sociology of housing* (1965); editor of *Family and marriage* (1963).

Harald Uhlig D. Phil., Professor of Geography, University of Giessen, Germany. Formerly lecturer at the University of Cologne and visiting lecturer at the University of North Staffs., Keele. Chairman of International Working Group for the terminology of the agricultural landscape. Editor *Types of field patterns*, vol. 1 (1967); *Typen der Bergbauern und Wanderlursten in Kaschmir und Jaunsar Bawar* (1961); articles in British and German geographical journals.

Desmond McCourt M.A., Ph.D., Reader in Geography, New University of Ulster. Formerly head of department of Geography at Magee University College, Londonderry. Author of articles on settlement evolution in archaeological, geographical and folk journals.

Pierre Flatrès Professor of Geography, Université de Lille. Formerly at Université de Rennes. Author of *Géographie rurale de quatre contrées celtiques* (1957); *La péninsule de Corraun: étude morphologique* (1957); *La France de l'Ouest* (1964); papers on settlement geography and planning.

Emrys George Bowen M.A., F.S.A., Emeritus Professor of Geography and Anthropology, University of Wales. Past President of the Institute of British Geographers, the Geographical Association and the Cambrian Archaeological Association. Author of *Wales: a study in geography and history* (1941); *The settlement of the Celtic saints in Wales* (1956); *Saints, seaways and settlements in Celtic lands* (1969); editor of *Wales: a physical, historical and regional geography* (1957).

John K. Wright (1891–1969), Director of American Geographical Society, 1938–49, and formerly librarian of the Society. President of the Association of American Geographers, 1946. Patron's Medal of the Royal Geographical Society, 1955. The author of many articles on human geography, some of which were collected in *Human nature and geography* (1967).

Andrew H. Clark M.A., Ph.D., Vernon C. Finch Research Professor at the University of Wisconsin, and Chairman of the department of Geography. Formerly at Rutgers University. Publications on human geography and North America.

Emrys Jones M.Sc., Ph.D., Professor of Geography, University of London, at the London School of Economics. Formerly lecturer in geography at Queen's University, Belfast. Formerly Fellow of the University of Wales and Fellow of the Rockefeller Foundation. Chairman of the Regional Studies Association. Author of *A social geography of Belfast* (1960); *Human geography* (1964); *Towns and cities* (1966); *Atlas of London and the London Region* (1969–70) editor, *Belfast in its regional setting* (1957); articles in sociological, planning and geographical journals.